DRAMA ON DRAMA

Drama on Drama

Dimensions of Theatricality on the Contemporary British Stage

Edited by

Nicole Boireau
Professor of English
University of Metz, France

First published in Great Britain 1997 by
MACMILLAN PRESS LTD
Houndmills, Basingstoke, Hampshire RG21 6XS and London
Companies and representatives throughout the world

A catalogue record for this book is available from the British Library.

ISBN 0–333–66972–X

First published in the United States of America 1997 by
ST. MARTIN'S PRESS, INC.,
Scholarly and Reference Division,
175 Fifth Avenue, New York, N.Y. 10010

ISBN 0–312–16541–2

Library of Congress Cataloging-in-Publication Data
Drama on drama : dimensions of theatricality on the contemporary
British stage / edited by Nicole Boireau.
p. cm.
Includes bibliographical references and index.
ISBN 0–312–16541–2 (cloth)
1. English drama—20th century—History and criticism.
2. Postmodernism (Literature)—Great Britain.   3. Self-consciousness
in literature.   4. Performing arts in literature.   5. Theater in
literature.   6. Acting in literature.   7. Drama—Technique.
I. Boireau, Nicole.
PR737.D73   1997
822'.91409—dc20   96–36456
                                                                CIP

This book is printed on paper suitable for recycling and made from fully managed and
sustained forest sources.

10   9   8   7   6   5   4   3   2   1
06   05   04   03   02   01   00   99   98   97

Printed and bound in Great Britain by
Antony Rowe Ltd, Chippenham, Wiltshire

Contents

Acknowledgements

Special thanks to Sarah Daniels and Catherina Pharoah for their help and to the University of Metz for having granted me a period of study leave.

I wish to express my deepest gratitude to Charmian Hearne of Macmillan for her invaluable assistance and advice at all stages.

N. B.

Notes on the Contributors

Elisabeth Angel-Perez is a lecturer in British theatre at the University of Paris-Sorbonne. She is the author of a PhD dissertation on the resurgence of medieval dramaturgy in contemporary English drama. She has published essays on playwrights from Christopher Marlowe and William Congreve to Howard Barker and Sam Shepard. She is also the author of a *History of English Literature* (Paris, 1994).

Nicole Boireau is Professor of English Literature at the University of Metz. She teaches theatre studies, British drama and fiction, feminism and theory of criticism. Her field of research is contemporary British drama. She has written a number of articles on postwar dramatists (Brenton, Daniels, Ayckbourn, Berkoff, Saunders, Shepard, and so on) and has contributed entries to *Histoire universelle des littératures* (Paris, 1993). She has co-edited 'Beyond Taboos', *Contemporary Theatre Review* (Vol. 5, 1996), with W. Lippke.

Ruby Cohn is Professor of Comparative Drama at the University of California (Davis). She has published many books on both British and American theatre, some hundred articles on different aspects of drama and a great number of theatre reviews. Among her most recent books: *New American Dramatists 1960–1990* (1991); *Retreats from Realism in Recent English Drama* (1991); *Anglo-American Interplay in Recent Drama* (1995).

Christine Dymkowski is Senior Lecturer in Drama and Theatre Studies at Royal Holloway, University of London. She is the author of *Harley Granville Barker: A Preface to Modern Shakespeare*, published by the Folger Shakespeare Library, in 1986, and has also written articles and papers on Edy Craig, Cicely Hamilton, Susan Glaspell, Caryl Churchill, Sarah Daniels and Timberlake Wertenbaker, as well as introductions to 13 plays by Eugene O'Neill, reissued by Nick Hern Books in ten separate volumes. She is currently completing a comprehensive theatre history edition of *The Tempest* for the Cambridge University Press and is theatre history editor of the New Variorum *Tempest* under the general editorship of Andrew Gurr.

John Elsom currently leads the MA course in Arts Criticism at City University. He was a founder of the Bush Theatre. He was the theatre critic of *The Listener* (1972–82), and a regular contributor to many papers. In the field of drama criticism he has published: *Theatre Outside London* (1969); *Erotic Theatre* (1972); *Post-war British Theatre* (1976 and 1980); *The History of the National Theatre* (with Nicholas Tomalin, 1978); *Post-war British Theatre Criticism* (1981); *Is Shakespeare Still Our Contemporary?* (1989); *Cold War Theatre* (1992). He has contributed postwar British theatre entries to *The Cambridge Guide to World Theatre* (1988, revised 1994), to *The Cambridge Guide to Literature in English* (1994) and to *The World Encyclopaedia of Contemporary Theatre* (1995). He is also the author of plays: *Peacemaker* (with Sally Mays, 1956); *How I Coped* (1969); *The Man of the Future is Dead* (1986); and *Malone Dies* (an adaptation of Samuel Beckett's novel, 1984).

Anne Fuchs is a lecturer in drama and theatre studies at the University of Nice–Sophia Antipolis. She has written many articles and papers on contemporary theatre and has specialized in South African drama. She is the author of *Playing the Market: The Market Theatre Johannesburg 1976–1986* (1992); she is the editor of *Theatre and Change in South Africa* (1996).

Maria Ghilardi-Santacatterina has interviewed Harold Pinter and reviewed his work for the Italian newspaper *Il Manifesto*. She is author of *Artists and the Creative City* (1995) and is Honorary Research Associate at the School of Arts and Humanities, De Montfort University, Leicester.

Albert-Reiner Glaap is Professor of English at the Heinrich Heine University in Düsseldorf. His main fields of interest and study have been contemporary Canadian, New Zealand and English literature and drama; methodology of English language teaching; and problems of literary translation. He has published numerous articles and books in these fields. He is the author of *Alan Ayckbourn. Denkwürdiges und Merkwürdiges. Zum Fünftzigsten Geburstag* (Reinbek, 1989). He was made an Officer of the British Empire in 1992.

Lizbeth Goodman is Lecturer in Literature at the Open University, where she directs the Gender, Politics, Performance Research Project and the Literature and Gender Forum, as well as the Shakespeare

Multi-Media Research Project in association with BBC Interactive Media. A native New Yorker who has studied and worked in the theatres of both the USA and the UK, her current work involves documentation and analysis of (mainly feminist and political) theatre and performance practice and their relationships to other media. Publications include *Contemporary Feminist Theatres* (1993), *Feminist Stages* (1996), *Literature and Gender* (1996), *Shakespeare, Aphra Behn and the Canon* (co-editor, 1996), and *Imagining Women: Cultural Representations and Gender* (co-editor, 1992).

Michel Morel is Professor of English Literature at the University of Nancy 2. His fields of research and teaching are critical theory and contemporary British fiction. He has published many articles in both fields and is currently writing a book on *L'acte critique*.

Klaus Peter Müller lectures at the University of Chemnitz. His fields of research and teaching are English and Canadian literature, literature and cultural identity, epistemology and literature, literature and anthropology, literary history, theories of literary criticism, translation theories and foreign language learning. He has written *Epiphanie. Begriff und Gestaltungsprinzip im Frühwerk von James Joyce* (1984); *Contemporary Canadian Short Stories* (1990); *Englisches Theater der Gegenwart* (1993); he has edited Howard Brenton's *The Genius* (1988); *Literaturübersetzen: Englisch, Entwürfe, Erkenntnisse, Erfahrungen* (with H. Friedl and A.-R. Glaap, 1992); *Anglistische Lehere Aktuell: Problems, Perspektiven, Erfahrungen* (with B. Korte, 1995).

Monique Prunet is Lecturer in English at the University of Paris-Sorbonne. She lectures on contemporary British Civilization and Economy. Her field of research is contemporary British Theatre from the 1960s to the present day. She has published a number of articles in various journals, and has given papers related to her field of research at many symposiums in France and in England. She is also co-author of *Initiation à la civilisation britannique* (1988, 3rd edn, 1995).

Aleks Sierz is theatre critic for the *Tribune* newspaper, and has also written on theatre for the *New Statesman* and the *Morning Star*. His work has appeared in *New Theatre Quarterly* and *Media, Culture and Society*. He has an MA in Arts Criticism from City University, London, and is cultural editor of *Red Pepper Magazine*.

Jean-Pierre Simard lectures at the University of Metz. He has combined an academic career with acting and directing for his own company in Saint-Etienne, a key city for popular theatre. He has written papers on the local working-class theatre and song culture. His thesis deals with John McGrath's contribution to popular theatre in Britain. He translates, adapts and directs contemporary British and American plays. He has written papers on British drama and is writing a book on British cinema. He combines a text analysis of plays and a reflection on the aesthetics of the stage and communication with audiences. He has written three plays and is a regular contributor to La Comédie de Saint-Etienne, a National Drama Centre.

Nicole Vigouroux-Frey is Professor of Drama and Cultural Studies at the University of Rennes (Haute-Bretagne). Her fields of teaching and research are English-speaking drama and media. She is responsible for a research programme on the Performing Arts. She is the Editor of the collection 'Le Spectaculaire': *Traduire le théâtre aujourd'hui?* (1993) and *Voix de femmes* (1994). She is the Editor of *Coup de Théâtre* and a member of the Socrates Network: Theatre Arts and Media. She holds a long-standing partnership with the CNRS (Arts du Spectacle).

Ann Wilson teaches in the Department of Drama, at the University of Guelph. Her academic interests focus on contemporary Canadian and British drama. She has published many articles in those fields. She is the co-editor of *Essays in Theatre/Etudes théâtrales*.

Preface
Nicole Boireau

This book addresses reflexivity in recent British drama. The pronounced taste of contemporary drama for self-examination seemed to offer an interesting object of study. Of course, the phenomenon is by no means a novelty. Thematic and structural reflexivity, namely drama as its own theme and organizing principle, or drama as discourse on and about itself within the play, has always been a major feature of the art of theatre. What possibly deserved further examination is the way reflexivity in contemporary drama relates to other concepts. The sense of distance inherent in drama is one of the main discoveries of twentieth-century theory, and reflexivity may be considered as the distancing device that contains them all. Yet, self-examination traditionally stands in danger of being treated like the bath water of narcissism and decadence. The desire to reassess contemporary drama in the light of such well-established although paradoxical notions motivated the writing of this book. Indeed, the extent of the reflexive obsession in the world of drama pleaded for an urgent re-examination of its premises. Although twentieth-century epistemology has left no terrain of thought unmapped there still seemed to be a sufficiently interesting challenge to add yet one more book of essays to the critical ocean. Far from putting an end to the multifaceted reflexivity debate, the wealth of existing material[1] on the subject has provided a stimulating basis for more questions to be raised and more answers to be given. Furthermore, the British stage of the last three decades has provided the contributors to this book with countless examples of metadramatic and metatheatrical practices, opening the way for a joint reflection on the nature of theatricality.

The art of theatre has never ceased to lay claim to its paradoxical nature: it says something about reality through the use of artificial conventions. Long ago, Hamlet's 'Mousetrap' made a definitive statement that truth comes through the world of illusion. Theatricality reveals the truth. The reality of the theatre lies in artifice. Drama posits the artificiality of its conventions within the framework of those same conventions. Drama and theatre are forced to meditate on the validity of their own medium within the limits imposed by that medium. The history of drama bears witness to the constancy of this phenomenon. Establishing the barrier of the fourth wall, recognizing and accepting the rules of the game, are the necessary rites of passage from ritualistic practices to representational drama. The existential relationship of actor and spectator was early acknowledged by the Greek Chorus. Baroque prologues, inductions and epilogues, relayed by their medieval predecessors, fulfilled a similar function. Among the most celebrated plays referring to themselves as plays are Shakespeare's *A Midsummer Night's Dream, Hamlet, The Taming of the Shrew* and Beaumont's *Knight of the Burning Pestle.* Renaissance and baroque theatre dramatized the essential duplicity inherent to its art. It combined the image of the world as theatre and the theatre as self-contained world, both spectacle and gaze of the *theatrum mundi.* The eighteenth-century taste for dramatic burlesques, rooted in a desire to copy and deride previous models, revealed again how easily drama could display its conventions.

The notion of reflexivity within contemporary drama takes multiple forms, which have been usefully analysed by major critics.[2] Some of these forms can be easily detected, such as the straightforward use of the 'play-within-the-play' or 'abyme'; the introduction of metadramatic discourse in the play; the thematic and self-conscious dramatization of theatrical conventions. Other devices may be less visible: for example, the exploration of role-playing within the role or the use of traditional dramatic forms in devised plays. The adaptation, translation, re-contextualization and transcoding of previous models (re-visiting, re-writing and re-playing tradition) make use of a yet more subtle hybridization in order to demythologize myths and create modern drama as a nexus of opposing forces. Recognizing the free interplay of forms, styles and performances, a dominant postmodern theoretical stance, is an experience shared by the playwright, the director and the spectator alike. Contemporary drama and theatre can be seen as one long continuous text echoing the changing geometry of twentieth-century culture, a new fractal architecture in which new forms endlessly generate further forms. Different modes of perception are called for, anticipating further forms. This dynamic principle, which is captured by the reflexive nature of contemporary art, is the central thesis of this book. Far from being marginal, the self-perpetuating and sometimes self-conscious mechanism of reflexivity has become the subject-matter and the organizing principle of many contemporary British plays and productions. The nature of theatricality itself emerges as the necessary corollary of such a study of contemporary British theatre. The extent of the phenomenon raises a number of questions. Is this compelling self-examination mere posturing? Can this ambiguous and playful interplay of texts, this proliferation of images-within-images support the exploration of serious issues? Or is drama in the process of locking itself up in the prison-house of its own conventions in order to evade important commitments? Is contemporary 'drama on drama' just one more form of art for art's sake? If daring drama is meant to achieve an ideological purpose by shattering ready-made assumptions, it seems that an honest and possibly iconoclastic critique of the clichéed notions of narcissism and decadence is crucially needed.

This book raises key questions and sets out to provide some tentative answers. The essays fall into three sections. Part I tells us a story of origins. The study of the reappropriation of the past foregrounds the need of contemporary dramatists to see history in a new perspective and to see it whole. The use of Greek myths, of medieval models, of Jacobean dramatic patterns and traditional Japanese forms in contemporary plays de-familiarizes present issues to better problematize them. Part II deals with the way in which major authors have stretched the mould of realism to breaking-point and generated new modes of perception. Samuel Beckett, Harold Pinter, Timberlake Wertenbaker, Tom Stoppard and Caryl Churchill all explore the hidden truth of the theatrical medium within their plays. Part III focuses on the interplay of codes and consequently of ideologies in performance. Forceful voices emerge from John McGrath's potent monologue. The de-familiarizing process of writing across media is also a way of challenging ready-made sexist images. Distancing procedures are shown to clear the way for a revitalizing philosophy. The theatre companies devising drama on drama reaffirm a strong link with the community in which they are rooted. Further cross-fertilization of dramatic traditions derives from the translation and adaptation of foreign plays. Turning to the art of the musical, it can be seen as the ultimate self-referential, non-representational and unifying form containing all the previous metaphors. It should therefore close the circle.

The 15 original essays together cover the different forms of reflexivity: all converge on the revelatory power of contemporary British theatre. In becoming its own problematic issue, drama is

paradoxically revealed in these essays to contain an invigorating in-
built sense of history. The more drama reflects on its own medium,
the more it reactivates its own meaningful patterns and the more it
tells us about the world. The more it re-affirms its links with the
living community. This is the central discovery and message of this
volume.

Cutting across the various end-of-the-century critical schools, the
authors re-interrogate conceptual frameworks and re-assess their
validity. The 15 authors, all scholars from different countries, ensure a plurality of viewpoints on the central issue. They ensure a
non-chauvinistic approach is taken to British drama. Critical safety
in numbers and in geographical distance! So much for academic
credibility. However, attentive readers will not miss the hidden
agenda of the whole enterprise. They will read the subtext. Academic research is a worthy pretext for joint homage to the powerful
attraction of the British stage. The phenomenal enthusiasm British
theatre has consistently inspired over the years and throughout the
world is fully acknowledged in this tribute, where love of British
culture and commitment to British drama have chosen the guise of
criticism. Academics from all over the world reveal a unity of purpose. The desire for a permanence beyond shifting ideologies, or
for a unity of vision beyond postmodern fragmentation may perhaps be the possible prophetic statement of drama on drama at the
end of the century.

Notes

1. The appended general bibliography is selective.
2. Richard Hornby, Ruby Cohn (in *Retreats from Realism*) and Manfred
    Schmelling make very useful distinctions in their respective books
    (see General Bibliography).

Part I
Historical Perspectives

1

Greeks in Drama: Four Contemporary Issues
Nicole Vigouroux-Frey

Martin Esslin concluded his essay *An Anatomy of Drama* (1976) by stating that:

> Drama is as multifaceted in its images, as ambivalent in its meanings, as the world it mirrors. That is its main strength, its characteristic as a mode of expression – and its greatness.[1]

The present essay will concentrate on one specific facet, the classical Greek world of the great myths considered in four major plays of our time (1970–90) by four masters of the dramatic language: Wole Soyinka (*The Bacchae of Euripides*, 1973), Edward Bond (*The Woman*, 1978), Steven Berkoff (*Greek*, 1980) and Seamus Heaney (*The Cure at Troy*, 1990). We shall see that, in spite of the wide variety of attitudes and philosophies at play, there is a certain coherence of thought, a unified and permanent degree of historical consciousness, an awareness that each epoch requires to assert narrow cultural roots and to indulge in multifaceted experimentation, thus testing human behaviour in a series of given situations. The recurrent patterns strike us as almost deliberate scientific method, as experimental laboratory work. Bemused audiences have witnessed the dual process of re-creation, out of prior creation, have stood through the travestied reflexive metaphor of war and peace in an end-of-century process of interrogation, or rather in some form of decadent game echoing the increasing conflict of distorted beliefs and emotions, in an irrational society. Do we endlessly gild the steeple instead of strengthening the foundations? In a short essay, *History*,[2] Edward Bond's answer is quite obvious:

> Why are our days crumbling and our times violent? Because we gild steeples. But in history truth – like the physical laws of nature

– comes from the foundations. True culture is created there, not at the top.

The four plays considered use the Greek model in an attempt to break away, to scrape off the effete decay of materialistic values. The four playwrights excavate the past in an attempt to write about the future and to assert their vital preoccupations in one total form of society.

> War and peace are taken to be mutually exclusive. But perhaps what we call peace has really always been a part of war. [. . .] War and peace are the products of irrational society. They are Siamese twins trying to strangle one another.[3]

Two twined aspects of life, two masked competitors wrestling for both tragic and comic pre-eminence on stage.

FROM TRAVESTIED MYTHS . . .

Because of their initial commitment, the four playwrights in question broke the frames of reference, laying bare the mechanism and function of mythologies, introducing a metamyth as a view of illusion or theatrical metaphor. Distortion, monstrosity are enshrined in the four plays, in the 'cess-pit' of 'London in the grip of a plague' (*Greek*), in cannibalism and Nature's monstrous cycle of regeneration (*The Bacchae*), in Philoctetes' contemplation of his wounds (*The Cure at Troy*) or in the eventual defeat of the Greek imperialist slave culture because of a handful of weaklings (*The Woman*).

Why is it so? Our four dramatists have paved the way to a new approach in Drama and political commitment:

> Most serious drama from the Greek tragedies to Samuel Beckett is [. . .] a form of philosophising, not in abstract but in concrete terms.[4]

Greek myths such as the Trojan war and Oedipus' tragedy are still partially shared by all potential audiences in rational Western world thinking. They provide the ideological, aesthetic foundations of serious drama. A coherent world-view no longer works in periods like our own, because:

a wide variety of philosophers and attitudes to life co-exist and there is a high degree of historical consciousness, an awareness too that each epoch, each country is different.[5]

The blessed times in which a story-line was almost inevitably a legend, presumably known to the entire audience, are long gone. The narrow range of possibilities at work in Greek tragedy is but wishful thinking. The repeated ring of names conjures up frozen echoes, compelling the spectators to rack their brains for knowledge, to travel the forgotten paths of educated memory: Oedipus, Hecuba, Troy, Philoctetes, Dionysus function as sound ideograms rooting an old myth in a new, familiar context, in an individual present. The myth fugitively seems to revive out the unfrozen name, soon to be frozen again in the labyrinth of memory and . . . there's the rub: the restored word no longer befits the story-line. Oedipus explodes in Eddie Puss; Dionysus is purposely spelt in a more modern form as Dionysos; the Trojan war is shortened to five years; Philoctetes' island resembles a post H-bomb world. In other words, when finally restored to its original place, the borrowed element no longer fits into the original space.

Using myths implies acknowledging the world not as it is, but as it wants to be. Bertolt Brecht referred to an ambiguous word to describe a similar situation: *Einverständnis*, which means sharing partnership in the understanding of reality.

The four plays in question all show the original object distorted into some gigantic monstrosity.

The Bacchae of Euripides (Wole Soyinka), commissioned for performance by the National Theatre at the Old Vic (summer 1973), express a communal feast, a tumultuous celebration of life and nature. In the Introduction, Soyinka aptly identifies Dionysos and the magic mystery of life with the eternal rhythms of growth, decay and rejuvenation. But soon enough he drifts away from the original Greek pattern by introducing Christ figures, for instance in the second wedding scene. The final scene of *The Bacchae* also reveals Christian influences: Dionysus transforms the severed head of King Pentheus into a fountain of wine from which masters and slaves merrily drink together. In such scenes the play betrays obvious Christian influences. Soyinka also emphasized the relationship between Dionysus and Ogun (see Introduction to the play), Yoruba god of metal, of creativity, of the road, of wine and of war. The Mysteries of Ogun echo the Mysteries of Dionysus. Thus, under the cover of the Western myth, the Yoruba playwright implies other lessons, suggests other situations:

> The Phrygian god and his twinhood with Ogun exercise irresistible fascination. His thyrsus is physically and functionally parallelled by the *opa Ogun* borne by the male devotees of Ogun.[6]

The play, its overall message, can be equally understood by both Western and African audiences:

> The dionysiac impulse was not new. Dionysianism, essentially agrarian in origin, was the peasant's natural evocation of, and self-immersion in, the mysterious and forceful in nature. The Dionysiac is present, of course, in varied degrees of spiritual intensity in all religions.[7]

Distortion is at work. We shall consider its purpose.

The very title of Berkoff's play gives an immediate clue. *Greek* emphasizes the satirizing distortion of the myth transferred to the 'septic isle' controlled by Maggot Scratcher. A string of scorching epithets asserts the 'evidence of the British plague' and comforts Eddie in this nihilistic mission:

> Rid the world of half assed bastards clinging to their dark domain and keeping talent out by filling the entrances with their swollen carcasses and sagging mediocrity/let's blow them all sky high, or let us see them simply waste away as the millions come to us.
>
> (Act II, scene 1)

The decadent surroundings are carefully established as we understand the full meaning of Eddie Puss's name: Oedipus. Ten years have gone by since he killed his father and married his mother. The solver of riddles remains in blissful ignorance while his mother/wife rhapsodizes about their everlasting felicity:

> Ten years have flown away as Apollo's chariot hath with fiery stride lit up our summers, thawed our frosts and kissed our cheeks [. . .] whilst we, my man that is and me, for three thousand three hundred and sixty five times did celebrate our own ritual in nights of swooning.
>
> (Act II, scene 1)

The parody of the myth is clearly exposed if we refer to Margaret Rose's definition of parody, 'the critical refunctioning of performed litery material with comic effect'.[8]

Born out of the Thames, or rather fished out of the river after a mine explosion, Eddie forces the myth into final explosion, into darkness and oblivion.

Darkness and light, that is to say black and white as the negative and positive aspects of freedom and knowledge, also play an essential role in *The Woman* (Edward Bond). The drama imagines, re-creates the end of the Trojan war and what followed the tragic death of Priam. A Woman, Queen Hecuba, is the focal figure. It is enough to indicate the transgression of the traditional myth, to state the urgency of a new reading out of the parody of the initial situation. Those at the bottom of the pyramid, the downtrodden, appear to be at the top: women, miners, fishermen.

Interestingly enough, in an essay entitled 'A Story', published as a follow up to the play, Bond expounds one of the real purposes of this travestied myth:

And one day a young miner decided to go to see the palace and come back to the miners to tell them what sort of thing white was. [...] At the top he found the mine owner. [...] He said, 'I have come to see your palace. And please sir what is white?'
The mine owner smiled. 'Well . . .' he said, looking at the sooty miner. 'White? . . .' he mused for a moment and then smiled and pointed to his head. 'My face', he said, 'is white'. With a whoop of joy the miner reached out, cut it off and chopped it down the shaft to the miners.
It would be better for them if those who know what white is also knew what black is.[9]

The tale is sufficient to explain what Bond means when he describes *The Woman* as 'a socialist rhapsody' or when he claims that 'it celebrates the change and those who make it.'[10] The travestied symbol of the severed head is a fortunate echo to Pentheus' severed head in *The Bacchae*.

The paradox at work in Seamus Heaney's very title *The Cure at Troy*, seems to prolong the major symbols at play in *The Woman*, subtitled 'scenes of war and freedom'. *The Cure at Troy* was first performed at the Guildhall, Derry, on 1 October 1990; Seamus

Heaney was then director of the Field Day Theatre Company. In his version of Sophocles's *Philoctetes*, Heaney explores the ways in which victims of injustice may become devoted to the contemplation of their wounds; in a similar manner he displays the perpetrators who appear to be frozen in the justification of the system they have built. The subject matter could not possibly have been selected at random: the location, the time of the performance were precisely those of that 'irrational society' previouly described by Bond, 'a world of hardship and loss'. The versified version, the poetry of the rhythm, all concur; they prolong and epitomize Bond's assertion: 'An irrational society justifies its irrationalty with myths.'[11]

Myths revived and travestied serve a purpose. It is expressed through their dramatic function.

... TO MYTHS REVISITED

'Modern mythologies feed on the images engendered by materialistic values. The lurid colours of the end-of-the-century anxieties need more than bland images to be properly grasped in the theatre', Nicole Boireau claims.[12] The statement is a very apt guide-line to show what occurs in the re-construction of Greek myths on contemporary stages.

Edward Bond, for instance, is haunted by a sense of torment and urgency: injustice, suffering in a money-based competitive society turn human beings into 'ghosts in chains'. But, at the same time, he believes that 'freedom is possible'.[13] *The Woman*, he claims, may offer a temporary solution: it celebrates the world, it shows history as a moral force, it shows the woman and the miner as real characters, not as 'superhuman archetypes':

> This play is a story showing in the characters and actions of its protagonists the cause-and-effect of change – especially the stupidity of reaction and the strength of the understanding that opposes it. It celebrates the change and those who make it. That is what makes the play a socialist rhapsody.[14]

The very notion of 'socialist rhapsody' deserves our attention. It strikes us as a divergent contemporary interpretation of the modern type of 'epic theatre', a 'rhapsôdia' suited to our rational culture, devised by means of quoting out of the original context. The approach becomes primarily analytical, the value of the play is that of a 'play of moments', ordering scenes instead of unfolding a story. The strong impact of those privileged moments is meant to stir the cultural recognition of the audience, challenged into thinking. Queen Hecuba as the focal figure, initiating the parody of the original situation, provides us with a substitute for Brecht's celebrated alienation effect; the burlesque, carnival-like situation provides us with an uncanny, outrageous element forcing the spectators to rake their brains for the origin of that choice.

Techniques borrowed from the various entertainment arts, shifting geographical perspectives, all contribute to enhance the value of the subtitle: 'scenes of war and freedom' with its implicit contradictions. We endlessly travel from Greek Headquarters, outside Troy, to scenes inside Troy, ending up on an island with its grotto, peopled with some Hecuba/Prospero, some Man/Caliban and a generous catalogue of dwellers and intruders. The moments on the island successfully contribute to create the Brechtian type of fable through a series of flighting, self-contained scenes, definitely carrying the audience a long shot from the well-made Aristotelian drama. *The Woman* creates a 'rational theatre' against the grain, devising a series of scenic metaphors so as to tear the spectator away from the original myth in order to re-create a contemporary poetic epic. Hecuba's drowned body will be burnt on the quay, but its ultimate, grotesque lesson in subversion will be treasured up:

> She was caught in a fence like a piece of sheep's wool. When the spout passed over her I ripped out her hair and her eyes. Her tits were sticking up like knives. Her face was screwed up and her tongue – a long thin tongue – was poking out.
>
> (*The Woman*, Act II, scene 9)

The water metaphor, the aquatic reference makes Hecuba a perfect martyr and figurehead of rebellion, of socialism. Aptly enough, it is Ismene, the fallen princess in the myth, who recovers her composure to voice out the ultimate interpretation:

> *Ismene*:   Since you've loved me my mind's begun to clear. Even yesterday I was calm.

Man: I may disgust you.
Ismene: No, never.

(*The Woman*, Act II, scene 9)

The man who appeared on the island a few months earlier remains unnamed and will stay for ever 'deformed, short and [with] dark hair and pitted skin' (Act II, scene 2, stage directions). His body is crippled from working in the mine. He may have run away from slavery. It is clear enough that Bond has departed from the traditional myth and wandered through Shakespeare's proto-epic drama, the island of *The Tempest*. From a Brechtian 'epic' type of play, *The Woman* expands into a post-Brechtian neo-epic, burdened with the traditional meaning of the original myth as Bond takes up the original names. In her tragic sacrifice to the wrath of the gods, Hecuba enables the fallen princess and the dwarfed slave to live together in hope, freedom and dignity regained.

In both *The Bacchae of Euripides* (Wole Soyinka) and *The Cure at Troy* (Seamus Heaney), the conflict also seems to be centred around tyranny and freedom. The emphasis does not lie on unfolding a tragic fable. The plays appear as two poetic allegories of the process of a social and mental evolution. Yet, both dramatists do not choose to appear as daring as Bond. Travestied or bent, Myth and History remain essential, enshrined in an exemplary past. The perspective only seems to be modified.

The poetic lines of *The Cure at Troy* strangely make the play sound like a frozen legend, out of the present time; and yet, because it was performed at the Guildhall, Derry, on 1 October 1990 when Seamus Heaney was then director of the Field Day Theatre Company we know that Philoctetes' island is most likely Ireland, the island of all saints and kings, some present time Western version of divine Olympus. The message is almost too clear. Every time Heaney says 'Greek', we cannot help reading the epithet as 'Irish': a fratricidal conflict dividing and weakening Ireland, just as the Greeks would not defeat Troy unless they would combine all Greek talents. Ireland's moral wound echoes Philoctetes' flesh wound. The venom disables him, mars the picture of harmony: the worm is eating the fruit. The cure then becomes the potential reunion in favour of a more immanent cause, of a more imperative necessity. Whatever the origin of the wound, whatever the bitterness of treason and injury, the duty of man is but to serve the interest of his fellowmen, not as a Christian set on a divine mission, but as a mere human prerequisite. Individual satisfaction finds no cause in the face of common interest. The tragedy in question is no longer the tragedy of a man, it turns out to be the tragedy of a nation.

> *Neoptolemus*: What's the shame in working for a good thing?
> *Philoctetes*: But good for who? Me or my enemies? [. . .]
> *Neoptolemus*: Stop just licking your wounds. Start seeing things.
> (*The Cure*, p. 74)

Individuals cannot but comply with common cause. The History of mankind cannot be written on individual grounds. Justice, freedom, war and peace have no meaning unless geared with universal meaning. A recluse on a volcanic island (the symbol is quite telling), Philoctetes broods over vain schemes of vengeance, treasuring a precious bow, re-enacting Caliban's bitter delusion. The appeal of the theatrical effect of the play-within-the-play-that-was is quite potent. Soreness, lack of communication, misunderstanding, can but lead to failure. The last years of the on-dragging Irish conflict were painful to live. Seamus Heaney borrows W. H. Auden's lines to illustrate the mood of the opening of his play: 'You shall love your crooked neighbour with your crooked heart.'

The cold reception of *The Cure* indicated that the Irish audience knew the real significance, the political message of the metaphor. The Irish warriors were not just ready to bend the bow into a golden harp or a bard's lyre.

Wole Soyinka's *The Bacchae* 'belongs to that sparse body of plays which evoke awareness of a particular moment in people's history, yet imbue that moment with a hovering, eternal presence'.[15] In other words, Dionysianism is set in the context of labour migrations in a context of industrial economy, replacing the agrarian tradition, bringing along new customs just as the development of Americas and Indies introduced a new slave culture based on displacement, dispossession or suppression of identity. The Myth of a non-Olympian provides easy identification and wish-fulfilment, releasing the frustrated energy of the downtrodden. The process is similar to that of the second part in *The Woman*. Vengeance, punishment can be achieved through the presence of the god who becomes the champion of the masses: the message is purposely subversive: 'Pentheus' death restores a harmonious balance in Thebes and liberates the enslaved.'[16]

Dionysus is identified as a 'class-conscious myth.' Soyinka enhances the revolutionary undercurrent of the original myth and states his intention in the Introduction: he identifies Dionysus with the Yoruba revolutionary god Ogun (p. vi). The slave leader empha- sizes the revolutionary language of the long suffering. Tiresias, the seer, fulfils the past of the scapegoat in an attempt to avoid disrup- tion of order; in vain, Pentheus, the king, eventually becomes the ritual scapegoat. We find a total reversal of the initial conditions of the Myth and the meaning must have been fully significant in its African context. The exploited masses cannot be taken for granted for ever and ever. Soyinka presses them to enact their own socialist revolution. In that sense *The Bacchae* can be considered as an Af- rican socialist rhapsody in which self-discipline comes out of self- knowledge. The original is not contemplated starry-eyed. Bridges are not haphazardly thrown across continents; timelessness con- veys a sense of futurity.

> *Tiresias*:   Restraint is something people must practise themselves.
> It cannot be imposed. Those who have learnt self-discipline –
> the greatest Guarantee of human will and freedom – will not
> then lose it for losing themselves to Dionysos. Answer me, is
> control not built upon self-knowledge?
> *Pentheus*:   What if it is?
> *Tiresias*:   Dionysos grants self-knowledge. With that thought I
> leave you. There is still time.
>
> (p. 33)

We have reached the full significance of the Myth, the moment when history yields to nature, according to Barthes.[17]

The ritual abruptly turns into a play of challenge and conflict. Man reasserts his eternal self, craves for continuity and productiv- ity within group solidarity. This is the reason why the playwright could claim:

> I see *The Bacchae* as a prodigious, barbaric banquet, an insightful
> manifestation of the universal need of man to match himself
> against Nature. The more than hinted-at cannibalism corresponds
> to the periodic needs of humans to swill, gorge and copulate on a
> scale as huge as Nature's on her monstrous cycle of regeneration.
>
> (Introduction, p. xi)

Berkoff's *Greek* and its world of rampant mediocrity, grotesque distortion, transgressed taboos, lewd language and body yearning conveys a similar urgent need for Nature. It is the ultimate journey, back and forth from the origin. Breaking the frames of reference implies the existence of pre-existing models conveyed through History. The archetypal family of basic needs or of more sophisticated peer thoughts can be traced from the original vomit, the mine explosion. It is just another way of confessing naked thoughts, of excavating the past, of returning to man degree zero, of substituting the slave for the king. What else can we expect in the 'cess-pit' of a plagued London? Scum instead of models, travestied archetypes, carnivalizing? The tragic figure of Oedipus is carnavalized in the grimacing figure of Eddie Puss. A sudden cataclysm, a natural catastrophe, upsets our models and conventions, destroys our sets of references, turns everything upside down. Xenophobia, nostalgic allegiance to fascism are but the hidden side of a decayed oligarchy. Oedipus/Eddie Puss's plea for forgiveness appears as the ultimate expression of love and urgency:

> Eddie: We only love so it does not matter mother, mother it does not matter. Why should I tear my eyes out Greek style, why should you hang yourself/have you seen a child from a mother and son/no. Have I? No. Then how do we know that it's bad/ should I be so mortified? Who me? [...] Yeh I wanna climb back inside my mum. What's wrong with that? It's better than shoving a stick of dynamite up someone's ass and getting a medal for it. So I run back.
>
> (*Greek*, final scene)

Eddie asserts the triump of Nature over Myth and History spinning out a basically anti-Aristotelian type of theatre. Berkoff/Oedipus claims that the function of the theatre in society is to be an instrument of change appealing to the spectator's intellect. The 'unnamable loudly named', the absence of traditional theatre structure contribute to recreate an alienation effect and prolong Bond's, Soyinka's or Heaney's endeavours to promote a new epic drama.

Dramatists wish to make us feel that the performance of ancient plays could have happened in this century. The important impact to the audience is that they watch the play in a critical frame of mind:

> This is the famous *Verfremdungseffekt*. [...] It really means strange-making effects, in other words, a method by which the spectator

is kept detached from the action, safe against the temptation of being sucked into it.[18]

Four dramatists have thus offered their audiences a re-actualization of theatricality trimmed for consumption at the end of the twentieth century. Four serious pieces in an outrageous mode.

Notes

1. Martin Esslin, *An Anatomy of Drama* (New York: Hill and Wang, 1976), p. 118.
2. Edward Bond, *History*, in *Poems, Stories and Essays for* The Woman, in *Bond Plays: 3* (London: Methuen, 1987), p. 271.
3. Edward Bond, *Scenes of War and Freedom: A Short Essay*, in *Bond Plays: 3* (London, Methuen, 1987), pp. 293–5.
4. Martin Esslin, *An Anatomy of Drama*, op. cit., p. 22.
5. Martin Esslin, *An Anatomy of Drama*, op. cit., p. 56.
6. Wole Soyinka, *The Bacchae of Euripides*, Introduction (London: Methuen, 1973), p. vi.
7. Wole Soyinka, *The Bacchae of Euripides*, op. cit., p. vii.
8. Margaret Rose, *Parody/Meta-fiction* (London: Croom Helm, 1979), p. 59.
9. Edward Bond, *A Story*, op. cit., p. 273.
10. Edward Bond, *A Socialist Rhapsody*, op. cit., p. 270.
11. Edward Bond, *Scenes of War and Freedom*, op. cit., in *Bond Plays: 3*, p. 270.
12. Nicole Boireau, 'Beyond Taboos', *Contemporary Theatre Review* (London: Harwood Press, 1996), pp. 88–9.
13. Edward Bond, *Scenes of War and Freedom*, op. cit., p. 296.
14. Edward Bond, *A Socialist Rhapsody*, op. cit., p. 270.
15. Wole Soyinka, *The Bacchae of Euripides*, op. cit., p. vii.
16. Wiveca Sotto, 'Comets and Walking Corpses', in *Black American Literature Forum*, vol. 22, no. 3, autumn 1988, p. 688.
17. Roland Barthes, 'Le Mythe aujourd'hui' in *Mythologies* (Paris: coll. Points, Le Seuil, 1957), p. 215: 'Le mythe transforme l'histoire en nature'.
18. Martin Esslin, *An Anatomy of Drama*, op. cit., p. 65.

2

The Revival of Medieval Forms in Recent Political Drama

Elisabeth Angel-Perez

The Berliner Ensemble's visit to Britain in 1956 probably brought forward the biggest scenic revolution of the twentieth century. A new conception of the theatre swept the English stage. It was based on the rejection of naturalism as well as on the necessity to encompass the whole of a collectivity, instead of just a privileged minority. This visit of paramount importance invited theatre to ponder over a new definition of its own domain.

It is in this light that the revival of interest shown for the Middle Ages by the political dramatists of the 1970s is to be considered. Bertolt Brecht noted that the medieval theatre was altogether close to what he thought theatre should go back to. The medieval theatre is, so to speak, 'Brechtian' before its time. The Middle Ages therefore provided modern dramatists with an example of non-illusionistic drama. This technical interest for the unsophisticated Mysteries and Morality plays also led modern playwrights to seek their material in that remote period. Leaving aside the genuine revivals of medieval plays,[1] as well as the adaptations of medieval masterpieces,[2] most modern playwrights have had a go at rewriting medieval plays. In 1969, John Arden created *The Business of Good Government*, a modern Nativity play, and the same year Edward Bond came up with *Passion*, a rewriting of the biblical Passion. In 1975, David Edgar's *O Fair Jerusalem* put on stage the horrors of the Black Death of 1348, an epoch which also constituted the backdrop for Peter Barnes's *Red Noses* (1985). *Sunsets and Glories* (1990), by the same author, transposed the scene from fourteenth-century France to thirteenth-century Italy, whereas Howard Barker's *The Castle* (1985) and *The Last Supper* (1988) took it back to medieval England. It is quite clear that political theatre, like the phoenix born

15

again out of its own ashes, seems to find in its remote ancestor a way to rejuvenate.

As I shall argue in this chapter, it transpires that modern playwrights are not content with seeking their material in the Middle Ages: they expose the very mechanisms inherent in medieval drama that they find of use to fulfil their own theatrical purpose. Furthermore, recent political drama does not only reveal an explicit interest in these medieval theatrical techniques but it also uses them systematically, even if sometimes unintentionally. My point will be to show that resorting to medieval methodology is a widespread phenomenon that clearly singles out political drama as a definite genre.

The present study analyses the reasons why today's political theatre, while seemingly wanting to break with any kind of tradition, is, in its very essence, palimpsest: it 'grows' on a pre-existing form. The necessity for modern drama to write on drama appears as a means not only to investigate its own mechanisms but also to stage its own social and political preoccupations.

MEDIEVAL TECHNIQUES AT WORK IN RECENT POLITICAL DRAMA

The 1970s mark the heyday of political theatre in Britain. From the late 1960s onwards, governmental subsidies had enabled amateurs to have a try at creating theatre companies at the periphery of the big West End playhouses and of the aestheticism advocated by them. This so-called 'fringe' pioneered an alternative theatre whose characteristics can still be identified as the founding criteria of the more recent political theatre: in contrast with mainstream theatre, the fringe is usually the product of collective work. Technically, it is not centred on the character as a meaningful psychological entity (the Stanislavskian character), nor does it focus on the details of society. On the contrary, it is concerned with the notion of collectivity and group. Ideologically, political dramatists intend to reform society. Initiated by John Arden, Arnold Wesker and Edward Bond, political theatre has promoted such successful playwrights as David Hare, Howard Brenton, Caryl Churchill or Howard Barker, founder of the 'theatre of catastrophe'.

Although extremely diverse, the works of these dramatists all share a number of elements. Their conception of the theatre is precisely the one that prevailed in the medieval theatre. It is built on two golden rules. First, the theatre must above all be democratic; it must address everybody, the society at large, and no longer the happy few; its mission is to put on stage the whole of society in a complete historical cycle. Second, the mode of representation is non-naturalistic: theatre is not meant to delude the audience but to alert them. In the Middle Ages, theatre aimed to bring the spectator to religious conscience and today, theatre is the means to awaken political and social awareness.

Medieval theatre appears as a model to political theatre in all the aspects of its theatricality.

Theatrical space

Like the medieval theatre, political drama is both entertaining and didactic. Though the message to get across is different, the technical means to achieve the projected goals are similar. Hence political dramatists opt out of the conditions of the theatrical event adopted by the mainstream. They revive the medieval custom of 'delocalized' theatre already at work in the alternative theatre of the late 1960s and try to adapt the ubiquitous fringe and amateur theatre to the conditions of proper stages. They manage to find readily accessible venues like the street itself (after the Mobile Street Players), or more frequently pubs, churches or even factories (after Wesker and Center 42). John Arden initiated the movement with *The Business of Good Government* staged in St Michael's church in Brent Knoll (Somerset). Much later, in November 1985, David Edgar's community play, *Entertaining Strangers*, was performed by the inhabitants of Dorchester in St Mary's Church, each enacting more or less his own part. Later, in October 1987, a second version of the play was produced at the Cottesloe Auditorium of the National Theatre. Edgar declared that he had to 'create some kind of metaphorical surrogate for the sheer power of Dorchester's numbers'.[3] Indeed, the original version, created by Ann Jellicoe, involved a cast of 180 people aged three to eighty-five. Furthermore, the political dramatists successfully try to promote daytime theatre, thus contributing to the integration of the theatrical event in everyday life. The famous London pub, the King's Head, has got into the habit of sheltering these special 'matinées'. The pub welcomed (and still does) lunchtime theatre: in 1970, Caryl Churchill's *Shreber's Nervous Illness* and Steven Berkoff's *Lunch* were, among many others, performed there.

Scenic Space

More convincing still is that the resurgence of medieval forms does not only affect the outer structure of the theatre. It contaminates the very stage technique implemented by the political dramatists. Political drama revives both the medieval mobile theatre (on pageant waggons) and the theatre-in-the-round.

Much influenced by the daring experiences of the community theatre in this field – notably Ann Jellicoe and her 'promenade performances' in Lyme Regis (*The Reckoning*,[4] *The Western Women*) and Welfare State's *Travels of Launcelot Quail*[5] – some of the most famous political dramatists have had a try at processional theatre. John Arden himself carried out this experiment with the cyclic *Non-Stop Connolly Show* and with *The Workhouse Donkey*, about which he declared:

> I would have been happy if it had been possible for *The Workhouse Donkey* to have lasted, say, six or seven or thirteen hours (excluding intervals), and for the audience to come and go through the performance, assisted perhaps by a printed synopsis of the play from which they could deduce those scenes and episodes which would interest them particularly, and those which they could afford to miss.
>
> (*Plays: One* [Methuen, 1977], p. 113.)

This experience is in many ways comparable to French director Ariane Mnouchkine's *1789* in Vincennes. The common purpose is to metaphorize the will to bring theatre down into the street.

The medieval theatre wanted to unite people in the adoration of Christ; political dramatists try to gather them around a political and artistic philosophy of life. Just like the medieval theatre-in-the-round, directly inspired by the antique *mappa mundi* (a sphere girdled with water), aimed at encompassing the whole of the Christian congregation, political theatre aims to encompass an aesthetic community. In 1968, Ed Berman's company, Inter-Action, performed John Arden's *The True History of Squire Jonathan* at the Ambiance Lunch-hour Theatre Club in London. The spectacle started with the audience having to step across a pool filled with water, the replica of the medieval moats or ditches that surrounded the theatrical area (*Castle of Perseverance*), and only this rite of initiation, this perambulatory, symbolic baptism, could obtain entry to the aesthetic community. David Hare conceived the set of *A Map of the World* (which opened in London at the Lyttleton Theatre on 20 January 1983) on the same device. The acting area was strictly framed by a circle of international newspapers, the objective being to contain the whole world in a macrorepresentation.

This ubiquitous theatre, allied with techniques of interaction between the spectator and the actors, reveals a wish to bring down the traditional barriers that separate the actors from the audience and to promote a global theatre.

Similarly in the Middle Ages, the aim of the theatre was not only to be accessible to everyone: theatre had to represent everyone at the same time. This is demonstrated in the way medieval theatre stages a whole cyclic history. In the Corpus Christi Cycles, the spectator is shown the whole cycle of biblical episodes, each echoing the other between the Old and the New Testaments. In the Morality plays, the central protagonist is also followed through a cycle – generally a moral one – that takes him from innocence to redemption, that is to regained innocence.

The stage projection of this will to show the whole of a community in a complete cycle consists of the pervasive and highly stylized device of 'simultaneous mansions.' This technique is at work both in the mobile and in the static theatre: the pageant waggons presented the audience at once with Heaven (the pageant upper level where God was generally sitting on a chair held by a system of pullies, enabling him to be brought down to earth), Hell (the street and its Hell mouth) and the intermediate space where man was seen to wander. The medieval rounds displayed yet a more blatant macrocosm or cosmogony with the different 'sedes' or 'scaffolds' towards which the sinner would head according to his moral itinerary.

Political theatre is animated by the same wish to show the whole of a situation at once and, to this effect, it resorts very frequently to simultaneous decors. In the preface to *Armstrong's Last Goodnight* (1964), John Arden explains that 'the play is intended to be played within the medieval convention of "simultaneous mansions". These are three in number and represent the Castle (for the Armstrongs), the Palace (for the Court), and the Forest (for the wild land of the borders)'. Howard Brenton's *Scott of the Antarctic or What God Didn't See* (1971) displays at once Heaven, Westminster Abbey and the sea; David Edgar's *O Fair Jerusalem* is built on a double localization which is not to be altered throughout the play: 'we are in a country church. In a corner, a table, representing the interior of a peasant's cottage'.[6] The emblematized space is the global space; there is no way out. One can easily trace the influence of Beckett (pathological immobility or paralysis of all the beckettian characters), reworking that of the tradition of Greek tragedy where the off-stage, for the character, means death. The protagonist has to make do with what is at his disposal and the audience, while presented with all the aspects of a situation, has to find the solution within the limits of a given universe. This cubist conception of the stage (use of simultaneous mansions; theatre-in-the-round) is widely used even in mainstream dramaturgy now: the works of such scenographers as Jocelyn Herbert (Royal Court) John Napier (*Cats* and Peter Barnes's *The Ruling Class*) or even Ralph Koltai (R.S.C) show it clearly.

AGAINST NATURALISM

The globalizing ambition can only be achieved at the expense of verisimilitude. Hence, medieval theatre is non-naturalistic. It resorts to the very methods and techniques which, in the twentieth century, were theorized by Bertolt Brecht whose key-notion is the 'A-effect' (Alienation-effect). As for political theatre, it is obviously a post-Brechtian theatre whose main credo belongs to the same range: distanciation. In both theatres, space, time, characterization and language all receive a similarly non-naturalistic treatment.

Metatheatre: the distanciated languages

Both dramas confess their theatrical – hence artificial – nature from the very outset of the play. Whereas a Nuntius or Messenger came to 'make room' and clear a 'platea' for the 'game' to take place, political theatre rehabilitates the prologue as a systematic device.[7] The prologue sets the rules of the game and enjoys a privileged status where the audience, acknowledged as such, is directly addressed and the convention of 'the fourth wall'[8] abolished. In Howard Barker's *The Last Supper*, Ella and Dora, the student and the teacher, deliver the prologue as if by way of answer to the medieval 'I am Alpha et Omega, the beginning and the end':

> *Ella:* We found God after all
> Thinking he had disappeared.

Dora: He had not disappeared
      We found him after all
      Like the vagrant under the wall
      He was only out of sight.
Ella: He stood up in the light
      Of all our shame and said
      In the beam of our shame
      Rubbed his eyes and said.
Dora: I am not dead
      I am the public [. . .]
Dora/Ella: Laugh you bastards, this is my creation, laugh.

                  (*The Last Supper* [London, John Calder, 1988])

The novelty in this play consists not in repudiating Nietzsche nor in developing anew the Shakespearian metaphor 'all the world's a stage' but in consecrating the origin of the theatre as liturgical and religious. 'Light' and 'beam' send us back to the light of the genesis and to the footlights of the theatre. The ambivalence of the word 'creation' accounts for and invites this metadiscourse.

Even more convincing is David Edgar's second version of *Entertaining Strangers.*[9] The first tableau of the play is constituted by a theatrical inset which is no other than a mummers' play, with its St George-cum-Dragon episode:

Presenter:
Make room! Make room for us to sport,
For in this place we do resort.
We have not come to laugh or jeer,
But for a pocketful of money and a skinful of beer.
And if you believe not what I say:
Enter old Father Christmas! Clear the way!

Whenever sympathy (illusion) threatens to come back, a rhythmic rupture occurs that irrevocably confronts the spectator with the artificiality (pre-fabrication) of the situation: hence political theatre follows the medieval example and makes an abundant use of such devices as the 'open technique', in the words of J. W. Robinson[10] – direct address to the audience, a vestigial manifestation of the art of preaching[11] – or the 'collective speech' where several characters recite exactly the same words at the same time, in chorus, and therefore provide the audience with information concerning their ideological or moral clan while reminding them forcefully of the illusion of the theatre. This technique is frequently used by most political playwrights, as a means to reinforce the sense of class-bound characters. John Arden often resorts to this device, notably in the prologue and epilogue of *Vandaleur's Folly* or in *The Non-Stop Connolly Show*:

> 1st Employer: We need men
> 3rd Employer: We need women
> 2nd Employer: We need men –
> Grabitall: Ssh – you don't mention Home Rule! You forget your-
> selves gentlemen!
> Employers: Ssh – ssh – we forgot ourselves. [. . .] But Mr Grabit-
> all, nonetheless, sorr . . .
> Because of *da-da* domination
> Upon the trade of our poor *da-da*,
> Creating ruinous competition
> We're put into the sad position –
> (*The Non-Stop Connolly Show*, 1977 [Methuen 1986], p. 70.)

David Edgar uses it in *O Fair Jerusalem* (I, iv, p. 245) while Howard Barker emphasizes the comic, because highly unrealistic and anti-illusionistic, turn of the device.[12]

Sympathy and empathy combine to create a dialectic drama which at once 'shows' and 'tells': illusion is first created and then destroyed. The same purpose is ascribed to the systematic use of hyperformalized languages (poetry, music), a technique shared by both political drama and Mystery and Morality plays. Arden and McGrath compose real ballad-plays (notably Arden's *Serjeant Musgrave's Dance, Armstrong's Last Goodnight* or McGrath's *The Cheviot, the Stag and the Black, Black Oil*) and Bond indulges in writing musical plays (*Restoration*) or proper operas (*The Cat, We Come to the River*). The musical intermezzi constitute an echo to the religious singing that disrupted the dramatic action in the medieval theatre. Their function is similar: they paradoxically highlight a dramatic apex while at the same time breaking the illusion that may have captured the audience. Such privileged moments constitute a show within the show, a spectacular and specular overbid, while insisting on the didactic mission of theatre. The epic (told) disrupts the dramatic (shown) in a dialectic theatre.

Distanciated characters

Just as the language is intended to perform the double-edged function of creating the plot while confessing its artificiality, the character also carries the divergent vectors of distanciation. In the Mystery and Morality plays, the character is archetypal; it stands for the moral category or for the cosmic order to which it belongs: it is obvious in the allegorical Morality plays where Mankind, Humanum Genus, or Everyman are seen to come across Mischief or Death or Mercy; yet this function is also relevant when applied to the Cycles, in which one can already distinguish the types of characters that will pervade the whole history of the theatre: Herod, for instance, is the archetypal villain; most of the time he belongs to tragedy;[13] on the other hand, Mak in the *Second Shepherd's Play* (Towneley 13), embodies the 'comedy villain'; the 'olde cuckolde' Joseph, as well as Noah, contribute to the creation of the type of the 'senex', while Mrs Noah in the Wakefield pageant (Towneley 3) can be identified with the old shrew. In the medieval theatre, all the characters can be regarded as the symbol of the group they epitomize, while in political theatre, the characters are deconstructed as psychologically true and stand as the embodiment of a social type on the stage; they stand as a synecdoche of their vocation or social position: their social function reads as their only surname, like Bondwoman in John Arden's *The Island of the Mighty* (1974) or Grabitall in *The Non-Stop Connolly Show*.

Furthermore, we know that in professional medieval troupes, the same actor performed several characters (doubling) and that in amateur creations, the same character was often played by several actors throughout the lengthy performances of the cycles (up to 15 Virgin Maries, 26 Christs and 10 Gods in the York Cycle). This discontinuity prevented the spectator from granting the characters their sympathy. In political theatre, the polymorphy of the character is not only a practical exigency but also rather an aesthetic choice which serves to destroy the illusion of bourgeois theatre. Heterogeneous characterization is therefore often associated with a revival in the use of masks (Arden's *The Island of the Mighty*, *The Non-Stop Connolly Show*; Brenton's *Christie in Love*, Peter Barnes's *Red Noses*). In medieval drama, masks are used to single out the character on account of a particular goodness or of a disease of the soul.[14] In political theatre, they are an expressionist way to metaphorize a social condition or frame of mind:

The large cast can be contained by a basic company of about a dozen actors, who will each have to play many different roles, not necessarily in their own sex: but stylized, easily-changed, strongly-defined costumes, and possibly stock-masks for recurrent social types (i.e. bourgeois politicians, employers, military officers, etc.) would greatly assist this technique.

(John Arden, *The Non-Stop Connolly Show*, pp. vi–vii)

This short survey clearly reveals that political dramatists constantly resort to medieval themes and techniques as a way to convey their sense of a new dramaturgy and their will to address new situations.

EXPLORING THE PARADOX

How is it that political theatre grows, like an epiphenomenon, on so semiotically opposed a dramaturgy as that of the Middle Ages? The morphological replicability is clear; yet the messages the two theatres want to convey are opposed. While the medieval theatre, directly born of the liturgical drama, has no other mission than to reinforce the established order and the imminence of the divine law on the congregation, political theatre is essentially an atheistic agitprop theatre. Why has it returned to the most ritualized and sacralized dramatic forms to achieve a dramaturgy of subversion? Could one question the *bona fides* of the medieval theatre and wonder if one could detect, even though only scarcely, vestigial traces of a pagan and superstitious thought in Christian medieval drama? The Vices and Devils do certainly show what one shouldn't do . . . yet they do it! Even through a confessed Lord of Misrule, what is 'forbidden' is nevertheless produced on the stage. True as it may be, this is not good enough a reason to explain such as systematic aesthetic bias.

The Middle Ages have never been as popular as they have for the last 20 years. Add to the small selection of the plays I mentioned before such plays as John Arden's *Armstrong's Last Goodnight* (Scottish border in the early sixteenth century) or *The Island of the Mighty* (Britain in the Arthurian days), Peter Barnes's *Noonday Demons* (AD 4th century) or David Rudkin's *The Saxon Shore* (AD 4th century), and it becomes obvious that the Middle Ages continue to exert their fascination on contemporary English playwrights and audiences. Moreover, the huge success of novels and films set at the same periods of history (from bestseller *The Mist of Avallon* to John

Boorman's *Excalibur* or even of *Monty Python and The Holy Grail*) illustrates the general public's revived interest in the period.

Neither is this particular taste for the 'exoticism' of so remote a period enough to account for the enormous surge of the Middle-Ages-set-plays offered to the public during the 1970s. The reasons that account for the revival of the Middle Ages in contemporary political theatre are many. Among others, they combine an attraction for the society of another economic era along with an interest in the origins of the vernacular theatre at a time when theatre, like all other arts, is busy defining its own domain.

From a historical interest to historicization: Means of introspection

That contemporary political dramatists became interested in this particular period of history is indeed significant: it allows them to go back to the one period of modern history that predates the advent of capitalism. The Middle Ages is a pre-capitalistic period,[15] hence it provides the dramatists with 'direct' access to the very basis of the system they reject.

Furthermore, this taste came precisely to match one of the techniques of awareness advocated by Bertolt Brecht and known under the generic name of 'historicization'. This technique aims at providing the audience with a better, because more objective, understanding of a situation by presenting a scenic illustration of a similar issue set in a different period of time. The Middle Ages, because of their temporal remoteness, enter contemporary drama as a political tool.

Post-1960 theatre has indeed been sharing the major postmodernist preoccupation: theatre tries to elucidate the theatrical event; in doing so, it goes back to the very origins of vernacular drama. Hence the interest for the period is not only centred on the social and economic aspects of the time, but also on the very way theatre was made at that time so as to cope with those realities. Theatre becomes the subject-matter of the political contemporay plays in their political and ontological quest.

Theatrical insets: the medieval play at work in political drama

The central question of the role of the artist in society, and more specifically of the playwright and his plays, is inextricably associated with political theatre by essence. This most prominent issue is given voice to in the many theatrical insets to be found in political theatre. Peter Barnes, David Edgar and Edward Bond, among many others, could be singled out as most representative examples. The mummers' play that opens the second version of *Entertaining Strangers* (1988) acts much as an eye-opener. Its presence reveals Edgar's social and theatrical preoccupation. It is in itself the pith of political theatre: the action of the mummers' play being always centred on a symbolic death giving way to a resurrection (like the sun), its presence in Edgar's play epitomizes the rejuvenation of political theatre by medieval theatre. From sheer parody to palimpsest, the theatrical inset shows that literature is universal: its aim is to go on telling us the same thing (non-relevance of a historical vision of literature?).

This is even more visible in *O Fair Jerusalem*[16] whose hypotexts are all taken from medieval literature. Not only does the play include several proper plays-within-a-play – a mixture of Morality and Mystery play with allegories and collective speech, later a parody of *Everyman* (p. 302) – but its dramaturgic bases all emerge from medieval imagery: the different times are those of the major religious festivals (Easter, Whitsun, Corpus Christi, Passion Sunday, and so on); the singer is but an alternative version of the Nuntius of a medieval play; at times he speaks in alliterative poetry ('Kneels in his coldest of cold cells contrite' [. . .] 'And great with groaning good each tree was bent', p. 253); the play is set in a church where three monks are seen using a curtain to carry out their ritual covering and uncovering of the cross, hence sending us back to the liturgical origins of drama; the monks resent deeply men's betrayal in Jesus' Death: using the sheep metaphor (p. 232), they make a definite allusion to the thief of the sheep in the *Secunda Pastorum* of the Wakefield Cycle; the knight that appears on the stage is 'dressed in green' (p. 234) and the love story that binds him to the Lady is yet another version of the Lancelot–Gwenever version. The second part of the play, set in 1948, is centred on the theatre play to commemorate the 600th anniversary of the Black Death. The diverse levels of theatrical insets become properly vertiginous.

Barnes's use of the theatrical insets is likewise systematic. In *Red Noses* (1985), two parodical insets can be found. The first act provides us with a parody of *Everyman*, whereas the second act offers us a revolutionary Nativity Play. Barnes holds that the true topic of his play is 'the birth of the show biz'.[17] While Barnes carries out his parody of these two medieval genres (Morality and Mystery plays), he also stages the public's reaction to them. The Morality *Everyman* is found not revolutionary enough – 'they haven't shown the world as 'tis or how we can change it' (I, xi) – whereas the nativity parody is seen as too revolutionary – "Tisn't funny till we throw out the old rubbish and gold and silver rust. Then it'll be funny'(II, ix). As Bernard Dukore has it, it entails that the Pope slaughters, as Herod the innocents, all the actors.

Last, in Edward Bond's *The Fool*, the dislocation of the acts' and scenes' structure promotes a sequence of tableaux to be seen as almost autonomous entities. As a succession of playlets, they are echoed by the mummers' play given by Clare and his friends at the beginning of Act I. The mummers' play is not only proleptic in the way that it gives the spectator a hint at the technique followed by the archplay itself but it is also prophetic in that, in the words of Lou Lappin 'the play-within-a-play creates an ironic and prophetic counterpoint to the fate of Clare.'[18] Yet, if the technique of the theatrical inset is far from a brand new phenomenon – there is all about Europe a strong tradition of dramas on drama that appears in history almost as soon as drama itself (see Aristophanes' *The Birds* and *The Frogs*), develops in the shape of drama on ritual during the Middle Ages, to become a genre of its own from the end of the seventeenth to the eighteenth centuries (from Buckingham's *The Rehearsal* to Sheridan's *The Critic*), fostering the genres of satire, parody and burlesque up to the twentieth-century wit comedies of Tom Stoppard (*The Real Inspector Hound* or *Travesties* or *Rosencrantz and Guildenstern Are Dead*) – what's new with the modern political playwrights is that they turn the metonymical presence of the 'play within' into a political tool.

The political theatre of the 1970s rejects all forms of delusion: its ideological aim is to arouse a political consciousness among the people. Similarly, the structure it chooses to vectorize this ideology is as much deprived of theatrical illusion as theatre itself can allow. However, social realism is not projected on the stage through realism but through another form of stylization: a set of devices whose aim is to confess the artificiality of the theatre while turning this artificiality into yet another form of spectacle. While asserting the 'playful' and 'gameful' nature of their plays, the political dramatists break free from the established convention of mainstream theatre and pick up the threads of a long-forgotten practice: drama on drama.

Contemporary theatre explores its own nature – the seams do not only show, they are made conspicuous – and as such, it is part of postmodernist aesthetics. When political, the effect is enhanced. Political dramatists paradoxically resort to the primitive methods and ritualizations of a precapitalistic era so as to expose the intricacies of a postcapitalistic world. They ignore (through an aesthetic bias as well as for financial reasons) the sophisticated techniques of this half of the century and long to recover the might of a nascent theatricality.

These very distant, yet-so-close, dramatic poles share a common credo. Both the medieval and the recent political dramatists believe in the perfectibility of mankind. Medieval theatre aims to improve man; political drama, after Brecht, believes in the capacity of the artist to change the world. Once the hero of the Morality play has atoned for his sins, the spectator should do the same; once the revolution has taken place on the stage, it should go down to the street! To this effect, rite and ritualization of the myth remains the best didactic means. Political theatre revives the dramaturgy of medieval theatre as if, through the discrepancy between the complex society it stages (the signification) and the simplicity of the medium chosen to this effect (the significans), it could more vehemently express its non-adhesion to the social framework that subsidizes it. Because they build up their plays on medieval theatre, the political dramatists achieve a narcissistic, autotelic drama whose specular nature reactivates the worn-out ideologies.

Notes

1. Such as that of the Mystery plays at the Barbican (Tony Harrison's *Mysteries*) or at the York Festival (Meg Twycross).
2. In 1969, Pip Simmons and his Theatre Group, formerly Drury Lane Arts Lab, adapted Chaucer's *Pardoner's Tale* at the London Come Together Festival; in 1973, the Freehold Theatre put *Beowulf* on the boards.
3. David Edgar, *Entertaining Strangers*, 2nd edn (London: Methuen, 1988).
4. Ann Jellicoe's *The Reckoning* (1977) was set in a school playground. The action was set on 'three raised areas of scaffoldings for seats and three small raised stages. About a third of the audience sat, the rest promenaded with the action taking place among them.' Ann Jellicoe, preface to David Edgar, *Entertaining Strangers* (London: Methuen, 1986).
5. The theatre company named Welfare State specialized in combining

both processional drama and theatre-in-the-round. Their best-known creation bore the meaningful name of *The Travels of Launcelot Quail* and during a whole month Welfare State coordinated performances all along the Arthurian route between Glastonbury and Saint Michael's Mount. The trip was punctuated by theatrical stops where, under a round tent, Launcelot would have to fight against the modern monsters of unemployment or nuclear threat in the shape of dragons or of all kinds of fancy animals borrowed from the extraordinary medieval bestiary.

6. David Edgar, *Plays: One* (London: Methuen, 1987), p. 231.
7. Clifford Leech notes that the prologue disappears quite clearly at the end of the sixteenth century for the very reason that 'there was no simple (moral) generalisation to offer in the prologue and to come back to in the epilogue.' See 'Shakespeare's Prologues and Epilogues', *Studies in Honour of T. W. Balwin*, ed. Don Cameron Allen (Urbana: University of Illinois Press, 1958), especially pp. 154–7.
8. The concept of the fourth wall, that is the audience as fourth wall, is at work in most mainstream plays. It is one of the essential targets of Brecht's dramaturgy.
9. David Edgar, *Entertaining Strangers*, 2nd edn (London: Methuen, 1988), p. 1.
10. The term 'open technique' is taken from J. W. Robinson, *Medieval English Dramaturgy*, PhD, Glasgow University, 1961.
11. The similarities between the stage and the *artes predicandi* are numerous. The prologue acts as the sermon, it epitomizes the central meaning of the play which works as an 'exemplum.'
12. See, for instance, the Workmen or the two Thieves in *Golgo*, in *Seven Lears* and *Golgo* (London: John Calder, 1990).
13. Except in *The Shearmen* and *Taylors' Play* where he is presented in a puppet-like manner 'raging in the pageant and in the street also' (London: EETS 1957), p. 27.
14. Beautiful gilded masks for beauty and bounty, painted masks with spots for sin: see Meg Twycross and Sarah Carpenter, 'Masks in the Medieval Theatre' in *Medieval English Theatre*, 1, III (1981), pp. 29–36.
15. See Fernand Braudel, *Civilisation matérielle, Economie et Capitalisme 15ème et 18ème siècles*, Tome 2: 'Les Jeux de l'échange' (Paris: Armand Colin, 1979).
16. David Edgar, *O Fair Jerusalem*, in Edgar, *Plays One*.
17. In Bernard Dukore, *The Theatre of Peter Barnes* (London: Heinemann Educational, 1981), p. 39.
18. Lou Lappin, *The Art and Politics of Edward Bond* (New York: Peter Lang, 1987), p. 74.

3

Cultural Transformations of Subversive Jacobean Drama: Contemporary Sub-Versions of Tragedy, Comedy, and Tragicomedy
Klaus Peter Müller

A unique dialogue between the present and the past takes place in those plays written by contemporary playwrights that are either based on or are related in particular ways to the theatre of the seventeenth century. Current drama on drama of the past elucidates both our contemporary perspectives on drama and our various positions towards dramatic works of the past. Drama on drama of this kind provides the means for comparative analysis and highlights the differences and the similarities between the specific ages and the individual writers concerned.

What is it that attracts current writers to an old play? What is taken over from the original text? Which things are left out or are changed to catch the contemporary mood and to reflect present ways of thinking and writing drama? This chapter will try to give answers to these and similar questions that have been raised in the larger context of adaptations. Adaptations are the results of revisions, of temporal, spatial, individual and – generally speaking – cultural transformations. In re-viewed plays, the world is looked at from a new angle; the vision has changed, and a specific culture is transformed by the new perspective. Another, different cultural text has been created.

As the world, a specific culture, is not only reflected and represented in plays, but also (re-)created and (re-)constructed, each play reveals the basic elements of its culture, the fundamental forms in which meaning is created and expressed. This chapter will examine revisions of plays as cultural transformations of specific *forms of meaning*. Three most typical forms of drama have been selected for this purpose: tragedy, comedy and tragicomedy. These forms have different meanings in different cultural contexts. One could also say, they are different forms whose shape and meaning depend on the culture in which the forms appear.

Drama reveals what human beings see and do not see, what their vision of life is. Like literature and art in general, drama is an epistemological metaphor, a human construct that reveals the way in which human beings understand and describe the world they live in. The perspective chosen in this book and expressed by the term 'drama on drama' is particularly interesting in this epistemological and anthropological context, because it implies that human understanding has been re-shaped and re-viewed during the course of history. These re-visions of human understanding and of the creation of meaning are intriguing not only as literary phenomena of intertextuality but also as symptoms of the perennial human process of 'interpreting' and 'writing cultures.'[1] Through the perspective 'drama on drama' in the form of contemporary revisions of Jacobean drama, we are thus looking at particularly intriguing ways in which humanity has made meaning. We will see, how the meanings of the dramatic terms 'tragedy', 'comedy' and 'tragicomedy' are dependent upon the culture in which these words are used. For this purpose, three representative Jacobean plays will be compared with their contemporary revisions: Thomas Middleton's tragedy *Women Beware Women* (c.1621) and Howard Barker's 1986 version, Middleton's comedy *A Mad World My Masters* (c.1605–7) and Barrie Keeffe's 1977 revision, and William Shakespeare's tragicomedy or 'problem play' *Measure for Measure* (c.1604), which will be contrasted with Howard Brenton's play, first performed in 1972.

SUBVERSIVE SOCIAL TRAGEDY RE-*DEFINED*

As meanings are always defined within a particular culture, there can be no definitions that are universally correct. Thus, the Aristotelian concept of tragedy can only help as a counterfoil with the aid of which specific, culturally determined meanings can be differentiated. It is useful to know the basic Jacobean understanding of the word 'tragedy', but it is more important to see how the word

is actually applicable to a specific play, what the actual form of tragedy a certain writer has created is really like.

Aristotle's definition included 'an action that is serious' and complete in itself; tragedy should arouse 'pity and fear' and thus 'ac-
complish its catharsis of such emotions'. There might be a 'Peripety
or Discovery' in the action or not, but there should definitely be
a change in the hero's fortune 'from happiness to misery'. It is
extremely important for Aristotle that this misfortune 'is brought
upon him not by vice and depravity but by some error of judgement,'
the 'tragic flaw' or 'hamartia'.[2]

Jacobean tragedy can quite generally be characterized by its emphasis on society rather than on an individual tragic hero. J. W.
Lever (1971, p. xvii) thus speaks of *The Tragedy of State* and main-
tains that in Jacobean tragedy 'it is not primarily the conduct of the
individual, but of the society which assails him, that stands condemned'. Andrew Sanders (1994, p. 169) discusses 'the advent of a
theatrical new age' in the same context and characterizes the new
epoch by the very fact 'that drama can represent a shared and
deficient humanity rather than elevate and isolate the tragic hero'.
Alexander Leggatt's (1988, p. 147) description of Middleton's tragedy also emphasizes the lack of a tragic hero and concludes that
'the result is a tragedy that has many affinities with satiric comedy:
the wide focus, quite unlike Shakespeare's concentration on a single
hero; the heavy irony; the lack of any compensating dignity'.

Middleton's *Women Beware Women* indeed does not possess a tragic
hero. As in his comedies, the characters are after material gain. The
intrigues have as their aim the acquisition of money, property and
sex. There is no yearning in the protagonists for 'something more
basic and intangible' that defines tragic heroes for Leggatt (1988,
p. 56) and which he finds in Shakespeare: 'an assertion of their own
identities, in which their values, their destinies, and their relations
with other people are all bound up'. People's identities in *Women
Beware Women* are defined by their wealth and their social status.
Their world is dominated by a mercantile value system. Even human relations are 'reduced to commodity transactions' (Leggatt,
1988, p. 146).

The play emphasizes this materialistic aspect from the very
beginning. In the first scene, Leantio, a merchant's clerk, has just
returned from a business trip on which he married Bianca. He calls
her 'the most unvalued'st purchase' (I, l. 12), his 'treasure' (l. 14),
which he intends to hide in 'obscurest places' (l. 166), in order to

keep her 'from all men's eyes' (l. 170) and thus from attracting 'thieves' (l. 167). He fails, however, loses Bianca to the Duke and is comforted by Livia, a rich gentlewoman, who provides him with her love and wealth. But Leantio is killed by Livia's brother Hippolito, who wants to preserve the family's apparent honour and at the same time make it possible for the Duke to marry Bianca. As Livia seeks revenge and Bianca tries to kill the Duke's brother, the Cardinal, for speaking out against the marriage, the play ends with six persons killed. The Cardinal voices the play's moral at the end: 'Sin, what thou art these ruins show too piteously. / Two kings on one throne cannot sit together, / But one must needs down, for his title's wrong; / So where lust reigns, that prince cannot reign long' (V, 2, ll. 222–5).

There is no tragic hero in this play and only one motivation drives all characters on, the lust for physical and material possessions. This lust creates desires that are 'not so much grand passions as itches that need to be scratched' (Leggatt, 1988, p. 141). There is not any heroic or tragic action, and nobody experiences a tragic recognition. Leggatt (1988, p. 150) is, therefore, quite right, when he concludes that in Middleton, 'we are brought in the end to see not the characters' greatness but their littleness.'

Middleton's tragedy corresponds to Jacobean definitions of the genre above all in two respects: in its structure ('tragedies begin in calm and end in tempest'), and in its supposed effect on spectators, namely 'to terrify men from the like abhorred practices'.[3] The behaviour to be avoided is the one that characterizes the entire play and the whole of society as portrayed, which is the mean desire that dominates everybody and only too evidently leads to death. Bianca explicitly expresses the lethal effect of this desire once more in the final scene: 'So my desires are satisfied, / I feel death's power within me' (V, 2, ll. 200f).

The serious moral judgement expressed by the Cardinal in the play's final four lines applies to the whole of society. No compensating dignity is presented in the play itself. In this sense, the play avoids an open confrontation between good and bad qualities. But its presentation of evil is nevertheless subversive. *Women Beware Women* contains the 'subversive knowledge of political domination' that Jonathan Dollimore has depicted as the essential element of all *'Radical Tragedy'*.[4] As there is no outspoken, direct confrontation in the play itself, though, the degree of Middleton's subversiveness depends very much on the spectator's interpretation and evaluation

of the tragedy. Howard Barker's version is far more radical and does
not avoid confrontation.

Barker changes Middleton's five-act tragedy into a play with two
parts. This is in line with a widespread tendency in contemporary
plays where the two-act structure is almost predominant. This structure can be used to emphasize the identity, similarity or even mo-
notony in people's behaviour (as in Beckett's *Waiting for Godot*),
or to underline contrast, difference and change. Barker employs the
second of these two possibilities.

Part One of his play consists almost entirely of lines literally taken
over from Middleton. Barker makes extensive cuts, leaving out passages that repeat statements already made or that are metaphorical examples of the world view held by the characters. Lines that
explicitly speak of the main problem dealt with in the tragedy, such
as III, 3, l. 168, '[people] commend virtue, but who keeps it?', are
dropped. Barker also changes Middleton's verse into prose. But he
uses all the main characters, he keeps the imagery and preserves
most of the scene divisions up to the final scene in Part One. In this
Scene Eight, Barker rearranges passages from IV, 1 and IV, 3 in
Middleton's play, and he also makes the first change in the play's
plot by not having Leantio killed but rather have him speak the last
words of Part One, which are taken over from Middleton (IV, 1, l.
92, 94f, ll. 103f): 'Why, here's sin made and never a conscience put
to it! Why do I talk to thee of sense or virtue that art as dark as
death? To an ignorance darker than thy womb I leave thy perjured
soul. A plague will come!' (p. 18)

The seven scenes in Part Two are all Barker's inventions. There
are significant changes in the plot and the characterization as well
as in the dramatic and tragic quality of the play. The language now
is contemporary and typical of Barker's outspokenness with regard
to sexuality. Leantio is 'undressed' on the stage at the beginning of
Part Two and speaks about his relationship with Livia: 'We fuck the
day to death. And suffocate the night with tossing. Time stands
still, she says so. Rolls back, even. As for the bed, it's our whole
territory, the footboard and the headboard are the horizons of our
estate, rank with the flood of flesh. Oh, beautiful odour of the utter
fuck!' (p. 19)

Livia has undergone a 'Transformation' (p. 19). She now despises
'this bunting clinging to a dirty world' (p. 19) and the 'thin and
sour longings' of its inhabitants. This world 'hates passion', which
is exactly what Livia has found. It makes her hate her former life,

and she expresses her new will at the end of Scene One in Part Two: 'All hate your lives and change the world!' (p. 20) The Ward, who was an imbecile in Part One and throughout Middleton's play, is also changed. He was 'less coarse-spoken' (p. 23) before, and he now – like Livia – expresses his hate for people's 'shallow ardours' (p. 22); he finds in the people around him common 'human vice' and recognizes them as 'beasts' (p. 23). His wife Isabella is very surprised about this change and about her father, who 'gladly sells me to an idiot, but finding he has mind, is all a-scuttle to rescue me' (p. 24).

Mind and passion, great desires, are qualities that are not accepted in this society. They are the features put into the foreground in Part Two of Barker's play, and they change some of the characters into people who through these attributes possess a redeeming power and a compensating dignity. Livia is the person most emphatically changed. She wants no longer to tease society, but radically change it. She now even loathes 'wit', and in her new condition she feels 'utterly alive' (p. 27). What for a man like Hippolito is 'madness' (p. 26) in her, is presented in the play as 'health', as no longer being 'utterly corrupt', but as being 'alive' and determined to alter society (p. 27).

The need to change society is explicitly voiced in the play by Sordido, another character Barker has considerably transformed. Sordido rants about conformity in the present society, where everybody says 'Yes' to everything 'and no is only fit for whispering.' He recognizes that Livia, too, is 'a no'. Their opposition to conformism, shallow ardours, thin and sour longings is the reason why both of them are 'no democrat[s]' (p. 28). Their great passion makes them violent, and they intend to alter the society by doing violence to the person who represents society best, Bianca.

Violence is of great importance in all of Barker's plays. The truism that we live in an extremely brutal society has led him to use savagery abundantly in his work.[5] This has raised much criticism. Violence on stage is indeed a great problem intellectually, aesthetically and also ethically. Our own time has become especially alert to violence towards women, and it is, therefore, helpful to learn what a woman thinks about this element in Barker's plays. Ruth Shade (1984) shows that it is absolutely necessary to see individual acts of violence in their contexts, both in society and in Barker.

Barker is quite aware of this problem, and he has Livia and Leantio discuss it in Scene Six. While Livia is convinced that they will 'save'

Bianca through violence, Leantio is not so sure: 'Save her! By rape!
Since when was rape salvation?'. Livia's answer puts the violent
act into the context of Barker's idea of tragedy as the 'Theatre of
Catastrophe':

> Leantio, whole cliffs of lies fall down in storms. By this catas-
> trophe she'll grope for knowledge her ambition hides from her.
> And simultaneously, Sordido's crime will rock the state off its
> foundations, which is erected on such lies as ducal marriages.
> [. . .] We liberate her from herself, and at the same stroke, un-
> leash contempt on all we've come to hate.
>
> (p. 30)

After the act, committed by Sordido who is killed by the Duke
for spoiling his 'property' (p. 33), Bianca forgives Livia, rejects the
Duke, experiences utter loneliness, but acknowledges that 'Catastrophe is also birth'. While she lost her identity at the end in
Middleton's play, she has now become aware of her own responsibility for her identity and declares: 'I have to find my life!' (p. 36).
There is no moralizing at the end of this play and no solution to
any of the problems presented. Whereas traditional tragedy was
often 'a restatement of public morality', Barker (1989, p. 54f) insists
that in his 'theatre of Catastrophe there is no restoration of certi-
tudes.' It is rather 'the audience which is freed into authority'. 'The
audience itself must be encouraged to discover meaning, and in
so doing, begin some form of moral reconstruction' (Barker, 1989,
p. 49).

Barker gives his audience 'rights of interpretation'. Just as the
dramatist's only obligation is 'to his own imagination', the audience is led to use its imaginative faculties productively, constructively and in new ways (Barker, 1989, p. 48). There is no intention
of tailoring the spectators' thoughts to an ideology or to anything
that could provide comfort and the feeling of security. Imagination
is recognized by the Cardinal in *Women Beware Women* (p. 30) as the
only real danger to society. In Barker's theory of the theatre, it has
an equally central position as the decisive quality both in the playwright and the audience. It is connected with 'complexity, ambiguity, and [. . .] potential disorder' (Barker, 1989, p. 31). 'An artist
uses imagination to speculate about life as it is lived, and proposes,
consciously or unconsciously, life as it might be lived' (Barker, 1989,
p. 33).

Barker's theatre does not offer solutions to problems of reality; it does not even try to describe reality objectively, but rather notices 'the absence of objective truths' (Barker, 1989, p. 80). Positively speaking, it is 'life imagined, it is possibility and not reproduction' (Barker, 1989, p. 28). His, therefore, is not a realistic theatre. Livia also explicitly rejects 'Realism', but she embraces action (p. 30). The action Barker's drama wants to induce in the spectator is a changed perception of life. This demands a new type of tragedy: 'We require a different form of tragedy in which the audience is encouraged, not by facile optimism or useless reconciliation, but by the spectacle of extreme struggle and the affirmation of human creativity. Failure is unimportant, the attempt is all' (Barker, 1989, p. 24).

Barker's new tragedy does not represent any specific truth. It also does not mirror life. Often it paradoxically 'derives its meaning precisely from the dissolution of coherent meaning' (Barker, 1989, p. 54). It thus is ambiguous and controversial, and – like all great art for Barker – it does not imitate life, but it complicates it (Barker, 1989, pp. 29–35). The audience is called upon to re-imagine reality in new ways. An imaginative reconstruction of reality is the most important objective of this new drama. It is to be achieved by the beauty and terror of the catastrophe: 'The audience, forced to review, re-feel, a 'wrong' action, is provoked and alerted, and launched unwillingly into consideration of morality, rather than subdued by the false solidarities of critical realism' (Barker, 1989, p. 62).

'Morality' and 'reconstruction,' or 'moral reconstruction' (Barker, 1989, p. 49) are key words in the poetics of this new tragedy. In imaginative catastrophe, in tragedy that abounds with terror and beauty and thus incites the audience to use its own imagination, 'lies the possibility of reconstruction' for Barker (1989, p. 55). Barker thus belongs into the context of constructivism as it is currently discussed in various areas of the humanities and the sciences. He has warned the author of this article against too much idealism in this context, but constructivism is not more idealistic than he is himself. Rather, it – like Barker – is idealistic and realistic at the same time.[6]

With his emphasis on strong audience participation, on the need for spectators to re-view traditional ways of perceiving and understanding the world, and with his unusual insistence on the need for a new *tragic* theatre, Howard Barker's position is very uncommon and even sometimes termed 'elitist'.[7] At a time when people have spoken of the 'Death of Tragedy'[8] and when the most successful theatrical form is the musical, Barker's insistence on tragedy deserves particular attention. For him, it is not the form that expresses conventional morality, the dominant ideology or a permanent, ahistorical truth. Rather, it is the form that tries to break with conventions, to overcome conformism and to bring about changes in all areas of contemporay culture. This culture is authoritarian for Barker; it is 'a culture of banality' trying to stifle imagination. It is 'philistine', rigid and simplistic, and, therefore, 'the complexity of tragedy becomes a source of resistance' (Barker, 1989, pp. 12, 14).

Barker chose Middleton's play because of 'its obsessive linkage between money, power and sex,' thus because of the traditional elements of the city comedy.[9] The society for him is almost identical with the country Middleton faced: 'England in this era is a money and squalor society, also. The connections were obvious' (Barker, 1989, p. 23). But Barker's definition of 'tragedy' is substantially different from Middleton's. His tragic form is not only subversive, but seeks explicit confrontation and outspokenly demands radical change. Barker is clearly not willing to 'tolerate the deforming social effects' of the society depicted. He has stronger characters with grand passions, desires and visions of alternative lives. And he underlines the constructive and imaginative capacities of human beings that can bring about a different society, a new world and a less materialistic culture: 'I always insist people can be saved' (Barker, 1989, p. 23).

SELF-REFLEXIVE, PARADOXICAL COMEDY RE-*PLAYED*

Like his tragedy, Middleton's city comedies 'present a low view of humanity' (Leggatt, 1988, p. 147). The plot is again concerned with sex, money and power, and the characters represent an even greater range of the social stratum. Comedy is meant not only to entertain but also to instruct. Thomas Heywood's 'definition of the comedy' describes it as a 'discourse consisting of divers institutions, comprehending civil and domestic things, in which is taught what in our lives and manners is to be followed, what to be avoided'.[10] Ben Jonson calls a comedy 'an image of the times [sporting] with human follies', and Middleton's comedy has even been described as being ' "photographic", [...] it introduces us to the low life of the time.' Middleton is thus to a certain extent 'a great recorder.'[11]

Middleton's comedy *A Mad World, My Masters* records the follies of his time and presents them as madness. It is important to notice that 'madness' has remained a highly significant motif in literature, which in our time has been used in very serious contexts rather than in an atmosphere of comic fun.[12] The 'masters' in the play are people like Master Harebrain, a citizen, who, like Leantio, tries to keep his wife from having social contacts and confines her to his house so that she says about herself: 'I am a prisoner yet, o' th' master's side' (I, 2, p. 106).

But the masters are by no means autonomous and free. On the contrary, they are mastered themselves by the very things they use to subdue others. Mistress Harebrain makes this clear for the audience in the same context in which she speaks about her own confinement: 'My husband's jealousy, / That masters him, as he doth master me' (I, 2, pp. 107f). Middleton's play makes extensive use of this principle, one that has been known since Terence's comedy *Heauton-timorumenos* (163 BC) and is expressed in the title of the ancient work which can be translated as: 'He who punishes himself'. The principle (and the title) means that the same thing which people greedily strive for is also that by which they themselves will suffer. A similar paradox is thus at work in Middleton's comedy to that found in his tragedy: the stubborn endeavour to possess something and preserve it eventually and necessarily leads to loss and destruction. Mistress Harebrain is confronted with this paradoxical situation without grasping its intellectual scope when she asks herself: 'What shall become of me? My own thoughts doom me!' (IV, 4, p. 44). Follywit is the last person in the play to learn that he has been caught by tricks very similar to his own: 'Tricks are repaid, I see' (V, 2, p. 287). The last two lines of the play express the moral connected with this principle: 'Who lives by cunning, mark it, his fate's cast; / When he has gull'd all, then is himself the last' (V, 2, pp. 297f).

The comedy makes fun of desperate and futile attempts of human beings who try to conduct their lives without observing the basic rules of human behaviour. It is folly and madness not to know or not to acknowledge those rules of life that people should know, be aware of and obey in their actions. Master Penitent Brothel, a country gentleman, names the values that his time has come to disregard and has replaced with their opposites: 'None for religion, all for pleasure burn. / Hot zeal into hot lust is now transform'd, / Grace into painting, charity into clothes, / Faith into false hair, and put off as often' (IV, 4, pp. 61–4). He also presents the solution: 'There's nothing but our virtue knows a mean' (IV, 4, p. 65). This is the contemporary and traditional solution to all the extremes presented in tragedy and comedy: the idea of the Aristotelian 'mean' in connection with the concept of Christian faith, hope and charity.[13]

In Act Four of Middleton's *A Mad World, My Masters* most of the characters seem to relent: Penitent Brothel, Mistress Harebrain, Sir Bounteous Progress and the Courtesan seem to have given up their sexual desires. Only Follywit persists and continues to act in accordance with his name. He even asks, 'shall I be madder now than ever I have been?' (IV, 5, pp. 11f), and unknowingly he is, by marrying the Courtesan whom he takes to be a virgin. Act Four ends with renewed emphasis on the values propagated by this comedy, when the Mother congratulates her daughter on her marriage: 'Thou'st wedded youth and strength, and wealth will fall: Last thou'rt made honest.' The Courtesan concludes: 'And that's worth 'em all' (IV, 5, pp. 140–2).

Middleton's choice of a dramatic form that allows him to go beyond this ending of Act Four is a most subtle one, the play within the play. This play is staged by Follywit, who is extremely ingenious in this situation and turns reality into a play. He is the only actor who is aware of this staging of reality, of which he is at the same time the director. His company, who does not know that they are acting, consists of his friends who have just been arrested by a constable. By pretending that this arrest is only a theatrical performance, Follywit avoids disgrace for himself and his wife, because the spectators do not know that the acting is reality. Through this device, Middleton again emphasizes the delusion of his characters who take reality for sport, for 'fiction' (IV, 5, p. 99), and for that which in truth it is not. It is them who are 'in a wood' (V, 2, p. 143), who are mad and confused. In the end, the characters are even forced to admit this: 'none here but was deceiv'd in't' (V, 2, p. 178).

But Middleton's irony goes even beyond this point of revealing the characters' delusion and madness. The masters in the play are not the masters of the play. The 'Masters' of the play's title are above all the spectators of Middleton's comedy. Sir Bounteous has already given an indication of this, when addressing these masters on a bare stage describing his own situation: 'An old man's venery is very chargeable, my masters; there's much cookery belongs to't' (IV, 2, pp. 30f). In the end, Sir Bounteous praises the actors' wit and describes the audience's response to the play in the play in such a way that it is clearly also a comment on the play itself, on Middleton's wit and on the spectators of *A Mad World, My Masters*: 'Troth, I commend their wits. Before our faces make us asses, while we sit still and only laugh at ourselves!' (V, 2, pp. 180f).

The self-reflexive and double-faced element that already exists in the basic paradox of the play, the *Heautontimorumenos* situation where the person who gratifies himself also punishes himself through the same means, is thus repeated through and in the play itself. The play not only entertains its spectators; it chides them at the same time, and by the very same things that are also experienced as funny. This paradoxical double-facedness is the foundation of the irony that permeates Middleton's entire comedy. It underlies and underlines the twin intentions of the comedy to entertain and to instruct.

Gulling and thus involving the audience is also a key element in Barrie Keeffe's version of *A Mad World, My Masters*. In his 'Author's Note' to the play, Keeffe emphasizes the need to adapt the script to local concerns, current affairs and the news of the day, as well as to national idiosyncrasies. He especially liked the Canadian 'opening "con"' in getting an audience not known to stand for God Save The Queen before a play to do just that. It involved playing enough of "O Canada" until the entire house was on its feet before switching to Britain's National anthem' (no p.). Keeffe is thus utterly aware of the relevance of cultural contexts in any appeal to an audience's response. And he also consciously makes fun of these cultural peculiarities. He plays with them in order to put a distance between the audience and their ordinary, 'natural' response to cultural signifiers.

Keeffe's playing with cultural signifiers begins with the play's title, which evokes the tradition of the city comedy, and it continues in the list of the *dramatis personae*, where this tradition is taken up as well but is altered to include cultural and historical changes: there is '*a gentleman of The City*', but also '*a gentleman of the press*', '*a superintendent of Scotland Yard*', '*a Trades Union official*', and '*a most noble nobelwoman*'. Humorous wordplay and a historical extension of the traditional list of characters mark Keeffe's use of the cultural signifier 'city comedy'.

Keeffe does not employ any of Middleton's characters. He creates a new plot, and his language is the colloquial English of the 1970s. Keeffe also changes Middleton's five-act structure into a two-act

form. Act One has nine scenes, Act Two eight. The play is set in the
north of London, in Hackney.

As there are new characters, there are also a new social structure and new jobs: the occupations of the policeman, the Trades
Union official and the journalist in the modern sense of the term
were created in the nineteenth century, while the 'social worker'
(p. 9), Janet, and the 'chairman of a vast consortium' (p. 54), Horace
Claughton, her father and the gentleman of the City, are representatives of the twentieth century. So is Bill Sprightly, the professional
sportsman, who, however, neither practises nor takes part in any
competition. In addition, there are still grandmothers, mothers,
fathers, and children, but we are already past 'the disintegration of
closely knit working class families' and in the age of 'the nuclear
family' (p. 9).

The 'social problems have escalated' (p. 9), and problems exist now
that the seventeenth century did not know, such as drug addiction,
pill popping, 'asset stripping' (p. 12), and immigration. There are
new food and drinks characteristic of this culture, such as 'bacon
sandwiches and Nescaff' (p. 11), 'Remy Martin' (p. 15), or 'Johnny
Walker Black Label' (p. 29). In fact, the play abounds with cultural
signifiers that Keeffe uses in order to play with them and to characterize individual persons as well as the age itself: 'the cultural
revolution' (p. 31), 'Madam Mao' (p. 67), Dusty Springfield, Vanessa
Redgrave, the Sex Pistols, the Tremeloes, Graham Parker, 'hippies'
(p. 56), 'the Margaret Thatcher cabaret', 'MI5', Fiat 'Panda' (p. 55),
and so on.

The 'Silver Jubilee' of Elizabeth II in 1977 provides the specific
historical background to Keeffe's play, which the author began
writing in 1976. The plot is still concerned with the traditional elements of the city comedy: sex, money and power. An old woman,
Grandma Sprightly, and her working-class family try to get money
from a factory, an insurance company, or, to be more accurate, from
the representative of these companies, Claughton, the gentleman of
the city. Claughton is also the citizen about to be knighted. The
traditional motif of social mobility, especially of citizens trying to
enter the gentry, is thus used by Keeffe, too.

While there have been changes in the cultural context and the
cultural signifiers, the basic motives and actions of human beings
have remained the same: there is still lying and thieving, sex and
lust, pride and conceit. Money is confused with 'happiness' (p. 20),
and morality depends entirely on economic profitability: 'Where's

your sense of moral decency? – Under the terms of my company's contract' (p. 25). The citizen, the policeman, the journalist, the professional sportsman, the grandmother and mother do everything for money, fame and fortune. Even the persons who are not lured by money offer no positive alternatives: Charlie, the 'minstrel', is a drug addict, and Janet, the social worker and 'friend of the poor and needy', is a rich man's daughter doing a 'special social study [. . .] on bereavement' (p. 13). She cannot cope with this reality in which she has to deal with the social problems created by her father and the economy as well as the politics he represents (p. 72). She therefore tries to kill herself, but the sleeping pills she takes are in reality aphrodisiacs that make her 'feel so randy' (p. 73) that she becomes even more lustful than her father.

Delusions about reality are as frequent in Keeffe's play as in Middleton's comedy. The play within the play announced at the end of Act One and meant to bring Claughton down emphasizes the misapprehension of reality as strongly as the same device did in Middleton. Keeffe even uses this means twice. At the beginning of Act Two it consists of a hilarious mixture of the Nine O'Clock News on BBC-TV and a striptease show. Keeffe's combination of two very diverse components of contemporary culture is another example of the playfulness in his use of cultural signifiers. Combining opposite, contrastive or very divergent elements into one situation is also the general stock device of comedy and the comic. Freud (1940) has extensively shown that jokes and wittiness always combine reason and emotion, the conscious and the unconscious. Keeffe uses this combination, too, and he emphasizes the emotional, sexual element. He even farcically exaggerates it (pp. 50f).

The play within the play is successful as a device to delude Claughton and ruin his reputation, but as the material evidence of Claughton's corruption has been stolen, the trick has to be played again. At the end of Act Two, Keeffe succeeds in staging an even better play in the play in which Claughton is led to believe that he is taking part in a fancy-dress party organized by the Queen. Here he talks with a fake Prince Philip 'going to have a piss in the horse trough' and believes he has been informed by him that Prince Charles is 'a bloody Trotskyite'. He is enraptured: 'Wonderful, oh this is what I was born for. Exchanging bon mots with the Royal Family, ah yes' (p. 84).

His conversation with the fake Queen, 'the very Lady of the Camellias of [his] dreams' (p. 85) is full of comic wordplay and funny misunderstandings. The climax of the comedy is reached, however, when he meets the real Queen, Elizabeth II, who happens to be present at the same place, dressed '*in stable clothes*'. Claughton, of course, does not recognize her. For him, 'she looks like a stable char at some backstreet gymkhana', she is 'plebs', and the policeman muses whether she could be one of 'the terrorists about to strike'. Claughton tells her to 'stop that boring cliché' she keeps on using in public, 'So kind, so kind,' and warns her to take her 'filthy hands off [his] costume' (p. 86).

The whole situation abounds with comical elements based on the fundamental contrast between appearance and reality. As in Middleton, the audience knows the difference between the two and, therefore, enjoys the apparently discrepant behaviour of the characters. But in the contemporary play it is far easier for the spectators to sit comfortably in their seats and simply laugh about the performance without having the feeling that they are also involved in the action and that they – to use Sir Bounteous's words again – 'only laugh at [them]selves'. There is no real confrontation presented, and it is difficult to detect a subversive quality in this play.

The result of the action on the characters confirms the idea that nothing has changed: the policeman has received his reward from Claughton and is now enjoying a rest 'in the comfort of [his] mock Tudor mansion in the wog-free suburbs'. Everything is 'back to normal' (p. 93), the have-nots have even less than before, the women take more valium and librium, and Claughton has been adopted by the conservative party, 'he stands at the by-election'. Even the music played at the end suggests that everything will go on in the same way: '*Graham Parker's That's What They All Say*' (p. 94).

The play represents an attitude to human history that leaves little space for subversive action and changed, improved human behaviour. This attitude is expressed in Act One, Scene Four, by the journalist, the gossip columnist Fox: 'As long as there are politicians, there'll be corruption. As long as there are bishops, there'll be choirboys. As long as men have ambitions, and whores have cunts, I'll fill my seven columns every day' (p. 33). The play gives no clear indication that this is bad, a wrong idea, destructive to life, or in need of an alternative. Keeffe's comedy uses the elements of the city comedy to show that they are still dominant in contemporary life, and that in spite of variations in the outward appearance of our culture there has been no substantial transformation. In this play, he is very pessimistic about the possibility of any change at all, and he uses the traditional elements together with new cultural signifiers to produce a piece of drama that is at the same time indicative of contemporary culture and of the lasting characteristics of humanity. Keeffe *plays* with problems that he takes to be perennial, and he uses a form for his play, the comedy, that has lost its subversive quality because of Keeffe's world view, even though the form has preserved its entertaining characteristics.[14]

In this sense, 'play' is a key-term in Keeffe's revision of the city comedy tradition. There is, therefore, a postmodernist element in his play, although he regarded himself as a political writer and he talked about 'doing my bit for the revolution in trying to change people's attitudes', thus demonstrating 'the need for change'.[15] Subversion in a play is strongly a matter of interpretation which needs corroboration from the play itself, and Keeffe's *A Mad World, My Masters* clearly does not foreground subversive activities, even though his farcical comedy is probably meant to be a satire. But there is not really any self-reflexion in the play, nor does it work with paradox in the same way as Middleton. It is much stronger in *playing* with the comical, funny and entertaining elements of comedy, so that its instructive satirical potential can be shrugged off by those spectators who think the play is simply too unrealistic.

TRAGICOMIC PROBLEMS RE-*PRESENTED*

A historical survey of theatre plays reveals that drama represents attempts to come to terms with the same problems of humankind again and again. The forms in which this is done vary from age to age and culture to culture. One form in particular has been identified with perennial human problems and it has been regarded as being particularly representative of these problems and of human life because it combines the classical forms, tragedy and comedy, resulting in tragicomedy. John Fletcher gave an appropriately vague definition of this form in his preface to *The Faithful Shepherdess* (c.1608): 'A tragicomedy is not so called in respect of mirth and killing, but in respect it wants deaths, which is enough to make it no tragedy, yet brings some near it, which is enough to make it no comedy.'

Shakespeare's tragicomedies are also called 'problem plays'.[16] They represent a 'serious and realistic treatment of a distressing complication in human life, but without a tragic outcome'.[17] *Measure for*

Measure is a good example of the problem play and an obvious mixture of tragedy and comedy in Fletcher's sense. It also mixes scenes of low life with representations of the aristocracy and ruling class. Its theme is the relation of justice to mercy. The theme is dramatically dealt with at both the social and the individual level. The Duke of Vienna is presented to the audience in order 'Of government the properties to unfold' (I, 1, p. 3). These include 'the terms [f]or common justice' (I, 1, pp. 10f) and the qualities that have also been used in poetics of tragedy and comedy: 'terror' and 'love' (I, 1, l. 19). The Duke is equally concerned as an individual with the two elements of the theme, justice and mercy. Personal involvement is even stronger in his deputy, Angelo. Shakespeare's play is extremely subversive by showing how rulers, heads of state, are subjects to their own decisions and liable to fail both in their official functions and as individual human beings.

Money is of no obvious importance in the play, but sex certainly is, and power is the most significant motif.[18] The state only seems to be powerful enough to define and execute its own idea of justice. The play shows the need for balance, measure for measure in the sense of the Aristotelian mean that has already been mentioned above in connection with Middleton's comedy.[19] The contrasts and antinomies juxtaposed and resolved in the play again reflect the Aristotelian and Christian tradition.

The play must also be seen, however, in 'a new trend of dramatic theory' combining elements of (romantic) comedies (where 'Shakespeare had dramatized a range of attitudes to love') and tragedy. Guarini's 'Compendio della Poesia Tragicomica (1601)' defined the form as a 'close blend or fusion of seeming disparates'. The measuring of extremes and the blending of seeming disparates that is already expressed in the name of this dramatic form, the tragicomedy, is equally essential for its content and the underlying world-view. Lever concludes that the form in Shakespeare's *Measure for Measure* 'is a close blend of tragic and comic elements, so carefully patterned as to suggest a conscious experiment in the new medium of tragicomedy'.[20]

Shakespeare laid 'extraordinary emphasis [...] upon the role of true authority, whose intervention alone supplies the equipoise needed to counter the forces of negation' (Lever, 1967, p. lx). This emphasis is the reason for the play's structure that is seriously criticized by Tillyard (1970, p. 122) as consisting of two parts where 'the first [is] incomparably the better half of the play'. I agree to a certain extent with Lever (1967, p. lxii), who notices the same division but sees it in the context of the play's form, where in the first part 'there was a progressive mounting of tension between opposed characters and conflicting principles [up to] the total impasse in III.i [when] the motion was reversed by the Duke's direct intervention'. The Duke now acts as moderator 'tirelessly engaged in "passing from side to side", "working amongst contraries" and bringing about the "reconciliation of enemies, harmony," and "above all, the comic order of things".'

But Lever does not sufficiently notice the fact that the Duke's concept of 'measure for measure' expressed in V, 1, pp. 407–9 ('An Angelo for Claudio; death for death. / Haste still pays haste, and leisure answers leisure; / Like doth quit like, and Measure still for Measure') is the Old Testament idea of 'justice' of Leviticus 24.20: 'Breach for breach, eye for eye, tooth for tooth: as he hath caused a blemish in a man, so shall it be done to him again'. Shakespeare's play, however, goes beyond this position, based on the authority of the law and the commandments of the Old Testament, to the New Testament's concept of Charity expressed by Christ's Sermon on the Mount. Charity, the highest value in the New Testament, asks people to behave in a merciful and very paradoxical way, namely to 'Love your enemies, bless them that curse you, do good to them that hate you, and pray for them which despitefully use you, and persecute you' (Matthew, 5, v. 44).

This is exactly what Isabella and Mariana do. Their behaviour is thus as subversive as Antigone's in its lack of respect for the law of the secular authority. Isabella's pleading for Angelo's life, although she thinks that her brother has died through Angelo's corruption, emphasizes the ethical paradox of the play in an extreme way. The much disputed and usually severely critized decision of Shakespeare not to have the Duke tell Isabella straight away that her brother has been saved (IV, 3, ll. 107–10) can thus be explained as an extremely significant dramatic device: since Isabella believes her brother to be dead, her plea to save Angelo is far more weighty and impressive than it would be, if she knew of his survival. It is most certainly this dramatic quality that induced Shakespeare to have a person do something that at a realistic level seems stupid and cruel. This device gives additional prominence to Isabella's plea and thus underlines once more the play's paradoxical emphasis on mercy over mere justice.

Howard Brenton's *Measure for Measure* contains no such redeeming elements. The Duke, just as Angelo, is 'a Dictator', Claudio is 'a Star' with Juliet as his 'Fan', Isabella is 'a Bible Sister', Lucio is now called Jerky Joe and is a 'Blue-Movie Maker', Pompey 'a Strip Club Owner,' Mrs Overdone 'a Brothel Owner'. The parts of Isabella and Claudio are 'for black actors', and the play is set 'in England, now' (p. 90). The black actors are signifiers of the new culture depicted in the play, and so are the other parts. Brenton takes over from Shakespeare but changes to denote the world of the 1970s as he sees it.

In contemporary colloquial language, Angelo at the end of Scene One summarizes an idea expressed in more genteel words in Shakespeare's play. The old style, 'We must not make a scarecrow of the law, / Setting it up to fear the birds of prey [. . .]' (II, 1, ll. 1f), is transformed into: 'The old man let the country go to the dogs. There will be a sense of purpose, there will be law in the country, there will be order' (p. 93). Brenton thus takes over characters, ideas, and great parts of the plot from the Jacobean play, but he adapts them to his view of the contemporary world. He also changes the five-act structure into a two-act play with nine and seven scenes respectively.

Like Keeffe, Brenton employs contemporary media. The Duke makes a public announcement on television about his decision to withdraw. Angelo does the same when he describes the condition of the law he finds in this country. His description is literally taken over from the Duke's own comment on the state of law to the Friar: 'As fond fathers / Having bound up the threatening twigs of birch, / Only to stick it in their children's sight / For terror not to use, in time the rod / Becomes more mocked than feared, so all our laws / Dead to infliction to themselves are dead, / The baby beats the nurse and quite athwart / Goes all decorum'. His conclusion is then spoken in contemporary prosaic terms: 'I intend to rectify this deplorable state of affairs. Speedily.'[21]

The scenes of low life are staged in a strip club, and the film industry produces blue movies. Claudio is a rock star, and Juliet, one of his fans, is 'gonna have his baby'. Journalism is described as '[g]utter press', and the police are again shown to be subject to bribery (pp. 99ff). The official charge against Claudio is 'a conglomerate charge. Obscene behaviour. [. . .] Performing a lewd act. Performing a lewd act likely to cause public outrage. Likely to cause depravity in minors. Likely to be offensive to married people. Likely to be offensive to religious conscience. Then there's the whole perverted angle. [. . .] Then there's the rape'. Jerky's confirmation that 'the girl was willing' because '[s]he's his chick' does not count (p. 101). As it is impossible to transfer the charge against Claudio in Shakespeare directly into the 1970s, Brenton turns it into a downright farce. The farcical element is continued when the Duke sees a psychiatrist about 'Sex' and answers in Shakespeare's words: 'Believe not that the dribbling dart of love / Can pierce a complete bosom [. . .]' (p. 102; I, 3, ll. 2–6). The Duke is now called 'Maurice' by the doctor, and he is 'hiding' and '[s]ulking in a fashionable psychiatrist's Belgravia flat,' wondering why he has given up power (p. 103). He is suffering from an identity crisis, one which is presented, however, not in a serious, but rather a farcical way. The farce underlines the point that the Duke embodied complete power, and that through his abdication he has given himself 'away to nothing'. As his doctor says, he might just as well 'lie down in [his] grave' (p. 105). What might be seen as tragic, a person's loss of identity and meaning in life, is here represented as funny and even farcical.

Having learned about Angelo's deceit, the Duke lays a plot to catch his successor. The play aptly and impressively demonstrates how Brenton mixes Shakespeare's language and elements of the old plot with new phrasings plus contemporary know-how and technology. Brenton's Act One ends with such a mixture, using lines from the Duke's speech at the end of Act Three in Shakespeare (III, 2, ll. 270–5):

Craft against vice I must apply. / Vice against vice. / With Angelo tonight shall lie / Not Isabella / But a replica. / A camera's lens / Shall see his sins, / So disguise shall by th' disguised / Pay with falsehood, false extracting / And perform an old contracting. (*Exultant*) Ha! Back in politics! the old adrenalin flowing! Haven't felt so good in years!

(p. 132)

The Duke's 'work of Providence' (p. 135), however, is literally 'getting out of hand' (p. 149) and turns into a farce, in which Angelo takes Isabella for a 'common whore' and recognizes the situation as a 'trap, for men of good will. An act, worked out by [her] pimp to snare innocent members of the public.' But he nevertheless takes his trousers off and wants to 'get on with it' (p. 155). Mrs Overdone takes over from Isabella without Angelo becoming aware of this, and the farce is built up to its first climax, in which Angelo recognizes that a 'grotesque humiliation' has been foisted on him (p. 159). But there is a second climax in this farce in which Angelo outdoes the Duke once more, who already thinks he will 'resume the management of the country' (p. 160). The head of the killed prisoner, whom the Duke believes to be Ragozine (as in Shakespeare), is in fact that of Claudio. Angelo has had Claudio killed, and he has brought policemen with him who arrest all on the Duke's side. The farce goes on to a third stage, a kind of anticlimax, when in the final scene everybody except Angelo and the Duke have left the country on the 'S.S. Political Utopia' and say goodbye to England, 'this bleeding country of old men.' This is called 'A happy end' (pp. 163f).

The Shakespearean conflict between mercy and justice has been transformed into a play where mercy is of no importance at all and justice is turned into farce. The comic elements have been stressed, and the tragic possibilities in the problem have been rejected. History in Brenton's play repeats itself; not as tragedy, though, nor as tragicomedy, but as farce.[22] It is extremely difficult to detect any paradox in his view of history, even though a paradox is explicitly suggested by Angelo at the end of the play:

> I offer this view of history. It is a paradox. The old order, unchecked, will bring forth a new and far harsher form of itself. [. . .] I find myself to be that new order. Unchecked. Therefore, I will proceed to fashion the England of my dreams. And you will learn that where power has rested, there it **shall** rest. For a thousand years.
>
> (p. 163)

A paradox combines seeming opposites, or, as Guarini said in his description of tragicomedy, it blends 'seeming disparates'. Angelo's view of history contains no opposites. It knows only of one power growing stronger and 'harsher' all the time for the very reason that it is 'unchecked' by any opposing force. Brenton leaves out the tragic elements in the problem portrayed, and he also avoids the paradoxical combination of opposites. He thus makes significant changes to the original text.

At the end of Act One, he takes over Shakespeare's 'Craft against vice I must apply.' But he adds to this 'Vice against vice', which is not in Shakespeare and which here does not mean that by deceit 'correction and instruction' will be brought about (III, 2, l. 31). This is not Shakespeare's paradoxical 'charity in sin' (II, 4, l. 63). The Duke and Angelo in Brenton are both 'Dictators', and the one evil simply fights against the other for supremacy. Neither will create the opposite of vice. Such an opposing pole is simply missing from the play.

It is thus not surprising that the scene which is most explicit about paradox in Shakespeare is most radically changed in Brenton. In the conversation between the Duke and Claudio about life and death, in which the Duke admonishes Claudio to 'Be absolute for death' (III, 1, l. 5), Claudio comes to know the basic paradox of human existence: 'To sue to live, I find I seek to die, / And seeking death, find life.' (III, 1, ll. 42f). Brenton has Claudio respond to the Duke in very different and very decisive terms:

> 'Be absolute for death'? What a childish remark. What a remark for a grown man to make. Be absolute for life, yes. [...] Be absolute for man, yes. [...] Absolute for women, little girls, little boys, pig on a farm, pussy cat, dog and animal or thing living. Seen a dead man? (*The* DUKE *nods, with a grunt.*) How can you BE anything for what a dead man is? 'Cept maybe a little ... (*with a sniff*) nauseous. Sad.

> (p. 125)

This is in all likelihood the position for life subscribed to by Brenton himself, but it significantly leaves out the paradoxical two-sidedness of the Jacobean and Shakespearean attitude that has characterized human life and history up to the present (Cf. Müller, 1993a). There is no substantial paradox left in this play, which also lacks tragic elements and is, therefore, not a tragicomedy, but a political, satirical farce.

PARADOXICAL SUBVERSIONS OF GENERIC FORMS OF MEANING

Even though Howard Brenton's play is intended to be directly political and utterly controversial (Bull, 1984, pp. 44–6), it clearly lacks the complexity found in Shakespeare. The problems Brenton represents are real ones, but the form used is far from realistic. In fact, none of the contemporary plays analysed tends to realism. Reality has become more and more of a problem for playwrights, and so have the forms through which it is represented. This does not always lead to increased complexity, however. In fact, a certain tendency in contemporary adaptations of Shakespearean plays towards reductive, or even simplistic revisions, or politically indifferent aesthetic play has already been noted.[23] The other tendency observed by some critics, the elimination of comic elements and a preference for tragedy, is not confirmed by Brenton. His revision has transformed Shakespeare's highly complex tragicomedy into a political farce that does not measure extremes and combine seeming opposites but increases the comic elements at the expense of all tragedy and paradox.

Nor has the self-reflexive, paradoxical and highly subversive quality of Middleton's comedy been maintained by its successor. Even though Barrie Keeffe, too, intends to involve spectators in a process of recognition and understanding, his dramatic form favours exaggeration and entertainment and thus results too easily in complacent laughter and indifferent, non-committal play.

Strangely enough, of the plays and forms selected in this article, it is in tragedy that contemporary drama on drama has found its most compelling form of meaning. Middleton's subversive tragedy has been turned into a controversial form outspokenly looking for confrontation and most active audience participation. Barker's tragedy is the form which is least characterized by explicit material cultural signifiers, such as, for instance, contemporary technology in Keeffe and Brenton. It is more concerned with the 'permanent human feelings' T. S. Eliot (Kermode, 1975, p. 192) saw represented in Middleton, with grand passions and the human desire to (re-) create one's own life. Barker emphasizes the creative and imaginative qualities of human beings in such a way that he is significantly characteristic of his culture in its emphasis on cognitivism and constructivism. He does not tolerate the consoling qualities of tragedy (which were of great importance in Aristotle's concept of *catharsis*), 'the reassertion of existing moral values' (Barker, 1989, p. 90), but he incites to resistance to traditional forms of perceiving, understanding and representing reality. Barker's form most strongly demands a moral and cultural reconstruction. Paradoxically, but perhaps not surprisingly (precisely because of the paradoxical quality of human life), it is a form that has so far usually been regarded as deconstructive, offensive and indecent. Maybe Kenneth Muir's (1970, p. 20) statement applies to Barker, too: 'The more moral [a dramatist] is, the more indecent he will be.'

It remains to be seen, whether the irony involved in human history and the paradoxical quality of human life will foster the creative and imaginative qualities that undeniably exist, or whether irony and paradox will lead to the eternal dominance of destructiveness that is most clearly portrayed by Keeffe. The different forms of meaning described in this survey certainly offer and represent the subversive possibility of creative human constructions of cultures. But they do it in significantly diverse ways that are characteristic of the individual author and his view of the culture in which he lives.

Raymond Williams (1979, p. 45) commented on the significance of 'tragic experience': 'Tragic experience, because of its central importance, commonly attracts the fundamental beliefs and tensions of a period, and tragic theory is interesting mainly in this sense, that through it the shape and set of a particular culture is often deeply realised.' His statement is equally valid for 'comedy' and 'tragicomedy' as significant forms of creating and representing meaning, as shared discourses in a specific culture. In our age, the artist is no longer the sage, the prophet-poet, the legislator, or the wise wo/man inspired by absolute truths, but rather 'The Artist Infirm' (Barker, 1985, p. 24), creatively, though insecurely, involved in an endless quest for truths and meanings. Tragedy, comedy, and tragicomedy as three fundamental forms of meaning are in such an age always sub-versions in a perennial process of writing cultures that nevertheless reveal the fundamental values, tensions, problems, desires and hopes of these cultures.

Notes

1. Cf. Clifford and Marcus (1986); Geertz (1973).
2. Bywater's translation of Aristotle as quoted in Cuddon (1991, pp. 983f).
3. The quotations are from Thomas Heywood, *An Apology for Actors*, 1612, sigs. Fiv-F4r, as cited in Evans (1989, p. 67).

4. Cf. Dollimore (1989, p. XXI): '*Radical Tragedy* finds in this theatre a substantial challenge; not a vision of political freedom so much as a subversive knowledge of political domination, a knowledge which interrogated prevailing beliefs, submitted them to a kind of intellectual vandalism; radical in the sense of going to their roots and even pulling them up'. Dollimore objects to New Historical interpretations that 'potentially subversive social elements are *contained* in the process of being *rehearsed.*' I agree with his opinion that 'to contain a threat by rehearsing it one must first give it a voice, a part, a presence – in the theatre, as in the culture. Through this process the very condition of something's containment may constitute the terms of its challenge: opportunities of resistance become apparent, especially on the stage and even as the threat is being disempowered.' (ibid.)

5. Cf. Mottram (1993) and Rabey (1989).

6. Barker expressed his warning in a letter to me referring to my article 'Recasting the World on Stage' (1995), where I have tried to show how thoughts of constructivism and cognitivism are represented in contemporary plays and theories of drama.

7. Barker is realistic enough to acknowledge that not all people are keen on improving their imagination and expanding their perceptive capacities, and that is why he acknowledges that his kind of 'tragic theatre will be elitist' (Barker, 1989, p. 13). But he insists that there should be this 'Radical Elitism in the Theatre', which is connected with change, reconstruction, morality and subversion: 'I believe in a society of increasingly restricted options that a creative mind owes it to his fellow human beings to stretch himself and them, to give others the right to be amazed, the right even to be taken to the limits of tolerance and to strain and test morality at its source' (1989, pp. 29–35).

8. George Steiner (1961). See Paul Goetsch (1993) for a most recent discussion of the possibilities and forms of tragedy in our time.

9. Barker (1989, p. 22). Barker certainly did not choose Middleton in order to have him 'punished or pitied' as David Trotter (1986) thought after the performance. For the tradition of city comedy cf. Gibbons (1980), Leggatt (1973), Leinwand (1986), and Paster (1985, pp. 150–77).

10. Heywood, loc. cit. Cf. also Ben Jonson's prologue to his second version of *Every Man in His Humour* of 1616, where he equally emphasizes the fact that a comedy intends to teach and delight at the same time. Beyond such basics, 'theory of comedy remained thin until after Shakespeare's day' (Daniell, 1986, p. 102).

11. Jonson in the same prologue. The two previous quotations are from T. S. Eliot, 'Thomas Middleton', in: Kermode (1975, p. 194). Lynch (1926) proposes a view similar to Eliot's. Leinwand (1986, pp. 3–20) has a more cautious attitude about 'photographic' qualities of theatre and drama. He emphasizes what I would call the most important cultural signifiers, the shared discourse apparent in plays: 'The bond between theater and what we may call actuality (actual only insofar

as it is an already organized perception) is their shared discourse of types and conventions' (p. 15).

12. For an extended discussion of this motif in contemporary plays, cf. Borgmeier (1993). Glaap (1993) offers a view on current comedy.

13. Cf. Aristotle's *Nicomachean Ethics*, esp. ll. 1106a11–1107a27; the greatest Christian values, 'faith, hope, charity' (1 Corinthians, 13, v. 13); and the Christian form of expressing the fundamental paradox of human life: 'Whosoever shall seek to save his life shall lose it; and whosoever shall lose his life shall preserve it' (Luke 11, v. 33).

14. Cf. my criticism of another comedy that was even explicitly intended to be subversive, David Hare's and Howard Brenton's *Pravda* (Müller, 1986). David Edgar (1988, pp. 226–46) discusses the pessimism of playwrights in the late 1970s.

15. Itzin (1980, p. 248). See also Cohn (1980) and Müller (1993a) for discussions of 'play' in the context of contemporary drama.

16. Cf. Lascelles (1953); Lawrence (1969); Schanzer (1963); Tillyard (1970); Toole (1966).

17. Lawrence (1969, p. 25). Cf. Tillyard (1970, p. 13): 'The plays then are powerfully united by a serious tone amounting at times to sombreness; they show a strong awareness of evil, without being predominantly pessimistic'. See also Styan (1962); Herrick (1962).

18. The play nevertheless talks about money, for instance in the context of the 'two usuries' (III, 2, l. 6), money-lending and lechery, resulting in interest and issue.

19. Cf. J. W. Lever's note in his edition of the play (Shakespeare, 1967, p. 3), where he says about the title that it is 'a commonplace signifying (i) just retribution and reward, or the just exaction of revenge' and '(ii) moderation or temperance as a virtue.' Lever also quotes Matthew VII.2 and thus refers to the Christian background.

20. The quotations are from Lever (1967, pp. lix–lxi). Lever (1967, p. lxi) cites Guarini's definition of tragicomedy as taking 'from tragedy "its great characters, but not its great action; a likely story, but not a true one; [. . .] delight, not sadness; danger, not death"; and from comedy "laughter that was not dissolute, modest attractions, a well-tied knot, a happy reversal, and, above all, the comic order of things".'

21. Brenton (1989, p. 98) and Shakespeare (I, 3, ll. 23–31). Why Brenton leaves out the line before 'The baby beats the nurse' is at first not easy to understand. The line uses two words printed in capital letters that are extremely important in both Brenton's and Shakespeare's plays: 'And Liberty plucks Justice by the nose' (I, 3, l. 29). But Brenton in fact extinguishes any sense of liberty in his play, whereas in Shakespeare liberty is generated through the very paradox of human behaviour, by which people are not forced to act in just one way, they can paradoxically also do the opposite.

22. Cf. Marx's statement 'at the start of *The Eighteenth Brumaire of Louis Bonaparte* [. . .] that the events and even the personages of history occur not once but twice, "the first time as tragedy, the second as farce"' (Edgar, 1988, p. 10). Edgar underlines Marx's point that farce

is not simply fun, but 'all about unexpected nakedness and hasty disguise,' about human pain and disastrous discrepancies between appearance and reality. Farce is thus 'a highly serious business.'

23. Cf. Broich (1980); Cohn (1976); Plett (1982); and the specific emphasis on subversions in Novy (1993).

Bibliography

Barker, Howard, *Don't Exaggerate (Desire and Abuse)* (London: Calder, 1985).

——, *Women Beware Women* (London: Calder, 1986).

——, *Arguments for a Theatre* (London: Calder, 1989).

Borgmeier, Raimund, 'Journeys Through Madness: Welten des Wahnsinns im zeitgenössischen englischen Drama', in: Müller, *Englisches Theater der Gegenwart. Geschichte(n) und Strukturen* (Tübingen: Narr, 1993), pp. 389–411.

Brenton, Howard, *Three Plays: A Sky Blue Life, How Beautiful with Badges, Measure for Measure*, ed. by John Bull (Sheffield: Sheffield Academic Press, 1989).

Broich, Ulrich, 'Charles Marowitz, *Measure for Measure*', in: Horst Prießnitz (ed.), *Anglo-amerikanische Shakespeare-Bearbeitungen des 20. Jahrhunderts* (Darmstadt: Wiss. Buchgesellschaft, 1980), pp. 114–29.

Bull, John, *New British Political Dramatists* (London: Macmillan, 1984).

Clifford, James and George E. Marcus (eds), *Writing Culture. The Poetics and Politics of Ethnography* (Berkeley: University of California Press, 1986).

Cohn, Ruby, *Modern Shakespeare Off-shoots* (Princeton University Press, 1976).

——, *Just Play: Beckett's Theater* (Princeton University Press, 1980).

Cuddon, J. A., *The Penguin Dictionary of Literary Terms and Literary Theory* (Harmondsworth: Penguin, 3rd edn, 1991).

Daniell, David, 'Shakespeare and the traditions of comedy', in: Stanley Wells (ed.), *The Cambridge Companion to Shakespeare Studies* (Cambridge: University Press, 1986), pp. 101–21.

Dollimore, Jonathan, *Radical Tragedy: Religion, Ideology and Power in the Drama of Shakespeare and His Contemporaries* (New York: Harvester Wheatsheaf, 2nd edn, 1989).

Edgar, David, *The Second Time as Farce: Reflections on the Drama of Mean Times* (London: Lawrence & Wishart, 1988).

Evans, G. Blakemore (ed.), *Elizabethan-Jacobean Drama* (London: Black, 1989).

Freud, Sigmund, *Jokes and Their Relation to the Unconscious* (London: Imago, 1940).

Geertz, Clifford, *The Interpretation of Cultures* (New York: Basic Books, 1973).

Gibbons, Brian, *Jacobean City Comedy: A Study of Satiric Plays by Jonson, Marston and Middleton* (London: Methuen, 2nd edn, 1980).

Glaap, Albert-Reiner, 'Ayckbourn, Frayn and all: Zur Entwicklung der englischen Komödie in den siebziger und achtziger Jahren', in: Klaus Peter Müller (ed.), *Englisches Theater der Gegenwart. Geschichte(n) und Strukturen* (Tübingen: Narr, 1993), pp. 341–63.

Goetsch, Paul, 'Die Tragödie in der Gegenwart', in: Klaus Peter Müller (ed.),

Klaus Peter Müller 57

Englisches Theater der Gegenwart. Geschichte(n) und Strukturen (Tübingen: Narr, 1993), pp. 365–86.

Herrick, Marvin T., *Tragicomedy: Its Origin and Development in Italy, France, and England* (Urbana: University of Illinois Press, 2nd edn, 1962).

Itzin, Catherine, *Stages in the Revolution: Political Theatre in Britain Since 1968* (London: Methuen, 1980).

Keeffe, Barrie, *A Mad World, My Masters* (London: Methuen, 1977).

Kermode, Frank (ed.), *Selected Prose of T. S. Eliot* (London: Faber & Faber, 1975).

Lascelles, Mary, *Shakespeare's 'Measure for Measure'* (London: Athlone Press, 1953).

Lawrence, William Witherle, *Shakespeare's Problem Comedies* (Harmondsworth: Penguin, 1969).

Leggatt, Alexander, *Citizen Comedy in the Age of Shakespeare* (Toronto: University Press, 1973).

——, *English Drama: Shakespeare to the Restoration, 1590–1660* (Burnt Mill: Longman, 1988).

Leinwand, Theodore B., *The City Staged: Jacobean Comedy, 1603–1613* (Madison: University of Wisconsin Press, 1986).

Lever, J. W., 'Introduction', in: Shakespeare, 1967, pp. XI–XCVIII.

——, *The Tragedy of State* (London: Methuen, 1971).

Lynch, Kathleen, *The Social Mode of Restoration Comedy* (New York: Macmillan, 1926).

Middleton, Thomas, *A Mad World, My Masters*, ed. by Standish Henning (Lincoln: University of Nebraska Press, 1965).

——, *Women Beware Women*, ed. by J. R. Murlyne (Manchester: University Press, 1981).

Mottram, Eric, 'History and the Perfectly Human: Howard Barker's Recent Plays', in: Klaus Peter Müller (ed.), *Englisches Theater der Gegenwart. Geschichte(n) und Strukturen* (Tübingen: Narr, 1993), pp. 453–77.

Müller, Klaus Peter, 'Culture, Politics, and Values in English Plays of the 1980s. Questions of definition, interpretation, and (self-)knowledge', *Englisch Amerikanische Studien* 1986, pp. 370–87.

——, 'More Than 'Just Play': The Creation of 'Fabulous History' in Beckett's Plays', in: Marius Buning and Lois Oppenheim (eds), *Beckett in the 1990s* (Amsterdam: Rodopi, 1993a), pp. 255–67.

——, 'Ein Lebenswerk über die Paradoxie menschlicher Geschichte(n): Samuel Becketts Drama', in: Müller (ed.), *Englisches Theater der Gegenwart. Geschichte(n) und Strukturen* (Tübingen: Narr, 1993b), pp. 479–520.

——, 'Recasting the World on Stage: The Freedom of Creating New Centres and Margins in Contemporary Theatre', in: Bernhard Reitz (ed.), *Centres and Margins* (Trier: Wiss. Verlag, 1995), pp. 9–29.

Muir, Kenneth, *The Comedy of Manners* (London: Hutchinson, 1970).

Novy, Marianne (ed.), *Cross-Cultural Performances: Differences in Women's Re-Visions of Shakespeare* (Urbana: University of Illinois Press, 1993).

Paster, Gail Kern, *The Idea of the City in the Age of Shakespeare* (Athens: University of Georgia Press, 1985).

Plett, Heinrich F., 'Shakespeare-Rezeption. Lesarten des *Hamlet* bei Kops,

Marowitz und Stoppard', in: Plett (ed.), *Englisches Drama von Beckett bis Bond* (München: Fink, 1982), pp. 204–49.

Rabey, David Ian, *Howard Barker. Politics and Desire: An Expository Study of his Drama and Poetry, 1969–87* (London: Macmillan, 1989).

Sanders, Andrew, *The Short Oxford History of English Literature* (Oxford: Clarendon Press, 1994).

Schanzer, Ernest, *The Problem Plays of Shakespeare* (New York: Schocken, 1963).

Shade, Ruth, 'All Passion Is a Risk. Howard Barker: Sex and Sexual Politics', *Gambit: International Theatre Review*, 41, 1984, pp. 101–10.

Shakespeare, William, *Measure for Measure*, ed. by J. W. Lever (London: Methuen, 1967) (*The Arden Shakespeare*).

Steiner, George, *The Death of Tragedy* (New York: Knopf, 1961).

Styan, John L., *The Dark Comedy* (Cambridge University Press, 1962).

Tillyard, E. M. W., *Shakespeare's Problem Plays* (Harmondsworth: Penguin, 1970).

Toole, William B., *Shakespeare's Problem Plays: Studies in form and meaning* (London: Mouton, 1966).

Trotter, David, 'An end to pageantry', *Times Literary Supplement*, 21 February 1986, p. 194.

Williams, Raymond, *Modern Tragedy* (London: Verso, 1979).

4

Women Beware Women by Howard Barker (with Thomas Middleton): The 'Terrible Consistency'
Michel Morel

All knowledge lies in instinct [. . .] It kills the soul not to exploit an inspiration.[1]

A pointedly designed semantic scandal, such is the arresting fruition of Barker's 'collaboration'[2] with Thomas Middleton. The author's use of hypertext[3] bridges the gap of centuries in a deliberately unsettling strategy of derivation, complementation and distortion. Culminating in the searching scandal of a liberating rape, the displacement of Middleton's argument foregrounds fundamentals which are inseparably theatrical and existential. In this disabusing hybridization lies the crux of the matter, the extraction of the 'terrible consistency' the author speaks of in the cryptic sequence of critical aphorisms prefaced to the play.[4] As he himself notices, his continuation of the original text is rendered optimistic, but this is only in comparison with Middleton's sombre constructions.[5] In reality, the whole enterprise is targeted beyond such surface alternatives. The anachronistic invention of a sixteenth-century stock-exchange shows well enough that the dramatist's approach to the past is not the antiquarian's. His is the example of an uncompromising appropriation of a Jacobean play in terms of a committed late twentieth-century argument. Indeed, the conception of human nature that underlies the undertaking can be said to be ahistorical. In this particular domain, I will take the text at its own words to try and attempt to assess the logic and the significance of such a manifestly universalizing stance.

Any summary of the two plays, even the shortest, will immediately make it clear exactly where Barker stands in his 'collaboration' with Middleton. In the earlier play, a double plot in five acts, involving two parallel series of sexual intrigues – one focused on the Duke, Bianca and her ousted husband, Leantio, the other centred on Isabella, her incestuous love affair with her uncle, Hippolito, and her forced union with the foolish Ward, with, as a mainspring between the two, Livia, the female Machiavel, and Leantio as her kept lover – culminate in the terminal Masque, in the course of which each protagonist meets his deserved death exactingly apportioned in accordance with the rigorous laws of poetic justice. The sole survivor is the speechifying cardinal who moralizes conclusively over the carnage. Barker's first act keeps the essentials of Acts I to III of Middleton's play, though giving precedence to the first plot, in anticipation of Bianca's transformation in the new second and final act. Along with his friend Sordido, the Ward, whose foolishness is no longer real but tactical, becomes the agent of Bianca's liberation. Curing fire by means of fire, Sordido rapes Bianca in the minutes that precede her public nuptials with the Duke. The 'catastrophe' shocks her into recognizing that the actual rape, of her own choosing, was her original seduction by her future husband. Sordido is killed, the Ward refuses his elevation to dukedom, and Livia and Leantio are nominated duke and duchess, the demoted and rejected Duke being left to conclude the play with: 'Don't love . . . ! Don't love . . . !'[6] As regards the cardinal, he remains trapped to the end in his unavailing discourses.

Everything in Barker's editing of the initial phases in Middleton's plots is made to contribute to the clarification of what becomes the central point of the new play: Bianca's seduction by the Duke is the telling epitome of a world which equates sexuality with money, rank and power: 'I discover in [Middleton] the man who knows love is also a commodity./The body as currency. Innocence pays no dividends. The orgasm is the deal.'[7] The changes in the new act all point in the same direction. The number of characters has been reduced, which entails a redistribution of cues. All subsidiary aspects have been eliminated, such as 'psychological' insights into the supposed logic of the secondary figures (their set speeches, the conceits they use, their asides, and in general most of the exchanges based on *quid pro quos* or dramatic irony); or again everything that might make the period dimension too obvious, like metrical verse, and would refer the spectator to an obsolete stage universe detrimental to the play's new strategy. Moreover, the language has been markedly trimmed so that the Jacobean ring is softened up and assuaged while still remaining distinctive, if only to make the brutal contrast between Act I and Act II centrally self-evident. Bianca's and Livia's coarse parlance has been attenuated and their freakish changes in mood and motivation have all but disappeared or assume a different meaning. All in all, one feels that any aspect liable to distract the spectator's attention away from the unifying thesis has been toned down or done away with. Such an adaptation might first seem to naturalize the text and make it more acceptable to a twentieth-century audience. In reality, the process is one of selection and of intensification, the final aim apparently being the flaunting of a theatrical mode of existence divested of all extraneous and secondary elements. For instance, the seduction of Bianca by the Duke, its jarring and distancing parallel with the chess game played the whole while by Livia and the old mother-in-law are preserved *in toto*, whereas the repulsive, but graphic cattle-market appraisal of Isabella's bodily charms is dropped altogether. The arbitrariness that refers one to types in the original text is rejected because it implies a psychological reduction which might blunt the new argument. It is no longer possible to pretend that the problem is one of aberrant idiosyncracies. The patterns and schemes that survive all suggest the presence of a concealed abstract gist. Each character's doing refers us, in the last resort, to the corrupt transactional or arbitrary side of the market of love – Bianca allowing herself to be seduced by a man nearly 40 years older than she is, Isabella thrown into Hippolito's incestuous arms, Livia deciding to purchase Leantio's love – while desire, no longer condemned by a sermonizing Cardinal or a hypocritical Bianca, remains untainted, and thus open to new developments and interpretations. The case in point is Livia. Though her scheming is left basically unchanged, her attitudes and words are sufficiently deviated and refocused to make her become the herald of passion in its affirmative and subversive dimension, as Act II systematically demonstrates. This minimal but central shift is typically condensed by Sordido into the rough formulation : 'You are a no, or you could not fuck like that'.[8] In contrast, Isabella remains strangely contradictory and muted, caught as she is between her uncle and a husband who, in the new play, will finally refuse to be committed. As for Bianca, her second act stance seems to be almost entirely derived from her dying cue in Act V of the original play: 'What make I here? these are all strangers to me'.[9] Nothing in Barker's revised first act allows us to foresee the coming mutation in her, but nothing prevents us from retrospectively considering it a definite possibility in the character attributed to her. She becomes a chrysalis in abeyance, and her moralistic baiting of the cardinal, the most disingenuous side of her former 'self', is sweepingly ditched in the new version.

Barker's intertextual strategy comes out in its specificity when compared with Wesker's rewriting of *The Merchant of Venice*, and Emma Tennant's thematic variations in *Woman Beware Woman*.[10] The difference is particularly clear when one considers the underlying relation between past and present central to the hypertextual derivation. Wesker turns the tables to redress what he considers, from his postholocaust point of view, a major historical injustice. In his plot, the Jews (and women) come morally out on top at the expense of the parasitical male bondage of the Italian aristocrats. His play can only be read as a polemical rewriting of *The Merchant of Venice*, the fragments of which intersperse the new work. The hypotext thus remains predominant both semantically and theatrically. It is the structural backdrop against which everything in the derivative text is to be understood and assessed. Emma Tennant's approach is quite different. She keeps the basic pattern but reduces it to a simple narrative and thematic line. The hypotext frames and sometimes misleads the reader's expectations, leaving the primeval essence of the revenge scheme unchanged. Yet, Emma Tennant's novel could be read independently. The text is the equivalent of a filmic remake, with the added complexity of hypotextual metafictional guidance. Nothing of the original play survives except the general argument of the dual plot. Intertextuality is valued only insofar as its fabulation makes the whole susceptible to postmodern equivocalness. The present alone is the focus of the intertextual transference.

Barker's collaboration is neither Wesker's revisionism, nor Tennant's appropriation. It has nothing to do either with Stoppard's surface word games. His construction is based on a sort of structural brinksmanship midway between past and present: 'To continually undermine the expected is the only way to alter people's perception', Barker declared in 1981.[11] And in 1984: 'I use history to hack away at comforting images of the past in order to evoke, to unlock feelings about the present.'[12] For him, man does not change, only circumstances. Hence the reversible relation he engages in with Middleton, which he terms 'collaboration'. He shakes up our assumptions about the cluster of implications and reciprocal effects between sexuality and society, while at the same time measuring the present against the past, and thus ascertaining where exactly the relevance of Middleton's version of it all lies. The edited first act is preparatory and structurally conducive to the second part of the demonstration. The new play can be seen or read independently, even though its texture remains dual and thus allows us to still hear part of Middleton's text. The relevance Barker refers himself to is not so much textual as historical, if history is the reconstructed sense of how it felt to be alive in past periods. The mutual focusing and targeting – of Act I by Act II, and vice versa – is the central means of a complex theatrical demonstration. In the resulting intensification, theatre and the social dimension of sexuality stand as two sides of the same coin.

'The orgasm is the deal' announces the foreword. Barker inverts Middleton's hypothesis while at the same time emphasizing its ruthless and abrasive truth. The rape in the play is perplexingly and exactingly tied up with purity. Sordido is 'thirty and pure' and this is his 'entrance'. And to make sure we do not miss the point, the newly freed Bianca is led to exclaim, like D. H. Lawrence's heroes, but also like resurrected Christ: 'Don't touch'.[13] Far from suggesting a Christian interpretation, for there is nothing Barker rejects more than the idea of redemption through suffering, the allusion is intrinsically blasphematory. It evinces the proud stance of the rebel and the affirmation of a resilient sense of individual moral integrity.[14] In this revolution, which is also a resolution, lies the 'catastrophe' of the play.

For Middleton and for Barker, Livia's stratagems are central, if only because the character resorts in both plays, and in both acts of Barker's version, to means that no end can ever quite vindicate. Her attitude is downright questionable, and the problem of her motivations cannot and will not be solved by any final reconciliation of contraries.[15] And yet Livia is the one who best expresses the paradox of the kind of hypothetical but assertive truth the text adumbrates. 'I will not be animal, but ecstasy' she says in Scene ii of Act II.[16] And later: 'My flesh is not a pond to drown your fears in. Desire's truth, Leantio, and compels it speak.'[17] True to her contradictory self, she persists to the end in her devious ways: 'Don't call me hypocrite, what I have dealt in I attend right to the finish.'[18] In the same way, the postcatastrophe Bianca will exclaim: 'I must be truthful. In cunt. If nowhere else, then there [...] Oh, God, I never felt so cold, such a deep cold and so alone'.[19] Bianca has thus achieved a kind of enlightenment which is very close to the one she reaches in Middleton's play. However, what she discovers is no longer despair but the confrontation of each invidual with the ordeal of her or his own truth. 'Catastrophe is also birth. [. . .] I have to find my life', she declares to the amazed Cardinal. Then she strikes Livia in the face, accompanying her cuff with a 'Thank you . . .' – in which one notices the absence of the exclamation mark which would have suggested a poorer because less ambivalent meaning – before being hurried away by Isabella.

Bianca has finally recovered her moral virginity, and the Duke's terminally mistaken repetition of 'Don't love . . . !' shows how far he is from ever simply sensing the possibility of such a far-reaching insight, and the complexity of the feelings that make it possible. From the final scenes of the play[20] comes the expression 'theatre of catastrophe' which Barker will henceforth use to characterize his own 'method', a method which conjoins the opposite aims of Brecht's theatre of distance and Artaud's theatre of violence. A catastrophe is etymologically a turning down, the upsetting of every surmise and expectation, a process that is also extraordinarily painful. Only because it hurts so hard, and not only the character, does the crisis here foster truth. The catastrophe Barker has in mind partakes of the nature of the ordeal, that is, an *ordalie*, that is, an *Urteil* or a judgement. At the end of his play, the characters seem to be placed on a sort of axiological scale; not a moral scale, but one which makes clear the degree of relative enlightenment each has achieved or not. At the top, stands Bianca, in her final and absolute repudiation of the venal link between love and power, and the Ward, who knows himself to be unfit to rule and declines any official function; at the bottom, the former Duke, who remains dead to such a logic, and Hippolito, who would sacrifice everything to the collective and the state. In between, we find Livia and Leantio, both of whom are left in a limbo of contradictions. If none of the *dramatis personae* is free of such contradictions, the text defines them all in reference to the controversial reversion to a stringent sense of purity of intention, a purity to be found only at the heart of the negative: 'Since when was rape salvation?' exclaims Leantio (p. 51), thus putting our own inner doubts and qualms into words. Part of the answer to these qualms lies in the nearly allegorical mode of existence attained by the characters in the concluding scenes. We are not far from an abstraction suggesting entities that refer us back to the Morality plays of yore. Only the values inferred and embodied on the stage remain problematic and contradictory. This does not mean they are flawed. The play merely demonstrates that to be living is to be, each individual in her or his own convoluted way, a tangled knot of contradictions. All the characters are extraordinarily outspoken. There is no word they cannot be found to pronounce, yet they are never more than tentative in their verbal gestures towards this kind of surmised truth. This is apparently what Barker appoints as a central aim to his theatre, a theatre not meant to provide answers, but only to clear the ground for the legitimate, if generally suppressed, questions. This is where the specificity of the genre comes into play, with the 'terrible consistency' the author assigns to it.

When we hear, or read, Leantio's liminal 'We fuck the day to death' at the beginning of Act II, the brutal passing and mutation from Jacobean to modern shocks us into an awareness which is very close to Brechtian alienation. In the character's altered and displaced utterance, two pacts of fiction are mutually foregrounded. Leantio's brutal explicitness makes us hear what remained hidden in the adapted but faithfully preserved Jacobean language of the first act. At the same time, the reined-in violence of that former language magnifies, by making it suddenly scandalous, the outspokenness of the 'new' characters. The conflicting nature of their scenic existence – they were Jacobean, they now become our contemporaries – not only makes all naturalization impossible but also endows those figures with a kind of two-tier and two-fold semiosis which is in itself intrinsically and intensely theatrical. A sort of structural double-entendre is inaugurated, which gives their various sayings a semantic brittleness, and makes it impossible to decide which exactly of the two imaginary worlds they belong to. They are surrounded by an aura of doubtfulness we can never quite forget; if only because their names are unchanged and they constantly refer to events and facts belonging to their 'prior' existences. Each new anachronism – Bianca being compared to Princess Diana, the allusions to buses, to the stock-exchange, among others – revives and intensifies the tension at the heart of this ambivalence. Diana is a modern-day Bianca, a Bianca who still remains, before she is raped, a pawn on Livia's chess-board. The theatrical dimension is thus validated in its generic legitimacy, since theatre as a genre based on mimicry lays bare what it impersonates in the very act of representing it.[21] Theatre is a mirror held up to nature 'to show virtue her own feature, scorn her own image, and the very age and body of the time his form and pressure [. . .]' as Hamlet says, this second and crucial part of the quotation being usually shelved as less important by most critics. In the modulation from Jacobean to modern, theatre is as it were squared. It becomes the representation of a representation, the baring of a baring, the extracted essence of what had already been made essential. The Jacobean patterns are anatomized and refined by the modern play, so that the twentieth-century theatrical schemes of life are at once mediated by and pitted against the theatrical schemes of Jacobean life. In the bringing together of two allied and yet opposed representations of reality, the second one being at a double remove, the line of acceptance is strained to the maximum. It is this constant straining of meaning through the structural double-entendre which allows us to intuit a kind of essential theatricality, which in turn refers us to the quintessence of life according to the text. And there precisely lies the 'consistency' of the fundamentals Barker wants us to recognize. The terror it holds in store for us is that such fundamentals are theatrically proved to be universal by their redoubled inscription in two absolutely autonomous historical realities.

What is intensified, made quintessential, through the squaring of theatre is the core of the power game in terms of human relations,[22] the sexual relationship: in this extreme of the penetration of self by self, the shock with the other[23] and with life is made absolutely climactic. Hence the use of rape to extract, invert and reclaim, for what truth it held, the rottenness of acceptance in the former seduced Bianca. Nobody is more knowledgeable than Livia in such matters: 'Oh, listen, our love plunged through all layers of affection, burst longing, split open desire, struck seams not of comfort but of truth.'[24] The splitting open and the seams she speaks of could be said to exemplify the relation established between the two plays. Theirs is a kind of superimposition, of 'verticality' of meaning not to be achieved by sheer juxtaposition, as in Stoppard's intertextual practices, but by an appropriation which continues the Jacobean text while subtly subverting it from within: '[. . .] I'm trying to get an epic quality which is vertical – or that's the only way I can think of it, which may be psychological or something. I want the scale, but I don't want the narrative unfolding the way it does in *Victory*,[25] for instance, any more. I'm tired of that', a pronouncement which is exactly contemporary to our play.[26] Such a verticality seems to me perfectly expressive of the derivative metatextuality Barker invents. To take only one example, perhaps the most glaring, and one which brings together the extremes of distance and catastrophe:

Sordido's name is kept unchanged though the character is now called the 'immaculate rebel'.[27] In the moment of what he terms his 'first entrance to the gateway of all life and death',[28] he, the virgin man, restores Bianca to her lost purity. And yet he remains 'Sordido', and his 'entrance', his unique action, amounts to outright violence, the price of which is instant death. In the very paradox of a saviour whose traumatic methods still justify the derogatory name is found both, and at once, the distance of Brecht and the violence of Artaud in their superimposed or 'vertical' copresence. The (sexual) semantic 'seam' that unites Jacobean to contemporary runs in a similar way through every single element in the second act. It is the foundation of a kind of historical bivocalism that puts face to face and confronts two ways and states of life, and leaves us in awe at the spectacle of a permanence demonstrated both in spite, and by means, of the passing of centuries.

On the basis of this postulated permanence, the play imposes upon us a semantic catastrophe whose disruptive aggressiveness remains latent throughout the second act, a catastrophe in the sense of an unresolved tension that suggests nevertheless some sort of hoped for opening. The play cannot be said to progress towards a solution. It rather deepens its constitutive strategy. The process is one of elimination of all anecdotal elements, be they historical or 'psychological', to reach a central area of contradictoriness which endures and never changes. This ahistorical conception of life explains two contrary aspects of the work. The first one is the fact that the rape can still be seen, albeit paradoxically, as a moment of resolution and revelation that separates a darker before from a more enlightened after. Yet, one should also, and rather, see it as a restoration that does not solve anything but only repairs a maximum imbalance, and makes it possible for average life to start again on its own trundling way. Hence the second characteristic, the fact that language sometimes achieves a validity and forcefulness which seem to approximate the best in Shakespeare. Such as Sordido's 'And her protesting mouth was stopped not by a fist, but greed and glamour suffocated it',[29] or Livia's 'It kills the soul not to exploit an inspiration',[30] or 'No, life is alteration, the shedding of all things until at death there is no regret',[31] or Bianca's 'it eases my journey through this puddle of dead dreams'.[32]

In such moments, and with such vividness and depth, the text can be said to be essentially poetic. It is poetic in a general sense, because it brings out in all its clarity the extraordinary complexity

Drama on Drama

and compositeness of the relation of the individual to life and society. The medley of confused and confusing motivations which centre on the allied drives to sex and power is here laid open for us to see and understand, not to judge and condemn. In this regard, I take the metatextual unveiling in the play to be the equivalent of a prolonged and bitter epiphany which makes us confront the hidden and unaccepted truths of our paltry motivations. Barker wants 'to subvert preconceived notions – to worry away at people's conviction, if they have any conviction',[33] 'to restore the *word* to theatre' through poetry, 'by which [he] mean[s] the crafting of language'.[34] In that more specific domain of poetry, Barker strikes one as intensely original. One senses a profound honesty and freshness in his use of language, the same as the one achieved in many of Seamus Heaney's poems. He keeps up the unsparing plainness of Middleton, but purifies it semantically by saving it from all the excesses that referred the reader or the spectator to types. His resulting downrightness seems more disturbing because it is shown to be grounded in facts: it gives expression to what we know is in our minds, but dare not admit even to our private selves. It shows us the general truth in us under the disguises and cunning ways which the workings of ideology and the unconscious make us naturally resort to. Barker's metatheatre serves as a kind of sieve and intensifier to return us to basics that concern us directly, and this not through historically dated beings but through average representatives of the stubborn mass of ever unlearning beings we call humanity. The desperate appeals and summonses present in this play bring us very close to some of the contemporary British writers who use the novel for parallel purposes and with similar effects. In so far as his theatre is content to show what life is and entails, it can be said to be 'celebratory'.[35] In spite of the terrible consistency he itemizes so clinically, Barker is not without a curious tenderness for his characters – I am not talking of the person of the author but of the writer, what we nowadays call the implied author – because they are the helpless prey of life's ambivalences and imbalances, which immediately suggests that these imbalances are perhaps indicative of unsuspected processes of resilient equilibration.

Barker's play extracts in all perspicuousness for us, and forces us to see, what we had not seen, what makes the staple food of our everyday thoughts. What we call history allows us to look upon the past as a sort of formative stage instrumental to our own supposedly more mature consciousness.[36] Barker's use of intertextuality unsettles the presuppositions that feed this 'secret history in us'.[37] By keeping the actual words and sentences from the original play and forcing them into a new contemporary textual descent, he corners us into admitting that the behavioural logic of by-gone years is equivalent to ours, and that what we had condemned from the comfortable distance of the present as violent and unrefined, is just ours, fully ours, in different guises and ways. Unfortunately, one cannot help adding that it is not only ours potentially, but remains stringently topical, of the most up-to-date and commonly referred to topicality, the one the media thrive on. Such an inventive and committed use of the intertext is not for entertainment's sake, nor for intellectual brilliancy. It has the terrible seriousness T. S. Eliot attributes to the Elizabethan farce which he discovers in Marlowe's *The Jew of Malta*.[38]

Barker affirms that '[he does] not do research' for his historical plays and that 'they are an amalgam of intuitions'.[39] Yet he appeals to a refined sense of cultural awareness. True to the demanding seriousness of his purposes, he provocatively declares: 'I don't think there is a popular culture that is actually worthwhile.'[40] What he means is that his plays force the audience to feel and think, and that for him theatre is anything but escapism in the tradition of easy-going stage make-believe. And he also has some hope that audiences can be educated away from their television mores and habits, away from the woolly consensual values of inane, though well-meaning, humanism. He wants to startle his spectator into awareness. His characters stand 'against compromise and for the whole hog', as he claimed in 1981.[41] The 'hog', that is, 'refusing to settle for less than the whole' in matters of sexuality, but possibly in matters of life too. In this, Barker is at one with the generation of British writers now in their forties. His complex collaboration with Middleton is based on nothing less than the belief that 'the big things are the things (theatre) does best'[42] and that there is an audience for such an approach in this, our age of distance.

Notes

1. *Women Beware Women (with Thomas Middleton)* followed by *Pity in History*, John Calder (London, 1989), pp. 46, 52. All the references are to this edition. To avoid any confusion in the notes, Barker's text will be referred to as *Playscript 112*.

2. 'Livia: "By this catastrophe she'll grope for knowledge her ambition hides from her" ' (p. 51); 'Hippolito: "Oh, catastrophe!" / [. . .] Bianca: "Catastrophe is also birth" ' (pp. 60–1).

3. According to Gérard Genette's terminology, the intertext is constituted by the derivation of a 'hypertext' (Barker's play) from a 'hypotext' (Middleton's play). Gérard Genette, *Palimpsestes* (Paris: Seuil, 1982).

4. 'My characters have a terrible consistency', 'Barker on Middleton', in *Playscript 112*, fly-leaf (no page number).

5. 'Middleton's world is a sexual stock-exchange. And I redeem his lost souls. I, the pessimist, redeem his rotted kindness', *Playscript 112*, 'Barker on Middleton'.

6. *Playscript 112*, p. 61.

7. *Playscript 112*, 'Barker on Middleton'.

8. *Playscript 112*, p. 47.

9. Thomas Middleton, *Women Beware Women*, The New Mermaids (London, 1968), p. 111.

10. Arnold Wesker, *The Merchant* (London: Methuen, 1983); Emma Tennant, *Woman Beware Woman* (London: Faber & Faber, 1989 [1983]).

11. 'Howard Barker Interviewed by Malcolm Hay and Simon Trussler', *Theatre Quaterly*, 10.40, 1981, 7.

12. Tony Dunn, 'Interview with Howard Barker', *Gambit*, 11.41, 1984, 35.

13. *Playscript 112*, p. 55, and 'Touch me not', John, 20:17.

14. As in Pasolini's St Matthew film in which it is the revolutionary side of Christ that is preferentially selected and developed.

15. 'The contradictions are never resolved. How should they be, unless you are a religious or a political fanatic', Tony Dunn, op. cit., p. 44. And about *Victory* : 'The audience doesn't quite know where it ought to be, because the contradictions are insoluble [. . .] It's a theatre of openness. It invites choice, or it invites flight from choice', 'Howard Barker Interviewed by Finlay Donesky', *New Theatre Quarterly*, 11.8, 1986, p. 344.

16. *Playscript 112*, p. 45.

17. Ibid., p. 50.

18. Ibid., p. 55.

19. Ibid., p. 59.

20. Ibid., p. 51 and pp. 60–1.

21. In their French translation of Aristotle's *Poetics* (Paris: Seuil, 1980), Roselyne Dupont-Roc and Jean Lallot justify their choice of 'représentation' for 'mimesis' in preference to 'imitation' by the fact that the idea itself is fundamentally theatrical in origin and that it implies a reference to both the source object and the target object, the one embodied on the stage, while 'imitation' tends to refer us preferentially to the source object. According to them, theatre re-presents the facts of life it focuses upon.

22. 'Any amount of power a man will take, provided we permit it, that's the shit in him', 'Howard Barker: A Personal View', Ian McDiarmid, *Gambit*, 11.41, p. 53.

23. To use Emmanuel Levinas's terminology for whom the Other con-

fronts and forces the self in what amounts to a war of differences (*L'Humanisme de l'autre homme*, 1973).

24. *Playscript 112*, p. 53.
25. Howard Barker, *Victory: Choices in Reaction* (London: Calder, 1983).
26. Donesky, op. cit., p. 337.
27. *Playscript 112*, p. 53.
28. Ibid., p. 49.
29. Ibid., p. 52.
30. Ibid., p. 57.
31. Ibid., p. 56.
32. Ibid., p. 44.
33. Donesky, op. cit., p. 336.
34. Ibid., p. 337.
35. Tony Dunn, 'Interview with Howard Barker', op. cit., p. 44.
36. 'The way we approach history [...] is always with condescension [...] that we are entitled to look back as if through the telescope at lesser beings. That's always offended my sensibilities', Donesky, op. cit., p. 338.
37. Ibid., p. 338.
38. 'Christopher Marlowe' in *Selected Essays* (London, 1932), p. 123.
39. Tony Dunn, 'Interview with Howard Barker', op. cit., p. 34.
40. Donesky, op. cit., p. 340.
41. Malcolm Hay and Simon Trussler, op. cit., p. 10.
42. Tony Dunn, 'Interview with Howard Barker', op. cit., p. 38.

5

Japanese Theatrical Forms in Edward Bond's *The Bundle* and *Jackets*

Monique Prunet

In 1968 when Edward Bond's first play inspired by Japan, *Narrow Road to the Deep North*, was produced, many critics at the time found similarities with the various and different genres of Japanese theatre, from Noh to Kabuki and even Bunraku. According to Ronald Bryden, the theatre critic of *The Observer* at the time, Bond might have been influenced by the visiting Noh Theatre in London then. The scenes rapidly following one another through their presentation of a historical episode, appear to be more closely related to Kabuki than to Noh, in which action is told rather than represented on the stage. However, it seems to me that clear references to the techniques of the Noh theatre may be found in both *The Bundle* and *Jackets*.

NOH

A traditional Noh play rarely presents an action as it is taking place, but it recalls a past event through elaborate song and dance. According to Professor René Sieffert:

> The Noh is the poetic crystallization of a privileged moment in the life of a hero, detached from its spatiotemporal context and projected into a dream universe evoked and revealed by means of a witness who is the *waki*.[1]

The three elements of the traditional Noh theatre, according to the principles of the great master Zeami, may be traced in *The Bundle* and *Jackets*: the use of the two main Noh characters, the *shite* and the *waki*, the classical structure of a Noh play, *jo*, *ha* and *kyû*, or introduction, development and conclusion, and the three levels of understanding which lead to unity, the metaphysical aim of Noh. However, the two plays should not be considered as westernized Noh plays, because the main element of a Noh play, emotion expressed through dance, is absent from Bond's plays.

Indeed, the hero, the central character in each play, may appear as the *shite* of a Noh play, whether it be Wang in *The Bundle* or, in *Jackets*, Chiyo in Part One and Brian in Part Two. As to the *waki*, it would seem that in both plays, there is one character whose role, without being as passive as it might be in an actual Noh play, emphasizes the part played by the hero, the *shite*. However, I would like to point out that, whereas in a Japanese Noh the *shite* and the *waki* should be considered as actors impersonating the characters of the play, the actual characters of Wang, Chiyo and Brian may be interpreted by any western actor or actress, not specifically trained for a highly specialized part, as are Japanese Noh actors.

Traditionally, the *shite* is required to portray a wide range of characters, whether it be gods, great warriors, women or ghosts, whereas the *waki* roles are of three different kinds: Ministers, Priests and Common Men, including warriors, townsmen and villagers. It should also be remembered that in a Noh play the *waki* never represents a ghost, a demon, a god or a woman, unlike the *shite*.

In *The Bundle*, Wang and Basho may be considered respectively as the *shite* and the *waki*. Indeed, in scene 1, Basho presents himself as a poet on his way to enlightenment, in the same way as would the *waki* in a Noh play, a priest travelling to a shrine. In this scene, a bundle, the eponymous hero, a baby abandoned by the river, attracts Basho's attention. His refusal to take him on his journey and the decision by the ferryman to bring the child home appear to emphasize the role he will play in the future. At the beginning of scene 2, Wang, now 14 years old, does establish himself as the *shite* through his brilliant dialogue with the ferryman, who can be considered as his attendant or *tsure* in a Noh play.

In key scenes, such as scene 4, when Wang's nine years as Basho's servant have been completed, or in scene 10, the last in the play, the contrast between the roles of the *shite* and the *waki* is obvious. Whereas Wang, like a new Moses, has become the successful leader of the people's rebellion against the landowner, Basho has been abandoned and his failure appears as a catalyst to Wang's success. The uselessness of his life is illustrated by Wang's parable: the story of a man who wasted his life carrying on his back the king who has been dead for a long time. Basho wasted his own life in his vain quest for enlightenment. The future belongs to Wang, the *shite*, who, through political awareness, has been able to lead and channel the energy of popular power towards a better destiny.

In *Jackets*, two distinct sets of *shite* and *waki* are presented: in 'Part One: The Village School', Chiyo, the mother of the young boy Kotaro, may be considered as the *shite* and Genzo as the *waki*; in 'Part Two: The City', Brian is the *shite* and Phil the *waki*.

In Part One, although Chiyo is the first character to appear on the stage, whereas in a traditional Noh play, the *waki* makes his entrance first, she indeed plays the part of the *shite*, the central character around whom the whole action of the play revolves: her role is pivotal, as she brings her son to be sacrificed, thus echoing Abraham's sacrifice of Isaac, but without the happy ending. Deprived of her action, Bond's message on society's cruelty to children would be lost. The importance of her role is explicitly made clear in the third scene, her monologue, 'Chiyo's Narration'. She reveals that her husband, Matsuo, Kotaro's father, and herself have decided to sacrifice their son in order to save Kan Shu, the young emperor, from Henba, a rebel general, who has ordered Matsuo to present him with the young prince's head as he knows that he is hidden by Genzo, the schoolmaster at whose school Chiyo has just taken her son. Her presence in the next two key scenes, 'The Identification' and 'The Proclamation', her finding on her son's desk the letter he wrote for his parents – stating that he is proud to die for a cause: 'Dearest mother you brought me here to die [. . .] It gave me great joy to learn that our prince still lived and even greater joy to learn that I would die for him'(p. 41) – and her commenting on his death with emotion but at the same time laughing, in contrast with her husband's crying,[2] put her into a specific category of *shite*. In Mad Woman or *Kyôjo Mono* plays, these *shite* impersonate deranged women, whose loss of a child has driven them mad. 'Chiyo's Narration' may recall the quest of the mad mother for her lost son in the Noh play *Sumidagawa*, put into music by Benjamin Britten under the title *Curlew River*, 'a parable for church performance'.[3]

As the *waki*, Genzo's part may be more active than the traditional *waki* in a Noh play. He falls into the category of *otoko-waki* or Common Men, as he is neither a Minister, nor a Priest. Indeed his role is instrumental in the accomplishment of Kotaro's ritual sacrifice: he is at the same time the harbinger of bad news – Henba's order 'to cut off the prince's head' (p. 22) – the decision-maker in choosing Kotaro's head to replace the young prince's and the executor of Henba's order. In drawing the audience's attention to the monstrous sacrifice, he emphasizes the *shite*'s grief and pride, thus stressing Bond's view on the barbarity of society.

As to Kotaro, the sacrificial victim in the play, his character is that of a *kokata* or 'child actor', of about ten years old, who accompanies the *shite*. A *kokata* often impersonates a high ranking person, such as the Emperor, symbolically represented by a child. A child's innocence and purity are meant to emphasize the character's dignity and power. Thus Kotaro's sacrifice is made all the more poignant as, through his death, he actually becomes the young emperor.

Part Two of *Jackets* mirrors the events of Part One, but takes place in contemporary England. Here the presentation may appear closer to the traditional Noh play, as Phil Lewis, the *waki*, makes his entrance first and welcomes home his school friend Brian Tebham, a soldier in uniform who, as the central character, is the *shite*. As a townsman, Phil belongs to the category of *otoko-waki*. In scene 4, 'The Street', and scene 5, 'The Canal Path', the dialogue between the two young men ending in Brian's dramatic suicide, may appear as the traditional exchanges between *shite* and *waki*, the relation of a tale leading to the *kuse-mai* or story dance. Scene 2, 'The Padre's Office', and scene 3, 'The same – Later', have already made clear the purposes of the tragic encounter between Brian and Phil: in a city torn by riots, the commanding officer has decided to sacrifice a soldier whose killing by the rebels will provide an incentive for repression.

Throughout the play, even in the last scene, 'Mrs Lewis's Kitchen', Brian's presence may be felt, as that of a ghost hovering over the characters. His corpse in scene 6, 'The Police Station', where the two mothers, Mrs Lewis and Mrs Tebham, as if in another Solomon's judgement episode, have to identify the victim, may be considered as the traditional ghostly apparition of the *shite* at the end of a Noh play.

As to the structure of both *The Bundle* and *Jackets*, it seems to be close to the classical Noh structure, albeit the fact that a traditional Noh performance includes five plays, the first being the introduction or *jo*, the next three the development or *ha* and the last one the conclusion or *kyû*. However each of the two plays unfolds according to such a pattern which will be illustrated by a few appropriate examples from each play.

In *The Bundle*, the introductory scene may be considered as a replica of the historical scene as related by the actual Basho: abandoning the young child, the future Wang, constitutes a serious error of judgment by the poet–philosopher, an error fraught with unpredictable consequences, because the abandoned child later plays a leading role and exercises power. Should Basho have taken care of him, there would have been no play! As remarked by Errol Durbach about Bond's *Narrow Road to the Deep North*, in other plays dealing with the same topic – *Oedipus Rex, The Winter's Tale*, or *The Caucasian Chalk Circle* – the abandoned child is eventually rescued. But Basho's refusal weighs tragically on society in both cases:

> Basho, ironically in search of enlightenment, merely negates the civilizing values implicit in his calling. The consequences of his regression form the action of the play, for the future of the child contains – both literally and figuratively – the future of the entire society; jeopardize the one, and the other will collapse.[4]

Scene 4 repeats the initial abandonment scene: in attempting to keep Wang with him, Basho asks him to take in the child he has just found by the river and to bring him up in order to achieve enlightenment. However, the poet himself refuses to be burdened with such a responsibility, and so does Wang who hurls the child into the river (p. 29).

In *Jackets*, it is clear from the first scene of Part One, 'The New Pupil', that hierarchy and blind obedience to orders from a superior, here Chiyo, are of paramount importance. Obeying one's elders and betters, whether it be your own mother, the schoolmaster, a mighty warrior such as Henba, is not to be delayed because disobedience would immediately entail retribution of some kind. The schoolboys are scared of the schoolmaster's authority (p. 20) as is further demonstrated when Genzo enters (p. 21). Genzo and Tonami, his wife, are themselves scared of Henba who has demanded the young emperor's head. Orders spiralling down from those who in power have to be complied with, for fear of dreadful sanctions.

Social differences are emphasized through the contrast between the mountain pupils' popular speech and rough manners and Kotaro's. Pride in serving one's masters is closely associated to obedience to the ruling class. At the end of the first scene, after having decided that Kotaro's head will be presented as Kan Shu's, Genzo makes it clear that it is an honour for Kotaro to have been chosen as a sacred victim:

That boy's lucky! He was born above his rank – now he'll die
above it: killed by an officer's sword! He came to learn. I'd've
taught him to die for his country.

(p. 25)

In the first scene of Part Two, 'Mrs Lewis's kitchen', law and order
still inspire fear, in spite of the street riots: when the doorbell rings,
Mrs Tebham and Mrs Lewis are both scared of the police (p. 57).
Instead, Brian Tebham walks in, but his army uniform immediately
isolates him from his school mate, cutting him off from his roots
and turning him into an enemy of his own class.

The following scenes, 'The Padre's Office' and 'The same – later',
reveal even more blatantly the differences separating the rulers from
the ruled. The officer's contempt for the Brian Tebhams of this world
equals the Padre's cynicism. Brian will be immolated in the name
of King and country, so that the established order may prevail. But
whereas in Part One, Kotaro knew about his sacrifice which he
considered as an honour, Brian ignores that he has become the bait
of a machiavellian plot, until he meets Phil in 'The Canal Path'
scene.

The *kyû* or finale of a traditional Noh play brings the play to its
conclusion with an accelerated tempo. In *The Bundle*, Basho's flight
away from the rebels in scene 9 eventually takes him back to Wang
in scene 10: he is now a pathetic figure on a journey to nowhere,
contrasting with Wang's triumph. *Jackets* offers a double-faced conclusion: established order and authority have been maintained at
the end of Part One, whereas after Brian's death, Phil's decision to
fight on may be the first step towards revolutionizing society.

According to Zeami, the three levels of understanding leading
to unity, the metaphysical aim of Noh through the perfection of
acting – what he calls the 'flower' – appeal to the senses of sight
and hearing and to the spirit. The first level involves elements of
violence including death. In a traditional Noh play, they are made
clear through fast dances and brilliant costumes. In both *The Bundle*
and *Jackets*, violence is a counterpoint to the whole argument. In
The Bundle, it may be expressed in deeds, such as Wang hurling the
baby into the river in scene 4, or in words such as the soldiers'
brutal comments when drowning the ferryman in scene 9. In Part
One of *Jackets* violence ranges from Henba's threats, in 'The Show'
scene, when he is interrogating the schoolboys and humiliating them
– a scene which is not to be found in the original Japanese play – to

Kotaro's execution which, although not seen on the stage, is made all the more visual through the display of the boy's severed head. In Part Two, actual death takes place on the stage when Brian shoots himself, but the atmosphere is highly evocative of social unrest, aggravated by the looming threat of military retaliation.

The second level of understanding is related to the sense of hearing through music, chant and the actual words. In my opinion, the power of the dialogues and images play a far more important role in both plays than the songs included in *Jackets*. When, in scene 4 of *The Bundle*, Wang declares to the abandoned child: 'You've been lying there for hundreds of years. [...] You're as big as a mountain (p. 28). [...] Must the whole world lie by this river like a corpse?' (p. 29), the audience is hit by the impact of his anger and despair at his feeling of powerlessness. In the last scene of Part Two of *Jackets*, the officer announces that the military clampdown on the rioting city is going to take place that very night: 'The code's name's Fallen Warrior' (p. 93) is trumpeted with such cynicism and contempt that one might want to join forces with the rebels.

The spirituality of Noh, deriving from its religious sources and from Zen Buddhism, is expressed through a sense of the sacred. The appeal to the spirit is tightly woven into the texture of both plays, but aiming rather at political awareness than mysticism, hence the playwright's choice to transfer the events into the past of a foreign country in *The Bundle*, and to juxtapose two different ages and countries in *Jackets*. Both plays emphasize the rebirth and suffering of a human being: it happens almost literally in *The Bundle*, since Wang has been saved like Moses; in *Jackets*, Kotaro and Brian, the victims sacrificed in the name of ruthless power, are meant to focus the audience's attention on Bond's post-modernist vision of society. In the playwright's own words, 'theatre [...] can take things apart so that they subvert the past we know'.[5]

KABUKI

Kabuki theatre, derived from puppet theatre and the performances of a group of dancers led by Okuni, a former female temple dancer, at the beginning of the seventeenth century, is less ritualistic than Noh but it is nonetheless a highly stylized genre of Japanese theatre. Although dance is not the main characteristic of Bond's *The Bundle* and *Jackets*, other elements are present, which relate them to Kabuki.

Indeed, Joshua Logan's opinion on Kabuki: 'The Kabuki theater is universal and timeless and reaches the core of man',[6] may apply to both plays. Of course their production on a Western stage cannot include traditional elements of a Kabuki play, such as the swish of the *agemaku*, the curtain at the far end of the *hanamichi*,[7] or the *mie* which are dramatic poses used to express a climax of great emotional tension. But other elements in Kabuki may be traced in the two plays. Both belong to the category of *jidaimono* or history plays, although, in *The Bundle*, the characters do not belong to the samurai warriors and the upper classes, as they do in such plays; *The Bundle* and Part One of *Jackets* are also both set in a premodern Japan in which a set code of behaviour was the rule. Besides, the characters conform to a model or stylization of what they represent.

Unlike *sewamono* plays, which deal with the everyday life of the common people, *jidaimono* plays refer to a golden age of Japanese history, a pre-Edo period,[8] and the main characters belong to the samurai warriors and the upper classes. *Jackets* was inspired by the last episode, Act VI, of a famous Kabuki play, *Sugawara Denju Tenarai Kagami* or *Sugawara and the Secrets of Calligraphy*, first produced in 1746 as a *jôruri*[9] puppet play, written mainly by Takeda Izumo. The title of this episode is 'Terakoya' in the actual Kabuki play, 'The Village School' in Part One of *Jackets*. As to the events in Part Two, set in modern Europe,[10] they follow the Japanese pattern in an urban context, most probably a large industrial city in northern England.

The original Japanese play, *Sugawara Denju Tenarai Kagami*, tells the story of the exile of a tenth-century aristocrat, Sugawara-no-Michizane, whose name in the Kabuki play is Kanshojo. His son, Kanshusai, is saved by Kotaro's death. Bond has dramatically transformed Kanshojo into the dead Emperor, killed by the rebel Henba (Genba in the Kabuki play), and his son Kan Shu into a prince who may inherit his father's throne, thus turning Kotaro's sacrifice into blind devotion to a questionable figure of authority. One should recall the practice for Kabuki playwrights to set their story in a pre-Edo era, not only to emphasize the event but also mainly to evade the censorship imposed by the Shogunate. More recently, immediately after the Second World War, during the American occupation, the performance of the 'Terakoya' episode in the Kabuki play, *Sugawara Denju Tenarai Kagami*, was banned in Japan on its first night on 15 November 1945, and for two years, the ban was applied to about 20 other plays precisely because of the patriotic issues they raised.[11] Hence Bond's interest for this episode which he has used to stress his own concern about modern society's oppressive and violent nature:

> I write about violence as naturally as Jane Austen wrote about manners. Violence shapes and obsesses our society, and if we do not stop being violent we have no future. People who do not want writers to write about violence want to stop them writing about us and our time. It would be immoral not to write about violence.[12]

The Bundle and Part One of *Jackets* take place in premodern Japan, in a violent society in which a rigid code of behaviour was enforced both by the Shogunate and by the samurai's Bushido philosophy.[13] Although Part Two of *Jackets* is taking place in Margaret Thatcher's Britain, a strict code is applied so that law and order might prevail, even though the rank and file are denied any explanation: as the Officer explains to the Padre: 'Millions are sacrificed in war and they don't know. God doesn't mind' (p. 63). But whereas in premodern Japan, the warriors' code was based on honour in order not to lose face, in modern Britain, according to Bond, cynicism and manipulation prevail.

Bloodshed and actual violence are not frequently used on the stage in Kabuki plays, and *tachimawari* or fights are usually mimed and accompanied by *geza* or background music, rather than realistically performed. In both plays, there are few scenes of actual violence: except for Brian shooting himself at the end of 'The Canal Path' scene in Part Two of *Jackets*, no one is killed on the stage. But the impact of violence is brought forth otherwise.

In *The Bundle*, at the end of scene 8, when Basho orders the soldiers to throw the ferryman into the river for having betrayed him by dropping his pole into the water as a warning sign of danger to Wang, there is no trial, no evidence: justice administered by Basho has to be expeditive and to serve as an example. The poet–judge exits like Pontius Pilate, while the ferryman's groans can be heard in the wings, as he is being hit by the soldiers. At the same time his wife starts crying and the audience can hear 'the weak, persistent sound of her cry, on one note' (p. 69). Although it is not taking place on the actual stage, the summary execution of the ferryman, drowned as if he were a dangerous dog, is nonetheless made all the more poignant through a few splashes and his wife's cry. In scene 9, distant shots and bursts of firing underline the atmosphere of war and violence spreading across the country, contrasting with the sight of Basho writing at his desk.

Violence in *Jackets* is of a more visual kind. In Part One, at the beginning of 'The Identification' scene, Genzo, having carried out Henba's order, returns with the ritual headbox which contains Kotaro's head, supposed to be Kan Shu's: 'His robe and hands are spattered with blood' (p. 39). The execution of Henba's cruel order is realistically emphasized by the display of blood on the schoolmaster's clothes; whereas in the original Kabuki play, the audience can hear the sound of Genzo's sword off stage, in *Jackets*, there is no actual evidence of Kotaro's execution. Great emphasis is placed by Bond on the blood shed in order to save Kan Shu's life when Genzo tells how brave Kotaro was:

> Genzo opens his wrap to show his blood-stained robe.
> *Chiyo* (clutching the robe):   Kotaro's blood!
> *Genzo*:   He falls to the floor! His blood falls down on him –
> *Chiyo* (clutching the robe):   I smell him! In his blood! His skin!
> His breath! My boy! Kotaro! Kotaro!
>
> (p. 43)

Such gory details do not appear in traditional Kabuki, as horror is expressed through acting rather than visual display.

However, Bond's dramatic writing also emphasizes his purpose: to focus his audience's attention on violence in our society. In Part Two of *Jackets*, in 'The Canal Path' scene, the atmosphere of violence is summed up in a few words by Phil as he describes to Brian how he joined the rebels while looting a store:

> *Phil*:   I was in a store. Riot outside. Ground floor empty. Tailor's dummy on the stairs. Evenin jacket. Tried it on! Another dummy in the mirror: by the rails. Got a leather jacket. Went over. Bent down. Not a dummy: bloke tryin it on – shot in the stomach. I was in an evenin jacket strippin a corpse an there's a war goin on in the street. You can't live like that.
>
> (p. 74)

Phil's description stresses the incongruity of the situation, and throws an almost surrealistic light on the scene, in which he finds himself unable to distinguish between the living and the dead, a confusion emphasized by the interplay of mirrors.

An aspect of violence which belongs to traditional Japanese mores is self-inflicted: ritual suicide, *seppuku* or *harakiri*,[14] plays an important part in Kabuki plays. The most famous one is to be found in the 1748 play *Kanadehon Chûshingura*, known in the West as *The 47 Rônin*,[15] immortalized by Japanese film-makers, one of the most celebrated films being Mizoguchi's *Genroku Chûshingura* in 1941/42. In *Narrow Road to the Deep North*, Edward Bond presented a *seppuku* taking place on the stage: in the final scene, the young priest Kiro commits ritual suicide by the river just as a half-drowned anonymous man rises out of the water.

In Part Two of *Jackets*, Brian's suicide at the end of The Canal Path scene may be considered as a *seppuku*, although the young soldier shoots himself with the gun he has wrenched from Phil. Brian is trapped: he has no other alternative but death, because he would be shot as a traitor if he returned to his barracks and he has already betrayed his own class by joining the army. Although he uses a gun and not a dagger, one may find some similitude between the traditional etiquette of *seppuku* and his own choice: 'He crouches over the gun and shoots himself in the stomach' (p. 79). A few moments earlier, he had held the gun in front of his chest, but had not pulled the trigger. His death may lack the formality of *seppuku*, but nonetheless his courage is not to be questioned. Phil may appear as playing the part of the traditional assistant or *kaishaku-nin*, as he tries to stop Brian rocking and covers his body with his own leather jacket.

Kotaro's ritual execution and Brian's suicide, both embodying self-sacrifice, are the twin faces of ritual violence as performed in feudal Japan, thus providing a link through the two parts of the play and a mirror to each other.

Through its high level of stylization, Kabuki appears 'as a vehicle that carries us to the heart of reality. Through actors who are "human pieces of architecture" [. . .] we begin to see ourselves, for each character is an immense abstraction, or rather a character reduced to its essence'.[16] However, whereas in Kabuki, references are clearly obvious, fixed by tradition so that the audience may immediately identify and understand the meaning of each character through established conventions and a specific code, such as *mie* or dramatic poses, *roppo* or stylized exits, *serifu* or speech, *kata* or forms, in both *The Bundle* and *Jackets* Bond does not use such formalized beacons to signpost his dramatic purposes.

The characters in both plays are emblematic of a social class or function; they are the standard bearers of the playwright's ideas and of their strength. As in a Kabuki performance during which the *kakegoe* callers[17] encourage the actors and noisily display their satisfaction, Bond, according to Tony Coult, has aimed at developing a kind of relationship 'between performer and audience [. . .] in which the audience is an equal partner in the unfolding event'.[18]

In *The Bundle*, Wang is originally the same child found by Basho on a river-bank in *Narrow Road to the Deep North*. Whereas in the earlier play, the child grows into a cruel and ambitious tyrant, Shogo, in *The Bundle*, Wang becomes a revolutionary leader, the head of an army of the oppressed and dispossessed, who manages to overthrow the ruling landowner and to lay the foundation stone of a better society. The moment at the end of scene 4, when Wang ponders over the future of another abandoned child, is one of dramatic intensity through a growing suspense as Wang repetitively picks up the child and puts it down again. When he suddenly hurls it from the stage into the river, that is the audience, the same audience may literally receive it as a shock, as the white sheet wrapping the child, both a symbol of innocence and a shroud, unfurls from his hand. Thus the audience is at the same time compelled to participate into a cruel act and unable to prevent it. 'It is a perfect dramatic moment and a precise and extreme challenge to an audience's own ability to make judgements.'[19]

In Part One of *Jackets*, the symbol of power is embodied by Kan Shu, who proclaimed himself emperor, after Kotaro's ritual beheading. He is the running thread between the two parts of the play. Whereas he was only a voice in Part One, speaking from behind a screen, in Part Two, in the second scene taking place in the Padre's office, he enters, 'in Japanese Imperial regalia' (p. 65) and formally bows to the audience. His unexpected and anachronistic intrusion into late twentieth-century Britain dramatizes the opening dialogue between Brian and the Padre, all the more so since Kan Shu is invisible to them and his actions without any actual results. The audience's attention is thus focused on the counterpoint of events, the simultaneousness between the Padre's ominous words to Brian and Kan Shu's picking up Brian's rifle and shooting him, as if reality and nightmare telescoped together. Dramatic effect is further enhanced when the Padre warns Brian about his future meeting with his enemy: 'You stand face to face with an enemy who speaks your language and walks your streets but inhabits another world. He might be from Japan. Don't trust him' (p. 66). The irony is that authority, in the person of Kan Shu, the enemy from another age and another country, thirteenth-century Japan, and from Part One of the play, is at that very moment still present on the stage.

Owing to its origins, Kabuki developed dances at a high level of sophistication with a wide range of musical instruments. In the nineteenth century, dance and drama were further integrated, so that dance and music became the essential parts of Kabuki. The character *ka* in the word Kabuki means 'song' and includes all music, hence the importance of music, whether it be vocal or instrumental music. In both *The Bundle* and *Jackets*, Bond's use of poems or songs is highly reminiscent of Kabuki techniques.

In *The Bundle*, Basho's poems as read by him in scene 4 before Wang's departure, or by Wang himself at the end of scene 5 do indeed punctuate the play as would songs in Kabuki. To me, the most forceful and striking poem is Basho's haïku in scene 9 which carries the ferryman's death sentence:

The ferry pole fell
Deep in the dark water – poked
In the eye of god.

(p. 68)

Basho then orders the soldiers: 'The ferryman's son knows he could not drop the pole in mistake. Throw him in the river. To warn the rest' (p. 68). The innocent form of a classical poem has been warped as Bond has turned the poet's art into crime, thus adding a more powerful dramatic dimension to the sound of a pole falling into the water.

Jackets includes two songs for Part One and three for Part Two, which were sung by a chorus from the cast.[20] In the French production in Paris in March 1993, the play was performed to the background of Khaled's very loud oriental music and songs, thus extending the dramatic impact of the 'theatre events'[21] in Bond's own words. At the same time, in some scenes, a black dancer in a long black robe was moving about at the back of the stage, a sinister and ominous presence, the embodiment of the tragic fate awaiting the innocent. As in Kabuki, music and dance are part of the very fabric of the play, as acknowledged by Claudel:

I mean music as used by a dramatist and not by a musician, attempting not to create a sonorous tableau, but to jolt and move our emotions by purely rhythmic and sonorous means, more direct and more brutal than words.[22]

Traditionally colours, costumes and props are extensively used in Kabuki; in both plays those elements intensify a specific dramatic moment, although Bond's characters do not wear the traditional wigs and costumes. Indeed it would be difficult for a Western audience to understand why in the 'Terakoya' episode, instead of wearing the traditional samurai wig with a shaven crown, Matsuomaru wears a *gojunichi* or 'fifty-day' wig to indicate that he has not been able to go to the barber because of his poor health. Nor would the symbol of his name – *matsu* meaning pine tree – be made clear by his kimono decorated with a pine tree motif, and be obvious to uninitiated spectators.

In both parts of *Jackets*, the use of colours underlines dramatic events. In the Kabuki 'Terakoya' episode, Tonami, the schoolmaster's wife, wears a *kokumochi* or standard kimono for a samurai's wife, usually brown. In the 1993 Paris production of *Jackets*, the colours of the kimonos and robes worn by Genzo, Tonami and Chiyo included various shades of light brown, clashing with the dark Japanese armours worn by the rebel Henba and his soldiers. In the first scene of Part Two, 'Mrs Lewis's Kitchen', there is a strong contrast between the colours of the two dresses looted by Phil, which Mrs Tebham, Brian's mother, is trying on: from a brown one, she gets into a bright one, red in the Paris production, the colour of fire and blood, which heralds her future bereavement. Phil's leather jacket also becomes emblematic as it changes hands through the play. In 'The Canal Path' scene, Brian's black tie is a declaration of war and heralds his coming death as he should have worn a white one like Phil, as a symbol of peace: thus life and death are drawn in black and white, a pitiful reduction.

As to traditional Kabuki props, fans and swords, if the characters in the two plays do not use fans, in 'The Identification' scene of *Jackets*, Genzo draws his sword against Chiyo who is frantically looking for her son. Other props are fraught with symbolic significance. In *The Bundle*, the recurrent ringing of the ferry bell and the use of a bowl of water stress moments of dramatic intensity particularly in scene 8 (p. 64) when, after offering the bowl to the mutilated Tiger, the ferryman calmly puts it down at the same time as the ferry bell is heard, ominously signalling the presence of Wang and his friends with their bundle of rifles, waiting for the ferryman.

Severed heads are important props in Kabuki, hence the obser-
vance of ritual when Matsuo is presented with the traditional headbox, a great dramatic moment as the audience knows that the severed
head is Kotaro's.

Paul Claudel called the Kabuki theatre 'a veritable professional
school for the dramatist',[23] and indeed key elements of traditional
Japanese theatrical forms have been woven by the playwright into
the very texture of both *The Bundle* and *Jackets*. Less important than
Noh or Kabuki, the influence of Bunraku should not be neglected:
in both plays, the characters, emblematic of a social class or function – in *The Bundle*, the poet, the liberator, the peasants and the
fishermen or, in *Jackets*, the tyrant, the warrior and the schoolmaster
– appear to be manipulated as are the puppets in a Bunraku play.
However, manipulation may change hands as in *The Bundle*, when
the tyrant-landowner is replaced by the liberating hero, Wang. The
title of *Jackets* or *The Secret Hand*, explicitly reveals the playwright's
intentions. Weaving visual elements of Japanese tradition evocative of the classical *ukiyoe*,[24] emphasizing hierarchy, ritual and sacrifice, the past living into the present, Edward Bond's *The Bundle* and
Jackets epitomize the playwright's increasing political commitment
and his attachment to the theatre as a tool crucial to the transformation of society: 'All revolutions are written on the back of
the calendar'.[25]

Notes

1.	Quoted in English by Leonard C. Pronko in *Theater East & West: Per-
spectives Toward a Total Theater* (University of California Press, 1967),
p. 75, from René Sieffert, 'Le Théâtre japonais', in *Les Théâtres d'Asie*,
éd. Jean Jacquot (Paris: CNRS, 1961), p. 149.
2.	It is important to underline here the stage directions: 'Two masks:
Chiyo laughing and Matsuo crying' (p. 44), and: 'Slowly the masks
change. As Chiyo recites she begins to weep and Matsuo to laugh'
(p. 45), as if the two characters had actually become Noh characters
wearing the traditional masks representative of their respective parts.
3.	Quoted in Leonard C. Pronko, *Theatre East & West*, op. cit., p. 103.
4.	Errol Durbach, 'Herod in the Welfare State: *Kindermord* in the Plays
of Edward Bond', *Educational Theatre Journal*, 27, 4, 1975, p. 484.
5.	In 'Notes on Post-Modernism' in Edward Bond's *Two Post-Modern
Plays: Jackets & In the Company of Men with September* (London: Methuen
Drama, 1990), p. 243.
6.	Quoted in Leonard C. Pronko, *Theater East & West*, op. cit., p. 138.

7. The *hanamichi* is an extension running from the far left of the stage through the audience into a green room at the back of the theatre.
8. The Edo period was an era of peace and isolation from 1603 to 1868, during which the Tokugawa family provided the ruling shoguns. It was during the Edo period that Kabuki appeared and blossomed.
9. *Joruri*: music based on narration with shamisen accompaniment, usually called *gidayu*.
10. Note in Edward Bond, *Jackets*, op. cit., p. 4.
11. This is a reference from the text by Toshio Kawatake in the December 1995 issue of the Japanese journal *Bungei-Shunju*.
12. Edward Bond, *Plays: Two* (London: Eyre Methuen, 1978), 'Author's Preface' to *Lear*, p. ix.
13. Bushido was the code of the warrior in feudal Japan.
14. 'The word *seppuku* is a polite reading of the characters for what is known [. . .] in the West as *harakiri. Hara* means "belly" and kiri is from kiru, meaning "to cut"', in Ronald Cavaye, *Kabuki: A Pocket Guide* (Rutland, Vermont & Tokyo, Japan: Charles E. Tuttle Company, 1993), p. 57.
15. The *rônin* were masterless samurai.
16. This is Gilles Sandier's analysis in *Arts*, as cited in Leonard C. Pronko, *Theater East & West*, op. cit., p. 131.
17. *Kakegoe* callers are members of the audience who shout at specific moments during the performance to show their appreciation.
18. Tony Coult, *The Plays of Edward Bond* (London: Methuen, 1977, ed. 1979), p. 85.
19. Colin Chambers and Mike Prior, *Playwrights' Progress: Patterns of Postwar British Drama* (Oxford: Amber Lane Press, 1987), p. 167.
20. For details about the places where the songs were sung in the two British productions of the play in 1989, see Edward Bond, *Jackets*, op. cit., p. 5.
21. In 'Notes on Post-Modernism' in Edward Bond, *Jackets*, op. cit., p. 243.
22. Quoted in English by Leonard C. Pronko, op. cit., p. 153, in Paul Claudel, *Le Livre de Christophe Colomb* (Paris: Gallimard, 1935), p. 21.
23. Quotation in Leonard C. Pronko, *Theater East & West*, op. cit., p. 131.
24. *Ukiyoe*: Japanese prints.
25. In Edward Bond, 'Notes on Post-Modernism', op. cit., p. 244.

Bibliography

Artaud, Antonin, *Le théâtre et son double* (Paris: Gallimard, 1964).
Banu, Georges, *L'acteur qui ne revient pas: journées de théâtre au Japon* (Paris: Aubier, 1986).
Bond, Edward, *Plays: Two* (London: Eyre Methuen, 1978).
Bond, Edward, *The Bundle or New Narrow Road to the Deep North* (London: Eyre Methuen, 1978).

88 *Drama on Drama*

Bond, Edward, *Two Post-Modern Plays: Jackets, In the Company of Men with September* (London: Methuen Drama, 1990).

Cavaye, Ronald, *Kabuki: A Pocket Guide* (Rutland, Vermont & Tokyo, Japan: Charles E. Tuttle, 1993).

Chambers, Colin and Prior, Mike, *Playwrights' Progress: Patterns of Postwar British Drama* (Oxford: Amber Lane Press, 1987).

Coult, Tony, *The Plays of Edward Bond*, rev., expanded edn (London: Eyre Methuen, 1979).

Daiji, Maruoka and Yoshikoshi, Tatsuo, *Noh* (Osaka: Hoikusha, 1969).

Durbach, Errol, 'Herod in the Welfare State: *Kindermord* in the Plays of Edward Bond', *Educational Theatre Journal*, 27, 4, 1975, pp. 480–7.

Internationale de l'Imaginaire, Nouvelle Série – N°5, *La Scène et la Terre: Questions d'Ethnoscénologie* (Babel. Maison des cultures du monde, 1996).

Jacquot, Jean, ed. *Les Théâtres d'Asie* (Paris: Editions du Centre National de la Recherche scientifique, 1961).

Lesoualc'h, Théo, *Les rizières du théâtre japonais* (Paris: Denoël, 1978).

Pronko, Leonard C., *Theater East & West: Perspectives Toward a Total Theater* (Berkeley, Los Angeles & London: University of California Press, 1967).

Roberts, Philip, *Bond on File* (London & New York: Methuen, 1985).

Sieffert, René, ed. and trans., *Zéami: La Tradition secrète du nô, suivie d'une journée de nô*, 'Collection UNESCO d'oeuvres représentatives' (Paris: Gallimard, 1960).

Tessier, Max, *Images du Cinéma Japonais* (Paris: Henri Veyrier, 1990).

Trussler, Simon, *Edward Bond*, published for the British Council by Longman Group, 1976.

Part II
The Theatrical Is the Real

6

Now Converging, Now Diverging: Beckett's Metatheatre

Ruby Cohn

Almost all Beckett's plays allude to their genre, but the allusions mutate over half a century. From Pirandellian toying with the drama as drama, Beckett evolves toward the performativity of experience as an intense theatre experience in a continuous present tense. His characters tend to be performers, whose audience shrinks over the years from onstage observers to avatars of themselves. The several observers on Beckett's stage have themselves been observed by critics, but the following piece restricts itself to more ostentatious metadrama.[1]

As early as Beckett's 1937 fragmentary *Human Wishes* three women characters watch a silent drunk who unsteadily climbs the steps in the home of Dr Samuel Johnson, which they share. One of the three, Mrs Desmoulins, remarks: 'Now this is where a writer for the stage would have us speak no doubt.'[2] And Samuel Beckett, the neophyte writer for the stage, does indeed have them speak – incidentally about the drama of their day, but no further about the scene in which they figure. Instead, Mrs Williams evokes 'the ignorant public', which, predicting divisions in today's formal theatres, is distributed into gallery, pit and boxes. Beckett's only venture into another century sports three historical women who name three playwrights of their time – Oliver Goldsmith, Hugh Kelly and Arthur Murphy – of whom two were dead in 1784, the putative year of that scene of human wishes.

A decade later in his 1947 *Eleutheria*, the play Beckett came most to dislike, metadramatic commentary is far more copious. His self-styled 'drame bourgeois' parodies *the* dramatic genre of the bourgeoisie, the well-made play. Although the term was derogatory even in the nineteenth century, the tics of the well-made play have proved durable: detailed exposition; crises rising to climactic curtains; revelation of a secret in an obligatory scene; swift resolution. The well-made play upheld bourgeois decorum, which was sometimes baldly stated by a *raisonneur*. At no time did metadramatic remarks pierce the façade of this genre, as they did in vaudeville and pantomime.

From *Eleutheria*'s Greek title to its silent conclusion, Beckett's well-made play subverts its own form: the exposition not only brims with extraneous information but it also places servants and bourgeois on an equal plane; crises take place offstage, and the first two acts end on anti-climactic kisses; the staging is ingenious but not spectacular; the obligatory scene usurps most of the last act, and the resolution circles back to the initial situation: Victor Krap, the scion of his bourgeois family, remains alone in his bare hotel room. Moreover, phrases of metadramatic dialogue puncture Beckett's 'drame bourgeois', as do occasional scenic directions. One might argue that metadrama is Beckett's *raisonneur*; artifice is the decorum of *Eleutheria*.

Act I is set in the Krap living-room, where several characters lament the two-year absence of Victor Krap, who is dimly visible in his hotel room. His father, Henri Krap, quips metadramatically at the expense of his coevals: scepticism about the dramatic viability of his wife or his new brother-in-law, Dr Piouk; recognition that his wife's corpulent friend dominates the stage although she serves no purpose there. To a question about his own role, Henri Krap replies that it is over, and the questioner observes that he nevertheless remains on stage. At two junctures, however, Henri Krap rises above such facile irony. Old and ill, he is helped to his feet, but then proudly displays his ability to exit and enter on his own: 'Je sors! (*Il sort. Il rentre.*) Je rentre! Et je ressors! (*Il sort. . . .*)'. These phrases, with accompanying movements, are what I have called theatereality, since the theatre and the real actions virtually converge; the character and the actor momentarily coincide.[3] More telling theatereality is embedded in Henri Krap's Act I curtain line: 'Rideau. (*Immobilité de M. Krap.*)'. Only in Act II of *Eleutheria* do we learn that the curtain was a metaphor for death, since M. Krap dies between the acts.

His metadramatic sensitivity transfers to a nameless glazier who is said to resemble him.[4] Aware that he does not speak like a craftsman, Beckett's Glazier designates himself as 'un poète qui préfère s'ignorer'. He also prefers to ignore his metadramatic bent. Like M. Krap, the Glazier comments on the play in progress: his own lack of definition, the play's entertainment appeal, the time wasted on supernumeraries, and especially the senselessness of the ongoing action. Nevertheless the Glazier is intermittently caught up in that action, which gradually narrows down to a conflict between himself and the differently rational Dr Piouk. The latter offers a swift conclusion, that is either the protagonist Victor Krap will accept poison and commit suicide, or he will reject it and return to the bourgeois life of Krap. The Glazier is less concerned with conclusions than with motivations: 'Il faut lui trouver un sens, sinon il n'y a qu'à baisser le rideau.' This time, however, Beckett delays the curtain for four pages while he clears the stage of everyone but the Glazier and his young son, who are irrelevant to the plot.

Act III, where resolution is traditional in the well-made play, opens with the Glazier awakening Victor Krap from a nightmare, only to demand that he take credible shape as a character.[5] When the Krap servant Jacques thanks Victor for explaining himself (offstage) on the night of his father's death, the Glazier tries to penetrate that explanation, but he is interrupted by a spectator who climbs from his box-seat on to the stage. The Prompter then comes onstage to accuse them all of deviating from the text, which suddenly drops from the flies. After an exchange of recriminations with the Glazier, the Spectator summarizes the Piouk–Glazier dispute, notes that the play's author is Samuel Béquet, and finally rephrases the Glazier's wish to understand Victor's motivation. Toward this end, the Spectator summons a Chinese torturer onstage for a literally obligatory scene. In view of the stage confusion, Beckett remarks in a scenic direction: 'Pressentiment que la pièce tout entière pourrait s'achever de la meme façon' (p. 140). After this metadramatic byplay the Glazier, the Spectator, and the Torturer elicit a self-justification from a terrified Victor: 'C'est une vie mangée par sa liberté.' Although the Glazier and the Spectator echo one another's metadramatic distaste of Victor's words, they finally accept his fictional limitations. However, when the Spectator (followed by the Torturer) attempts to return to his box seat, the Glazier insists that they exit by the wings. His insistence underlines the obvious – that the Spectator is a type-character played by an actor. The mollified Glazier returns his attention to the plot in which Dr Piouk, abetted by Victor's fiancée, challenges the protagonist to choose between life and death. Refusing, Victor invokes theatre: 'On ne peut pas se voir mort. C'est du théâtre.' Only actors can see themselves dead, but Beckett's fictional Victor Krap chooses not to choose. In taking his leave, the Glazier kisses Victor's hand – a habitual gesture in the well-made play, but not on the part of a metadramatic commentator, who has the longest role in this particular quasi-bourgeois drama. *Eleutheria* contains Beckett's most patent metadramatic animadversions. The Spectator, the Prompter, and even the stage text derive from Pirandello, but the Glazier is more complex.[6] Windows recur in several Beckett works, and in this ill-made play a window is shivered by the shoe of Victor Krap, who has renounced the outer for the inner world, unaware that he is the protagonist of a play. The Glazier never repairs the window, as he wavers between participating in the plot and criticizing it, between rhythmic conversations with his son and subservience to more conventional dialogue, between espousing the rationalism of a plausible concatenation and delivering a clumsy kiss on the hand of the irrational protagonist with the oxymoronic name.

It still amazes me that a mere year elapsed between the sprawl of *Eleutheria* and the play that changed twentieth-century Western drama – *En attendant Godot*. Gone is exposition, conflict, obligatory scene, resolution. But shards of metadramatic commentary remain. Like Henri Krap and the Glazier of *Eleutheria*, Didi and Gogo disparage the play in which they play, declaring it inferior to pantomime, circus and music-hall. Gogo's complaints might echo in the minds of the audience: 'Nothing happens, nobody comes, nobody goes, it's awful!' In this vein, too, Didi reassures Pozzo: '... I have lived through this long day and I can assure you it is very near the end of its repertory'. As late as the end of Act II Gogo sneers: 'Some diversion!'

In *Human Wishes* Mrs Williams scorns 'The ignorant public'. In *Eleutheria* Dr Piouk assures Henri Krap that he might 'amuser les badauds', and the latter voices his contempt of that enterprise; Henri's alter ego the Glazier reiterates: 'Faut amuser les badauds!' Yet in neither play does a character address the audience directly, as do both friends in *Godot*. Gogo looks at us as he ironizes: 'Inspiring prospects'. Didi refers to us as 'that bog', and he therefore understands Gogo's reluctance to exit through the auditorium. Pozzo addresses an onstage audience, but his words include us all: 'Is everybody looking at me? ... Is everybody listening?' After Didi echoes Pozzo on the virtual simultaneity of birth and death, he also echoes him on the actual theatre audience: 'At me too someone is looking'. These lines hover at the boundary of theatereality, but a fictionally blind Pozzo stands squarely in that realm when he asks where they are: 'It isn't by any chance the place known as the Board?' Informed of the tree, Pozzo concludes that it is not the Board, although we see him on the actual stage board.[7] Above all, however, *Waiting for Godot* metadramatically underlines the stage varieties of waiting; to pass the time, the two friends engage in games, questions, contradictions, exercises, abuse – the stuff of vaudeville, to which they allude verbally.

Endgame is more formal. The title succinctly summarizes the action: the process of ending as a process of playing. The difficulty of filling stage time is more arduous in *Endgame* because the characters are in a more advanced state of decay. Since Clov alone is mobile, they have fewer resources with which to propel the action forward. Time passing is conveyed through a drizzle of vague but metadramatic 'things' and antecedentless pronouns: '*This* is not much fun; *this* is deadly; . . . *this* has gone on long enough; how can *it* end. The *thing* is impossible. Some*thing* is taking its course' [my emphasis]. Hamm asserts three times: 'We're getting on', but the very repetition paradoxically undermines the assertion. More anxious are the separate, identically worded pleas of Hamm and Clov: 'Keep going, can't you, keep going.' This is more subtle metadrama than the ostentatious derogations of *Eleutheria*.

The self-consciousness of playing crosses the threshold into theatereality. Hamm wrenches syntax to announce his role: 'Me to play.' A residual tragedian, he enunciates the terminology of formal drama – audition, dialogue, aside, soliloquy, underplot.[8] Clov's line might seem more neutral, but in the context of tragedy 'making an exit' demands gestural panache. As opposed to these several reminders of traditional dramatic action, a single observation lampoons the actual theatre audience – that of Clov when he views them through the glass: 'I see . . . a multitude . . . in transports . . . of joy. [*Pause.*] That's what I call a magnifier.'

Winnie of *Happy Days* also has a magnifier, which she aims not at the audience but on stage items – toothbrush inscription, pornographic postcard, and the emmet – all invisible to us. Less self-aware than her male predecessors in Beckett's drama, Winnie never acknowledges the theatre audience, and yet her phrases occasionally include us: 'I am not merely talking to myself. . . . Strange feeling that someone is looking at me. . . . Someone is looking at me still. Caring for me still. Eyes on my eyes.' Like her male predecessors, Winnie finds it hard to urge the action forward, and she exploits several resources – her props, her husband, misremembered quotations, nostalgic memories, and, like Hamm, a story. Her Shower–Cooker tale may be memory or story, but in either case Mr Shower–Cooker (whose name puns on *schauen* and *gucken*) is given words that an actual audience may echo: 'What does it mean? he says – What's it meant to mean?' It is a question that Winnie herself never asks; yet she has an obscure sentiment of being in a play, which is repeated night after night, with her glass unshattered and her parasol intact. In Act II of *Happy Days* Winnie converts her face to a prop – a fictional character involved in the actress's actual facial contortions. The adults of *Godot* consciously perform, and the males of *Endgame* perform or compose onstage; like Hamm, Winnie of *Happy Days* injects performance into her composition. When her fictional Millie is said to scream, it is Winnie who actually screams – in a transfer of terror. During her two determinedly happy days Winnie seeks to camouflage her terror, but only Millie's screams and her 'blaze of hellish light' convey her fear metadramatically.

A comparable fear, exploiting the stage discomfort of the live actors, suffuses the second half of *Play*, the play whose final form eluded Beckett for nearly two years. Beginning with *Play*, completed in 1963, Beckett's metadramatic touches depart from the binary scheme of earlier plays: on the one hand, disparagement of the stage action, and on the other, skepticism about the offstage audience (seasoned occasionally with a soupçon of theatereality). The former disappears, and the latter assumes new forms.[9] In a residual parody of the *raisonnneur* of the well-made play, however, M of *Play* advises us: 'Adulterers, take warning, never admit.' M's requests for posthiccup pardon ('That small word' of *Richard II*) may be a courtesy to the unmentioned audience, or that small word may be a verbal reflex without designee. More subtle is the metadramatic import of the fictional lawnmower to which both M and W2 call attention: 'A little rush, then another.' The lawnmower is fictional, but its rhythm is that of the speakers of *Play*, each one triggered by the spotlight into 'a little rush, then another' of words. Later W2 likens the action of the spotlight to 'a great roller. On a scorching day. The strain to get it moving, momentum coming – ... Kill it and strain again.'[10] In this theatereality the fictional embraces the actual verbal rhythm, as the light strains to maintain the momentum.

The printed text of *Play* divides the comprehensible dialogue into 1 and 2, but Beckett himself has spoken of the Narration and the Meditation.[11] Although the boundary is not so sharp as his terms imply, much of the Meditation flirts with theatereality. M speaks of a 'change', and we are aware of changed lighting and volume. W1 addresses the spotlight as 'you', but many of her remarks target us in the audience, who see the stage only by means of the spotlight. It is W1 who equates silence with darkness – quite accurately in *Play*. W2 echoes M's 'this' for her new state, and she echoes W1's 'you' for the spotlight. It is W2 who expands upon Pozzo's anxiety about an audience: 'Are you listening to me? Is anyone listening to me? Is anyone looking at me? Is anyone bothering about me at all?'[12] Breathes there an actor with soul so secure that she has not asked herself these very questions?

Toward the end of the Meditation the spotlight's movements grow erratic, cutting off speech mid-sentence and sometimes even mid-word. In the theatre he/it seems to be reacting to the doublets of the characters: W2 is merely skeptical: 'I doubt it.' W1 is unaccommodating: 'Get off me.' M is insulting: 'Mere eye.' Like us in the audience? The last comprehensible sentence in *Play* belongs to M: 'Am I as much as . . . being seen?' What with the dimming light, the rapid tempo, and the audience concentration required, he may well ask. Only retroactively do we realize that the spotlight of *Play* is a pervasive agent of theatereality; but then we see the play twice.

A decade passed before Beckett exploited *Play*'s range of theatereality, but between 1972 and 1983 his incisive stage images are enhanced by verbal portraits, with actor and character now converging, now diverging (to quote *Watt*'s Sam on fences). Gerry McCarthy has illuminated the way in which the actress playing Mouth of *Not I* (1972) undergoes the physical and psychological stress limned in her monologue. After the initial ad-libbing, the first comprehensible words are: 'out . . . into this world . . . this world . . . tiny little thing'. Fluttering in the spotlight is a tiny little thing, a woman's mouth, from which words come 'out' into this theatre world. The voluble monologuist is bereft of a body – 'whole body like gone' – so that we may, on reflection, appreciate her inability to designate her physical position. Even under the onslaught of the swift wordstream we may respond to her awareness of the physical process of speaking: 'all those contortions without which . . . no speech possible'. In this nuance of theatereality a few phrases are apposite both to narration and visual image. Unlike Winnie, however, who illustrates the screams in her story, Mouth enunciates an *in*ability to scream, which she punctuates by two screams. Like Winnie's cries, those of Mouth displace terror. More problematic

are Mouth's eight repetitions of 'Imagine!' These might be as inter-
jectional as M's 'pardon' of *Play*; or in another reading, that mono-
word in each play might be an injunction to the theatre audience
– to pardon, to imagine.

Although sound and light of *Not I* do not attain the status of
a character, they function theatereally. Mouth refers several times,
sometimes together and sometimes separately, to a buzzing sound
and to a beam or ray of light. Moreover, half the references to
buzzing are qualified as 'so-called' – so called by Mouth, but we
might prefer her synonym 'a stream of words', as we might call the
beam or ray a spotlight. Yet rhythmic repetition lures us into Mouth's
vocabulary for the image we see and hear about. Midway in the
anti-autobiographical monologue we learn that the buzzing is 'not
in the ears at all . . . in the skull', and that can be our sensation in
the audience. Toward the end of the monologue the brain is said to
seek sense in the words, wherever they are heard: 'the whole being
. . . hanging on its words' like an attentive *aud*ience. The wordstream
and lightbeam of *Not I* are at once a sporadic fictional image and a
pervasive physical presence – theatereality.[13]

In *Footfalls* (1975) we hear two live voices in a narrative evocation
of a visual image. Although Beckett has not labelled the scenes of
Footfalls with number or name, they nevertheless may be separated
into (1) the dialogue of M and V, (2) the monologue of V, (3) the
monologue of M, and (4) the final bare silence. The play opens on
the titular footfalls, with M pacing on the stage strip of board. After
a brief exchange between M and her invisible mother V, the latter
twice counts M's steps, replete with 'wheel' when she turns. The
dialogue continues, punctuated irregularly by M's footsteps back
and forth. By the time V asks: 'Will you never have done . . .
revolving it all?' we have seen M revolve seven times on the stage
strip – theatereality. In V's monologue, Beckett resurrects direct
address to the audience: '*See* how still. . . . *Let us watch her*. . . . *Watch*
how feat she wheels.' (my emphasis) A metadramatic effect arises
from V's demonstratives – 'this', 'here', and even 'floor here'. V
again counts M's steps as she builds a narrative about them. That
narrative ends on an assurance that May speaks, 'Tells how it was.'
when she 'fancies' she is alone.

It is unlikely that the M-actress 'fancies' herself speaking with-
out an audience for her monologue, which opens with the word
'Sequel' – a sequel in rhythm rather than plot; and in theatereality.
M then sketches someone who paces in a deserted church. New

details of theatereality, verbally parallelling the image, are preceded by a new introduction: 'The semblance.' M zeroes in on the woman we see and the light in which we see her – 'a palette of grays' (Brater, 1987, p. 66). Only then does M compose a narrative about a mother–daughter couple, a thematic sequel to the two previous mother–daughter scenes. Obviously oral and aural, the tale by M nevertheless twice interjects: 'the reader will remember' and cites *new* details. Although a church also figures in this section of M's narrative, the fancy takes a new form, teasing our imagination. For we never learn what Mrs W (double-you) fancies, since M's hesitant narrative shifts to Amy's absence from church, despite her audible 'Amen'. Theatereality has slipped into metatheatre; we hear an absent V in the first two scenes, but in the third scene the words of the absent mother are voiced by M, who composes a narrative about an absent daughter. Absence is omnipresent. The mother–daughter pairs are fictional in *Footfalls*, but the two different timbres of 'revolving it all' and the single 'faint tangle of pale grey tatters' who revolves at each end of the stage strip are pervasive theatereality.[14]

Play and *Not I* are essentially static events of theatereality, whereas the moving theatereality of *Footfalls* becomes the nucleus of its four scenes – the fourth entailing an absence of everything but light. *A Piece of Monologue* (1979) intensifies stillness on stage, while its theatereality contains an oppositional component. A motionless man is reflected in a standard lamp of the 'same height', and its 'skull-sized white globe' echoes his head. White-haired like the head of *That Time*, this full-length figure wears a white nightgown and white socks – perhaps bedsocks, since we also see 'white foot of pallet bed' on our right. These physical objects will be verbalized in the Speaker's narrative, in Beckett's familiar theatereal mode.

What is new is the stage stillness within a tease of verbal dynamism. At first the narrated man is 'Still as the lamp by his side', and his hair, gown, socks and foot of pallet bed are white or once white 'to take faint light'. Recalling earlier metadramatic commentary, Beckett's Speaker utters words that might refer to theatre: 'So nightly. . . . Night after night the same.' Within the still scene we first hear: 'Nothing stirring anywhere.' But soon the Speaker describes: 'The words falling from his mouth. Making do with his mouth.' Metadrama shades into theatereality when Speaker of *A Piece of Monologue* describes the very speech he utters: 'Parts lips and thrusts tongue between them.'

Larger gestures of the narrative speak only through words. Three times, Speaker offers scrupulous accounts of a man lighting an oil-lamp, while the stage figure is not only motionless, but the standard lamp is clearly lit by electricity. We also hear: 'Glimmer of brass bedrail.' 'The gleam of brass.' 'Brass bedrail catching light.' Yet the *white* foot of pallet bed is invariant on the right corner of the stage. Toward the end of Speaker's monologue words like 'frame' and 'fade' embrace painting and film as well as theatre, but other words enunciate *theate*reality: 'White hair catching light. White gown. White socks. White foot of pallet edge of frame stage left.' Unlike these textual designations, Beckett's scenic directions are frameless.

Onstage the white-clad speaker and the standard lamp are separated by two metres, or an approximation of the space that would be occupied by either of them toppled. Three times Speaker describes a burial in the rain, which lacks any visual analogue. The stage of *A Piece of Monologue* is bare, except for its two verticals and fragmented horizontal, but the narrated persona moves between birth and death, between white and black, between a windowed room and a dark gravescape, between ghosts of loved ones. As Porter Abbott has suggested, the three narrated scenes of light/life and death/burial parallel the birth and death of speech and performance, which we witness. The act of narration and what is narrated fuse incantatorily, with details that prompt us in the audience to look again and again at the still stark scene – invariant until the light begins to fade, when the actor articulates: 'Such as the light going now. Beginning to go. . . . Unutterably faint. The globe alone. Alone gone.'

Rarely produced, *A Piece of Monologue* stretches (or shrinks?) theatre to a frieze. Except for the final fade, the only stage movement is Speaker 'Making do with his mouth.' (Even this is the actor's choice, since Beckett had no objection to David Warrilow using a tape of the monologue.) Our urgent concentration evolves a dynamic tension between the moving words and the still image, fading in and out of the frame of theatereality.

Rockaby (1980) increases Beckett's control over that in-and-outness. Rather than the still image of *Monologue* we are confronted with a hypnotically regular rocking. As in *Monologue*, however, we hear a narrative about a busy being that only gradually converges in theatereality with the image we see. In *Rockaby* most of the words we hear are recorded; cued by a live 'More' from the rocking woman, four scenes are narrated. With marvellously creative perversity, a mechanical rock and a recorded voice blend in Beckett's only verse drama, and a woman who sits 'completely still' in 'constant' light shimmers in a palette of blacks of different textures.

Rockaby resembles *Footfalls* in its focus on visible movement, which is viewed in a verbal surround. *Rockaby* is, however, more deliberate in its progress toward theatereality. The first three 'More's evoke a woman who is 'all eyes' in a vain search for 'another like herself'. In those scenes she talks 'to herself/ whom else', but the live woman accompanies her recorded voice only in the line: 'Time she stopped.' Those three consonant-slowed syllables hover metadramatically over character and actress. In the fourth scene, however, we hear about what we have observed for some ten minutes: 'into the old rocker /mother rocker / . . . all in black /best black /sat and rocked'. The woman we see, in *her* best black, gradually converges with her fictional mother, and both seem to be embraced in the arms of the cradle–rocker–coffin.

The first three scenes chant, repeat, and permute Beckett's most limited dramatic vocabulary in his most musical diapason. Linda Ben-Zvi's calculations are instructive: 'Ironically, as the woman tires, the variety increases. There are nineteen new lines out of fifty-one [. . .] in Part 1, fifteen out of fifty-six in Part 2, nineteen out of fifty-seven in Part 3, and forty-three out of eighty-three in Part 4' (p. 177). A sizeable fraction of those 43 new lines parallel the mother and/or daughter of the narration with the rocking woman onstage. Part 4 retreats from the outside world 'high and low/ to and fro', and even from the windowed upstairs room. In her mother's footfalls, as it were, 'she' takes refuge in her rocker 'and rocked/rocked'. The conclusion of *Rockaby* inflects theatereality with delay. As the narrated mother is 'dead one night /in the rocker /in her best black /head fallen /and the rocker rocking', so the actress' head is 'slowly inclined' while the rocker rocks. In Billie Whitelaw's indelible performance, her face is that of a sleeping infant, so that mother and child fuse in a rockaby at once lullaby and elegy.[15]

Like its immediate predecessors in Beckett's drama, *Ohio Impromptu* (1981) plays an incisive image against a narrative that moves literally and figuratively. Reader and Listener, 'As alike in appearance as possible', are visually striking in their long black coats and long white hair. They sit on white armless chairs at the short and long sides, respectively, of a white table, so that we see Reader in profile and Listener full face. Two props enter Beckett's drama, for on the table are a 'black broad-brimmed hat' and an undescribed book 'open at last pages'. Reader reads from that book, but a silent Listener controls the tempo of reading with six pairs of raps on the table: one rap stops the word-flow, and the second rap permits continuation from the beginning of the truncated phrase.

In spite of its midwestern American title, the narrative of *Ohio Impromptu* is set near the Isle of Swans in Paris, where the narrated protagonist walks: 'In his long black coat . . . and old world Latin Quarter hat.' We might call this a subversion of theatereality because the stage men do not walk, and the visible hat covers no head. Soon the narrative introduces 'a worn volume', which is taken by a messenger from *his* 'long black coat', and from which he reads till dawn. The two men in the tale are dressed alike in the unusual garments of the men onstage, but the tale intrudes neither table nor chairs. In the narrative no one knocks, but the reader, having seen 'the dear face and heard the unspoken words', announces that he will not come again. When dawn breaks, the two men in the story 'sat on as though turned to stone', and the two men on stage 'raise their heads and look at each other. Unblinking. Expressionless'. As though turned to stone, in the cliché embedded in the reading. Although *Ohio Impromptu* has been said to close on a 'mute recognition scene' (Brater, 137), the recognition is ours – suffusing the black-and-white scene with the sadness of a 'Farewell to love' that is more mysterious than Krapp's tape of a quarter-century earlier.[16]

A play set in a theatre might seem like the logical terminus for Beckett, because his earlier drama enfolds metadramatic commentary, and his later drama plays fugues on theatereality. *Catastrophe* was written in 1982 in French for an Avignon evening in honor of the imprisoned Czech playwright Vaclav Havel. In its original Greek meaning *catastrophe* is a turning-point, but French and English concur on its modern meaning of disaster.[17] Beckett's *Catastrophe* is one long scene of theatereality, where fictional and physical action converge and diverge. The setting is an unnamed theatre; the characters (designated by initials, as in other Beckett late plays) are protagonist, director, stage manager, but the offstage lighting technician is playfully named Luke. Props are few: a chair and cigar for the director D, a plinth for the protagonist P, a pencil and notebook for the assistant stage manager A (who may light the director's cigars with matches or lighter, since that prop is unspecified). Costumes are more elaborate: the fur coat and toque of D, the overalls of A, the black robe over the ashgrey night attire of P. The lighting is announced 'in technical terms'.

Yet *all* the characters are played by actors, and the actual performance is a fictional rehearsal of 'Final touches to the last scene'. As always in theatereality the actual and the fictional *only nearly* converge. Under D's impatient instructions, A manipulates P as if he were a prop, rather than a human being. D's purpose is to offer a lamentable P for the pleasure of the audience – a contemporary compliance with Aristotelian pity and terror, as well as Beckettian habit. Toward that end, D objects to the position of P's hands, but accepts A's suggestion to join them. Never touching P himself, D instructs A to disrobe P, and to whiten his exposed flesh. From the stalls, D highhandedly rejects A's final suggestion that P '[. . .] raise his head [. . .] an instant [. . .] show his face'. Satisfied with P's misery, D admires his handiwork: 'Terrific! He'll have them on their feet. I can hear it from here'.[18] And we hear these final words of the play, followed by 'Distant storm of applause. P raises his head, fixes the audience. The applause falters, dies.'

I know of no denial that P's silent defiant gesture is a *triumphant* catastrophe, and yet there are gaps in this view. Attention is sometimes drawn to P's 'fibrous degeneration', which mirrors that of Beckett's actual hand, but the playwright's interminable cigar-smoking is mirrored in *D* onstage. P's head-raising is originally suggested by A, and that gesture might have been even more moving, if he were gagged, as in A's rejected suggestion. A is therefore an ambiguous figure, and her wiping of D's chair has been variously interpreted. The 'distant storm of applause' is also problematic. Since we are witnessing a fictional rehearsal, there is presumably no audience, and what we hear is what D imagines. Yet it is late in the play to enter the limited imagination of a satirized character like D. Puzzling as the recorded applause may be, it serves to make us self-conscious about *our* applause: if we echo D's imagination, we range ourselves with him; if we do not applaud, we fail to acknowledge P's rebellious gesture. In the few performances I have seen audiences *do* applaud, and I do not know whether that is theatereality, but *Catastrophe* marries tyranny to theatre:[19]

In *Catastrophe* Beckett comes full spiral from his early character's scorn for 'The ignorant public' in *Human Wishes* to challenge a contemporary audience, and to reflect metadramatically on the pain that bleeds through his plays. I have tried to isolate Beckett's palette of metadramatic hues, but he himself always enfolded it into a total experience. Beckett's metadrama inevitably embraces more than drama.

Notes

1. Quite differently, Bernard Beckerman in 'Beckett and the Act of Listening' and Katharine Worth in 'Beckett's Auditors: *Not I* to *Ohio Impromptu*' comment perceptively on Beckett's stage listeners. Both essays are found in *Beckett at 80*, ed. Enoch Brater. Matthijs Engelberts, 'Quelques thèses sur la narration et le théâtre chez Beckett', touches on the same subject in *Samuel Beckett Today/Aujourd'hui*, vol. 3. Despite its title, Godwin Uwah's *Pirandellism and Samuel Beckett's Plays* (Potomac, Md.: Scripta humanistica, 1989), does not discuss metatheatre.

2. Quotations from 'Human Wishes' come from *Disjecta*, ed. Ruby Cohn; from *Eleutheria* (Paris: Minuit, 1994). All other quotations from Beckett's plays are taken from *Samuel Beckett: The Complete Dramatic Works* (London: Faber & Faber, 1990).

3. In this essay I try to refine my discussion of theatereality, as sketched in *Just Play*, p. 28. I apologize for the neologism, but it does seem to me to embrace a technique, which I am less disposed than Steven Connor to enfold into 'clothed repetition'. Although reflexivity (sometimes and redundantly called self-reflexivity) is an overused keyword in recent Beckett criticism, his metadrama has received less attention. I view metadrama as a form of reflexivity, and theatereality is a distinctive form of metadrama. Beckett is far and away the dominant perpetrator of theatereality, but the device is not unique to him. There is no evidence for an actual crimson carpet that carried Agamemnon to his death, but its existence is not improbable in the *Oresteia*.

4. Beckett was probably familiar with Baudelaire's prose poem 'Le mauvais vitrier', but any recollection is oblique. Rather than the victimized glazier of Baudelaire, Beckett's glazier at times victimizes the protagonist, Victor Krap.

5. Beckett scholars will recognize this recurrent nightmare rooted in Beckett's own life; his father taught him to swim by coercing him to dive off a high board.

6. In *Just Play* I erroneously attached metadramatic commentary to the vaudeville tradition. Whereas that tradition underlies *Godot*, the remarks of *Eleutheria* target formal dramatic structure, in the wake of Pirandello, who also intrudes mention of his own play into *Six Characters*. McMillan and Fehsenfeld read *Eleutheria* as Beckett's 'Discourse on Dramatic Method', in which he rejects dramatic conventions. Although I agree that Beckett rejects conventional drama, I hope that

I have shown that he does so through metadramatic barbs at the well-made play. For a subtle reading of *Eleutheria*, especially in comparison to *Krapp's Last Tape*, see Abbott.

7. The line works better in the original French, since 'plateau' is not quite captured by 'board'.

8. Theatereality is more pronounced in Beckett's translation into English, which introduces the underplot and the exit.

9. I base my commentary on the plays as published in *The Complete Dramatic Works*, but Rosemary Pountney traces the evolution through manuscript stages of *Play*, *Not I*, and *Footfalls*.

10. In Beckett's production notebook for the Schiller Theater – Reading ms. 1730 – the verbal rhythm is related to the lawnmower. I quote the published text, but Billie Whitelaw notes that Beckett revised to: 'Kill it, strain again' (p. 78).

11. Paul Lawley has argued persuasively for a synoptic reading of the two parts, 'Beckett's dramatic counterpoint: a reading of "Play"', *Journal of Beckett Studies*, 9 (1984), pp. 25–41.

12. Beckett's Schiller production notebook lists the following, without a title: 'Being seen?/ Being heard?/ What being demanded?/ Will eye weary?/ Meaninglessness/ Loss of reason.' The first four questions are theatereal.

13. This crucial lyrical phrase is omitted from the Faber edition of Beckett's *Complete Dramatic Works*. In the American edition of *Footfalls* 'Sequel' and 'The semblance' are spoken only once.

14. This harmonizes with 'the schismatic self' analysed by Linda Ben-Zvi, 'The Schismatic Self in "A Piece of Monologue"', *Journal of Beckett Studies*, 7 (1982), pp. 7–18.

15. The excellent Hegedus–Pennebaker film failed to capture Billie Whitelaw's child-face at the end. Cf. Connor: '[. . .] the dramatic interest of [*Rockaby*] comes from the emerging relationship between what is described in the recorded monologue and what the audience sees before it' (p. 133).

16. Several critics have tried to gloss the 'impromptu' in the title, since every word and every gesture is studied. No one to my knowledge has suggested the analogy with a musical impromptu, with its three-part form: statement of theme, contrasting melody, modified return to theme. Although the six pairs of knocks do not fit this scheme neatly, they do move from 'Little is left to tell' through 'unspoken words' to a repetition of the 'little' and to the final modified theme: 'Nothing is left to tell', with no further speech after the second knock. For a subtle and complex reading of *A Piece of Monologue* see Abbott, ch. 8.

17. Bernold (1992, p. 106) claims that Beckett intended only the turning-point meaning, but this would violate his whole polyvalent practice. The word 'turning-point' figures in *That Time*.

18. The original French is more ambiguous: 'Il va faire un malheur.' It is fascinating to peruse the manuscript of *Catastrophe*; P's defiance evidently occurred to Beckett after he had typed a quasi-final draft, for it is added in ink.

19. Jackson writes perceptively of the ramifications of the tyranny of theatre. Keir Elam seems to me correct in his interpretation of the final and literal catastrophe of *Catastrophe*: 'The real conclusion comes afterwards, in the audience's own gesture, extending the catastrophic series (D's ending, P's ending, our ending) out into the world.' In *The Pleasure of Play* Bert O. States argues that the ending of *Catastrophe*, like tragic art in general 'does not quite make moral sense'. The character's pain is our voyeuristic pleasure. States arrives at this conclusion after a densely argued gloss on Aristotle.

Bibliography

Abbott, H. Porter, *Beckett Writing Beckett: The Author in the Autograph* (Ithaca: Cornell University Press, 1996).

Astier, Pierre, 'Beckett's *Ohio Impromptu*: A View from the Isle of Swans,' *Modern Drama*, 25, September 1982, pp. 331–41.

Ben-Zvi, Linda, *Samuel Beckett* (Boston: G. K. Hall, 1986).

Bernold, André, *L'Amitié de Beckett 1979–1989* (Paris: Hermann, 1992).

Blackman, Maurice, 'The Shaping of a Beckett Text: "Play",' *Journal of Beckett Studies*, 10, 1985, pp. 87–107.

Brater, Enoch, *Beyond Minimalism* (New York, Oxford University Press, 1987). ed. *Beckett at 80/ Beckett in Context* (New York, Oxford: 1986).

Connor, Steven, *Samuel Beckett: Repetition, Theory and Text* (Oxford: Blackwell, 1988).

Elam, Keir, 'Catastrophic Mistakes: Beckett, Havel, The End', *Samuel Beckett Today/Aujourd'hui*, No. 3, p. 16.

Fehsenfeld, Martha and McMillan, Dougald, *Beckett in the Theatre* (London: Calder, 1988).

Jackson, Shannon, 'Performing the Performance of Power in Beckett's *Catastrophe*,' *Journal of Dramatic Theory and Criticism*, 6, spring 1992, pp. 23–41.

Kalb, Jonathan, '*Rockaby* and the Art of Inadvertent Interpretation', *Modern Drama*, 30, December 1987, pp. 466–79.

Kennedy, Andrew, *Dramatic Dialogue: The Dialogue of Personal Encounter*, (London: Cambridge, 1983).

Knowlson, James, and Pilling, John, *Frescoes of the Skull: The Later Prose and Drama of Samuel Beckett* (London: Calder, 1979).

Lyons, Charles R., 'Perceiving *Rockaby* – As a Text, As a Text by Samuel Beckett, As a Text for Performance', *Comparative Drama*, 16, winter, 1982–3, pp. 297–311.

McCarthy, Gerry, 'On the Meaning of Performance in Samuel Beckett's *Not I*', *Modern Drama*, 33, December 1990, pp. 455–69.

Pountney, Rosmary, *Theatre of Shadows: Samuel Beckett's Drama 1956–1976* (Gerrards Cross: Colin Smythe, 1988).

States, Bert O., '*Catastrophe*: Beckett's Laboratory/Theatre', *Modern Drama*, 30, March 1987, pp. 14–22.

Whitelaw, Billie, *Billie Whitelaw . . . Who He?* (London: Hodder & Stoughton, 1995).

Of the many books on Beckett's drama, the following touch on his meta-drama, although I do not specifically cite them:

Gontarski, S. E., *The Intent of Undoing in Samuel Beckett's Dramatic Texts* (Bloomington: Indiana University Press, 1985).

Hauck, Gerhard, *Reductionism in Drama and the Theatre: The Case of Samuel Beckett* (Maryland: Scripta Humanistica 102, 1992).

Homan, Sidney, *Beckett's Theatres: Interpretations for Performance* (Lewisberg: Bucknell University Press, 1984).

McMullan, Anna, *Theatre on Trial: Samuel Beckett's Later Drama* (London: Routledge, 1993).

Morrison, Kristin, *Canters and Chronicles: The Use of Narrative in the Plays of Samuel Beckett and Harold Pinter* (Chicago University Press, 1983).

7

Pinter and the Pinteresque: An Author Trapped by His Own Image?

Maria Ghilardi-Santacatterina and Aleks Sierz

'But don't you remember the word games we all used to play?' asks Maria in Harold Pinter's *Moonlight*.[1] At such moments, the author is reminded by one of his creations of the infinite intertextual nexus in which his play is located, while, at another level, he is also sending out a cue to the audience, an invitation for them to call to mind the image they have of his work. Is this a case of self-reflexivity and/or of self-parody? Could it be that Pinter has become trapped by the Pinteresque? And who needs the Pinteresque, anyway?

Discussions of intertextuality often focus on the recognition that the text is a system which produces meaning, not by reflecting 'reality' but by its relationship to other texts. This raises the question of the positioning of the work in relation to the subject, and asks what kind of 'author' or 'reader' it constructs. Developed by Julia Kristeva from her translation of Bakhtin's concept of dialogism – 'the necessary relation of any utterance to other utterances' – intertextuality typically involves a 'mosaic of citations', a palimpsest of traces, a locus where other texts may be read. Meaning, a critic such as Umberto Eco would argue, comes from the diverse series of intertextual frames invoked in the 'reader', frames which authorize and orient interpretation, which fill in the gaps in the text, and guide the 'reader's' inferences about the text. For systematizers such as Gerard Genette, intertextuality – 'the effective co-presence of two texts' – is just one element in transtextuality, which refers to all that puts one text in relation to all other texts. Transtextuality also includes paratextuality (the relation between text and paratext, such as prefaces, dedications and book jackets), metatextuality (the critical relation between one text and another), architextuality (the generic taxonomies suggested by the title of a text), hypertextuality (the relation between one text and a previous text which it transforms).[2]

Self-allusion, parody and pastiche, unconscious echo, direct quotation, structural parallelism are all devices which commonly make up intertextuality in literature. They constitute a two-dimensional system in which texts talk to other texts. Theatre, however, is by its nature a three-dimensional intertextual system, which makes it hard to separate out its various elements: 'The presence of a multiplicity of signs – verbal, visual and audio – forces the spectator to follow the whole performance simultaneously. During a performance (as opposed to an act of reading) the spectator must accept an imposed pace.'[3] To construct meaning, the audience has to master the 'rules of the game', the decodification of one drama depending on familiarity with other drama. While each new play is necessarily related to other plays – whether because an author is influenced by other work, or because a director turns it into their own style or because an actor gives the character a slant which is typically theirs – intertextual relations are not just confined to other plays. The theatrical frame is never 'pure': any performance draws on any number of cultural references. Despite an apparent passivity, the members of the audience are actively making meaning out of what happens on stage.

For the audience, drama is a complex cultural experience:

> The language of theatre is possibly even more extensive than that normally ascribed to cinema. For not only must the text, mise-en-scène, lighting, performances, casting, music, effects, placing on the stage all be taken into account [. . .] but also the nature of the audience, the nature, social, geographical and physical, of the venue, the price of tickets, the availability of tickets, the nature and placing of the pre-publicity, where the nearest pub is [. . .] For when we discuss theatre, we are discussing a social event.[4]

If the image of the author results from a distillation of such intertextual relations, in Pinter's case the image has been subsumed by the idea of the Pinteresque, his name having passed into everyday language (as well as Pinteresque, the Oxford Shorter English Dictionary cites Pinterian and Pinterish). Regarded, since the death of Samuel Beckett, as 'Britain's greatest living playwright', Pinter's public image has been refracted through widely shared ideas about his work, which is often seen as composed of pauses, enigmas and menace. The Pinteresque applies to work that uses silences, inconclusive dialogue, ambiguous memory games and threatening visitations. The reiteration of clichés and the use of words as evasion is recognized as Pinteresque even by people who have never seen a Pinter play. But what the category of the Pinteresque conceals, however, are the differences in Pinter's dialogue between the early plays and the later work, with the tendency to reduce the idea of the Pinteresque to language, when it properly applies to the Weltanschauung embodied in his plays.

Such a highly charged image weighs heavily on the author. In December 1971, Pinter said: 'Harold Pinter sits on my damn back.' Then he answered the question: 'Who is Harold Pinter?' with: 'He's not me. He's someone else's creation.'[5] Yet Pinter's relationship with his own self-image has been more ambiguous than such a simple denial suggests. Could he be said to be a victim of his own image? When commentators tried to put him into the kitchen sink school, he said in 1961: 'What goes on in my plays is realistic, but what I'm doing is not realism.'[6] And although he may well have tired of reading that his plays were comedies of menace, you don't have to take his account of his own contribution to the image of the Pinteresque literally: 'Someone asked me what my work was "about". I replied with no thought at all and merely to frustrate this line of enquiry: "The weasel under the cocktail cabinet." That was a great mistake. Over the years I have seen that remark quoted in a number of learned columns [. . .] But for me the remark meant precisely nothing.'[7] The use of such a poetic image, however, is remarkably ambiguous because while deflecting inquiry, it paradoxically feeds back into a clichéd image of the Pinteresque. Today, on the other hand, even his good-humoured reaction to the word Pinteresque suggests the weary consciousness of an author resigned to his own self-image: ' "Oh, this dread word Pinteresque", Pinter complains, self-mockingly. "It makes people reach for their guns. Or behave as if they were going to church. It's highly regrettable." '[8]

When Pinter's *Moonlight* opened at the Almeida theatre, north London, on 7 September 1993, questions which derive from public perceptions of his image occupied much of the discourse about it. In the play, the stage is divided into three areas, each of which is a room belonging to a different house: in one, Andy, an ex-civil servant, lies dying in bed, his wife, Bel, beside him; in another, also with a bed, are his sons, Jake and Fred; in a third space above them, there is their sister, Bridget, who is probably dead and has a ghost-like appearance.[9] While Andy and Bel are unable to bring their sons to their father's death bed, the couple are visited by old friends Ralph and Maria. In ambiguous passages which call up memories, Andy seems to have had an affair with Maria, who may have had an affair with Bel, who might possibly have been intimate with Ralph. *Moonlight* is framed by a prologue and epilogue delivered by Bridget, while the whole stage is bathed in moonlight.

Because *Moonlight* is seen as a play by a 'difficult' author – a work that doesn't yield all of its meanings easily or lightly (especially as far as the epistemological status of Bridget is concerned) – the role of the critic is that of an essential mediator between the play and its audience. As the play's first interpreters, the critics were divided along the lines of whether they were enthusiasts or detractors. Not only did they use a range of intertextual devices (the favourite of the detractors being parody), but they also generally tried to elucidate the way this 'difficult' play was a drama-on-drama. The detractors were led by the *Evening Standard*'s Nicholas de Jongh. Starting with a put-down that attempted to mimic Pinter's terseness – 'Listen. It is the sound of Harold Pinter scraping the barrel [. . .]' – de Jongh argued that 'the play's themes recall many of Pinter's yesterdays: here is the old crisis of failed communications; people do not speak; they run talkative circles around each other; family life is a cluster of tensions and schisms; an erotic triangle is lyrically remembered; memory seems just a game people play' (8 September 1993). The banality of this elucidation of Pinter's intertextuality is a direct result of de Jongh's belief that Pinter's newest play is but a 'laboured imitation of his old great self'.

Charles Spencer of the *Telegraph* used another typical strategy – he accused the drama-on-drama in *Moonlight* of being self-parody. Pinter 'seems to be offering a deliberate send up of his own reputation for baffling an audience' (9 September 1993). In the *Independent*, meanwhile, David Lister began his review by using the mocking style beloved of Pinter's detractors, pointing out that *Moonlight* was 75 minutes long, rather than the 17, 8 or 40 minutes of his previous works. He finished his attack by using a phrase from the play as a summary of his reactions: ' "What is being said? What is being said here? [. . .] What finally is being said?" ' (8 September 1993). For a more down-market audience, Martin Hoyle of the *Mail on Sunday* served up the myth that Pinter had been suffering from writer's block, saying that his was 'a blocked talent going through the motions', capable only of producing 'a collection of Pinterisms to order: evasive gentility, shock four-letter words, mysterious codified exchanges' (12 September 1993).

By using such rhetorical devices, these critics tried to persuade their readers to join in a tired scepticism about Pinter that leaves the familiar image of the author largely untouched. His new play is located intertextually with his other work, but its difficulties and differences are ignored in favour of mockery, with the assumption remaining that the author has nothing new to say. The critics who appreciated the play had a harder task than that of the detractors. They had to show how the appearance of *Moonlight* forces us to reconsider established clichés about Pinter's career.

John Peter's thoughtful appreciation in *The Sunday Times* had the most space in which to do this. He began by relating *Moonlight* to other Pinter plays which take place at night, a time of 'peculiar, brooding intensity'. 'Night is when paths cross, when threats are made, when memories are most vivid but least reliable'. Comparing Andy of *Moonlight* to Deeley of *Old Times*, he elucidated the play's use of 'conversation as evasion'. But Peter also pointed out what was new in *Moonlight*: 'People are no longer seeking admittance, craving security or protecting their strongholds. This is a play about departure, about barely holding on, about letting go.' In the end, despite the evident pleasure he derived from the performance, even Peter could not resist damning with faint praise: 'This dark, elegiac play, studded with brutally and swaggeringly funny jokes, is one of Pinter's most haunting minor works.' That 'minor' reads like a stab in the guts (12 September 1993).

Pinter's official biographer, Michael Billington of the *Guardian*, began his review by saying that *Moonlight* 'will come as a shock to those who have lately pigeonholed him as a writer of bruising polemic'. Though it 'carries echoes of earlier Pinter plays, including *The Homecoming* and *No Man's Land*', it also breaks new ground and 'stirs the heart' with its 'direct confrontation with mortality' and its account of the gulf between parents and children. Billington pointed out that the director, David Leveaux, 'combines the concrete and the mysterious: the classic Pinter mix'. 'What makes this an extraordinary play is that Pinter both corrals his familiar themes – the subjectiveness of memory, the unknowability of one's lifelong partner, the gap between the certain present and the uncertain past – and extends his territory' (8 September 1993). The use of the word 'territory' is a particularly apt one, referring as it does to the characteristic territorial struggles of Pinter's previous work, such as *The Caretaker* and *No Man's Land*.

Benedict Nightingale of *The Times* was at first less generous. Although he welcomed *Moonlight* because it was about 'personal matters' and not about 'politics', he couldn't resist sneering at Pinter's political commitment. Pointing out that Ian Holm, who plays Andy in the play, was Lenny in the 1965 version of *The Homecoming*, he interpreted *Moonlight* as being about Pinter 'coming home to *The Homecoming*', while equating Andy with the earlier play's Max. After finally appreciating both the text and the production, Nightingale concluded that *Moonlight* 'marks a genuine return to form' (8 September 1993).

In arguing that the new play represents a return to a 'theatre theatrical', the *Spectator*'s Sheridan Morley said that *Moonlight* has 'all the ingredients of the Pinteresque: menace with mirth, the weasel under the cocktail cabinet, the roll-calls of long-forgotten names that may once have had some significance but are now used as an escape from dangerous conversation' (18 September 1993). Another critic, Clive Hirschorn of the *Sunday Express*, commented that the play's humour starts with the title, which 'is ironic' (12 September 1993). It was finally left to John Gross of the *Sunday Telegraph* to point out another aspect of drama-on-drama which is characteristic of Pinter, the many instances of 'vaudeville-style humour. The man who "didn't hide his blushes under a barrel"; the man who "never missed a day at night school"' (12 September 1993).

Critics can, of course, act as reporters of what goes on outside the theatrical frame. Paul Taylor in the *Independent* claimed that 'few people emerging from the theatre professed to have fully understood' *Moonlight*, before quoting representatives of the arts establishment such as Melvyn Bragg: ' "I'm still trying to work it out, but it was terrific, very good"' (9 September 1993). By contrast, Mark Amory in the *Independent on Sunday* gave plenty of clues on how to interpret the play's intertextual references: 'You get a stream of clichés, references, quotations (including one from *Hamlet*) and proper names [...] It's impossible to take it all in as you watch; one day, probably very soon, scholars will sort it out. Sometimes phrases seem all allusion and rhythm, bereft of sense – "gemless in Wall Street" may echo "Eyeless in Gaza" but stands for nothing' (12 September 1993). In an interview, Pinter used the same quotation from *Moonlight* to emphasize his awareness of intertextual games, saying: 'I'm well aware that my work is packed with literary references.'[10]

If one of the functions of reviews is to set out the terms of discourse about a production, the wide disparity of views about *Moonlight* indicates that there is more to the critics' disagreement than just a divergence in personal taste. The suspicion arises that this could be evidence of a fundamental split about how to locate Pinter's most recent play in relation to the rest of his work, and ultimately to his prevailing image. Most critics seemed unable to accept *Moonlight* on its own terms, preferring to see it as a self-parody, and its author as trapped inside the Pinteresque. They also attempted to control what was genuinely new in the play by prescribing how audiences should 'read' it. Quite rightly, they showed how the play is teeming with echoes from Pinter's previous work. In the dialogue between Andy and Bel there are distinct echoes of *Old Times, No Man's Land* and *Betrayal*, and the banter between Jake and Fred is a pared down Pinteresque language game. Familiar themes abound, such as the subjectiveness of memory, the impossibility of ever knowing anybody else, the gap between the certain present and the uncertain past, plus the verbal piss-taking humour. Fewer critics adequately grasped the newer elements in *Moonlight*, such as the gut-wrenching emotions expressed in Andy's anger and terror at approaching death, the presence of death in life, and the poetical, symbolist nature of Bridget's monologues.

A strong cultural image such as the Pinteresque structures, for better or worse, the aesthetic expectations of the audience. This is not a new phenomenon. With the original production of *Betrayal*, for example, people had become so used to regarding Pinter as enigmatic, that the clarity of the play's theme, its love triangle, struck them as banal, despite the sensitivity of the writing. With *Moonlight*, almost every review mentions mystery or enigma. Yet there is actually very little that is really enigmatic or mysterious about *Moonlight*, although it is by no means an 'easy' play.

Near its end, the following exchange is typical:

Andy: 'What's happening? (Pause) What is happening?'
Bel: 'Are you dying?'
Andy: 'Am I?'
Bel: 'Don't you know?'
Andy: 'No. I don't know. I don't know how it feels. How does it feel?'
Bel: 'I don't know.' (Pause)[11]

Not much mystery here. A man is dying, and is unprepared for death. The rhythm of the exchanges is recognizably Pinteresque and there is a noticeable aggression in both partners. But there is nothing enigmatic here. Instead, this passage conveys a universal human truth (that we are seldom prepared for death) in the clearest language.

One element of Andy's power to move the audience arose from an external intertextual dimension: by casting Ian Holm as Andy, the production chose an actor who had been absent from the stage for 17 years. As the reason for this was reported to be stage fright, his triumphant stage comeback mirrors Pinter's comeback as a writer of full-length plays. Both were seen as overcoming blocks. (Ian Holm was also to star in the 1994 revival of *Landscape*, directed by Pinter, at the National Theatre, and broadcast a year later on BBC2. Here there was a further aspect of drama-on-drama: his wife, Penelope Wilton, was cast as his stage spouse.)

The venue of *Moonlight* also sent out significant cultural signals. Very much Pinter's home ground, the Almeida is a sophisticated fringe theatre in Islington, far away from the West End, with a policy of producing a daring mix of classical and new work (including that of 'difficult' authors such as Howard Barker). It had already hosted revivals of *No Man's Land* in 1992 (with Pinter in the role of Hirst), *Betrayal* and *Mountain Language*, as well as the premiere of *Party Time*, all in 1991. With Pinter often spotted drinking at the bar, the first and second nights of *Moonlight* had the atmosphere of a private party, with the author acting as host. 'To celebrate the Almeida's association with Harold Pinter', there was an exhibition of photographs by Ivan Kyncl of past Pinter productions in the wine bar – and a selection was reproduced in the programme. Islington is an apt location for Pinter's work: it is often parodied as a left-wing borough, with 'trendy lefty' and 'champagne socialist' residents.

One last locus of intertextuality deserves mention: the published text of *Moonlight*. Whatever Pinter might have said about the brevity of his directly political work being irrelevant to its appreciation, the blurb on the back of the published text is unambiguous: '*Moonlight* is Harold Pinter's first full-length play since *Betrayal* in 1978.' Surely this couldn't have been published without his authorization. The first edition opens with the briefest of potted biographies: 'Harold Pinter was born in London in 1930. He is married to Antonia Fraser.' Is this a case of self-parody or a gesture of defiance? (The establishment never forgave an East End Jewish boy marrying into the aristocracy – the play, like *Party Time*, is dedicated to his wife.) The same page carried an erratum slip glued in after the work had been printed. It specified that the play's opening line: 'I can't sleep. There's no moon. It's so dark, I' should be changed to 'I can't sleep. There's no moon. It's so dark. I'. In other words, a comma is changed to a full stop, and therefore a pause. Putting this correction on the first page the reader comes across emphasizes Pinter's desire to remain in full control of his work – yet many saw in it an instance of unconscious self-parody, a relapse into the Pinteresque.

Although *Moonlight* is about the certainty of mortality and rage against the dying of the light (a metaphor perhaps for Pinter's fears about his death as an author), its successful opening at the Almeida began a week of activity that could be seen as a triumphal comeback. A few days after the first night, Pinter presented his papers – the manuscripts of 26 plays, 17 screenplays, plus sketches, prose and poetry – on an 'unprecedented' long-term loan to the British Library. By doing so, Pinter laid himself open to the possibility of being 'deconstructed' in terms of his image, making this an act of generosity with the risk of vulnerability. While this could be seen as a celebration of his status as Britain's leading playwright, at the same time he was dispelling the myth of the writer's block. To crown this momentous week, Pinter attended the first night of the transfer from the Royal Court to the West End of David Mamet's controversial hit *Oleanna*, which Pinter had directed.[12]

But there is more to drama-on-drama than the success or otherwise of one or two productions. Other factors, both biographical and political, come into play. Before the opening of *Moonlight*, it had been widely assumed that Pinter was suffering from writer's block, that the brevity of his directly political plays (such as *Mountain Language* and *Party Time*) was a sign that he was finished as a writer, only capable of 'dispatching curt, angry telegrams to the world's audiences on behalf of Amnesty International'.[13] More than once, Pinter has contested this image, pointing out that in 15 years of so-called writer's block he has produced six short plays (including *A Kind of Alaska*, *One for the Road* and *Party Time*) and eight film scripts (including *The French Lieutenant's Woman* and work on *The Remains of the Day*). At the same time, he admits that during the years between *Betrayal* (1978) and *Moonlight*, he had 'bumped into a brick wall' whenever he tried to write a full-length play.[14] Whatever the complex truth about Pinter's problems with writing, the myth of his writer's block has been eagerly embraced by those who were unable to accept that politics is an integral part of his work. Because the political plays of the 1980s and early 1990s did not fit in with their image of the Pinteresque, commentators have tended to dismiss them. A rare exception was the *Observer*'s Michael Coveney, who in his review of *Moonlight* said: 'Heretically, I hankered for the hard, cutting, political edge in the recent shorter plays' (12 September 1993). Whenever Pinter refused to be constrained by what the public expected of him, and tried to elude the constrictions of the Pinteresque, the establishment employed what he calls 'the established tradition of mockery of the artist in this country'.[15] Indeed, the myth of the 15-year writer's block could be interpreted as a metaphor, a way in which the anti-Harolds expressed disapproval, when so often it was the critics who were blocked, unable to accept his new political persona.

By itself, *Moonlight* could be viewed as one of several attempts at redefining Pinter's image in the 1990s. Two other productions, both of work from the earliest days of his career, in 1958, also seem to challenge received notions about the Pinteresque, albeit in different ways. Revivals of *The Birthday Party* at the National Theatre in 1994 and of *The Hothouse* at the Chichester Festival (transferring to the West End) in 1995 surprised audiences because the plays' comic side now far outweighed the ponderous, 'difficult' quality of menace. This challenge to traditional ideas about the Pinteresque also extends to a reinterpretation of the narrative of his artistic career. Until the 1990s, Pinter's career was divided into an 'early' period of comedies of menace or kitchen sink absurd drama (*The Birthday Party* to *The Homecoming*) followed by a 'middle' period of poetic drama and memory plays (*Landscape* to *Betrayal*) followed by a 'late' period of short polemical works (*One for the Road* to *Party Time*). This schema usually represented a political as well as aesthetic judgement. An early 'unpolitical' Pinter could be seen as declining into a 'late' propagandist. Or, in the words of Michael Billington's review of *The Hothouse*: 'Pinter is often thought of, misleadingly, as a pedlar of mystery and menace who only in the 1980s acquired a political conscience. But this exemplary revival proves [...] that he was, from the start, a dramatist with sharp antennae for the insidious corruption of power [...] We need to revise our notion of Pinter' (*Country Life*, 7 September 1995).

The highly acclaimed revival of *The Birthday Party*, directed by Sam Mendes, made use of several intertextual devices to reinterpret the play in an uncommonly light vein. From the first moment of the play, when we hear the 'diddly-diddly' theme tune reminiscent of *Housewife's Choice*, a 1950s' radio series, we are not so much in

Pinterland as in a nostalgic location where 'light entertainment' solicits canned laughter. Casting Dora Bryan as Meg added to the nostalgia – she is best know for playing 'silly, old bags' in kitchen sink dramas in the early 1960s. Amid all the guffaws, some members of the audience were puzzled by the discrepancy between Pinter's reputation and the style of the production. One spectator asked the person next to her: 'Is Pinter meant to be that funny? Strange, somehow I didn't think so.'

Mendes's recipe for this successful revival is his customary clarity. The movement and gestures of the actors are graphic, the dialogue is depleted of Pinteresque pauses and its rhythm has been naturalized in order to cue laughs. Under the bright sunshine of literalism, the sit-com achieves its easy effects, with only one problem: the end of the play. Here, Mendes's recipe threatens to fail – it is difficult to explain what has happened to Stanley and where he has been taken, and, most of all, why this is happening. By relying solely on the resources of the sit-com, there has been no build-up of ambiguity, no shades of questioning. As James Campbell wrote in *The Times Literary Supplement*: 'Beneath the surface conviviality there should surely rumble a tremor of menace' (25 March 1994). Instead, the taking away of Stanley by Goldberg and McCann could in this version be justifiably interpreted as a practical joke, at which audiences can laugh, but which has little emotional impact. The proliferation of images-within-images provided by the Mendes production weakens the political core of the play.

If the easy laughter of Mendes's *The Birthday Party*, while questioning the Pinteresque, could be seen as detracting meaning from the play, the revival of *The Hothouse*, directed by David Jones, proved instead that when Pinter himself questions the Pinteresque, a new dimension of meaning is acquired. Written in 1958, put aside until 1979, now revived again, *The Hothouse* was successful chiefly because Pinter played Roote, the colonel in charge of a psychiatric prison. It is worth noting that at the time Pinter wrote the play, very few people had heard of the punitive use of psychiatric prisons, and therefore the play had, from the start, an explicitly political message.[16] With Pinter in the central role, intertextual ironies abound: here is a famous human rights activist playing the role of an abuser of rights; an actor almost upstaging the author (both being the same person); an author famous for his short temper playing a character on the verge of a tantrum. Needless to say, such intertextual meanings depend on audience competence. At the end of the play, one American tourist in the audience asked an usher whether Pinter had played Roote. Clearly, this spectator grasped only a part of the available meanings. Though it could enjoy the humour, a less than competent audience would be unable to appreciate Pinter's latest struggle to free himself from his image.

The stress on the comic aspects rather than the humourless statu- esqueness of some previous productions comes from Pinter's col- laboration with David Jones. When they worked together on *Betrayal* and *Old Times* in 1983 and 1985, 'It was,' according to Jones, 'inter- esting for Harold to find that the nature of the beast could change in different productions, that there isn't only the one way to do his work.'[17] Of course, this is not the first time that there have been seismic shifts in the way Pinter has been interpreted on stage: while the early productions of his work, by directors such as Peter Hall, used a style that was influenced, as Pinter himself was, by Beckett, and emphasized the absurdist elements in his work, later revivals by directors such as Kevin Billington were somewhat more natu- ralistic. Billington, wrote John Elsom in 1978, 'refused to dwell on what used to be regarded as Pinter's distinctive style – the long ambiguous pauses, the hints of distant menace, "the weasel under the cocktail cabinet"'.[18] In *The Hothouse*, as in other recent revivals of his work, such as *No Man's Land* in 1992, Pinter's direct participa- tion (whether as actor or director) in the production enables him to handle the elements of self-parody and self-quotation, and to go beyond a mere self-reflexive exercise, in a way that results in new meaning. By declaring war on the 'difficult' side of his image, he is arguably making his political message clearer. Accessibility is per- haps the quality that best characterizes his new persona.

So who needs the Pinteresque? Not, it seems, Pinter himself. For him, the 1990s have proved that, in his own words, 'There is life in the old dog yet.'[19] All of his recent creative output shows a much more pluralistic persona than the old image allows. Do audiences need the Pinteresque? Reactions to his plays in the West End sug- gest that people are more than ready to accept the unPinteresque productions that foreground humour. Yet, as a study of the reviews of *Moonlight* shows, it is the critics who, after more than 30 years of Pinter plays, still have the most problems in accepting new variations in the intertextual universe of his plays. Perhaps it is the critics who need the Pinteresque much more than Pinter does. As Fred says in *Moonlight*: 'Any confusion that exists in that area rests entirely in you, old chap.'[20]

120   *Drama on Drama*

Notes

Place of publication is London unless otherwise stated.
1. Harold Pinter, *Moonlight* (Faber 1993), p. 16.
2. See M. M. Bakhtin, *The Dialogical Imagination* (Austin: University of Texas Press, 1981); Julia Kristeva, *Revolution in Poetic Language* (New York: Columbia University Press, 1984); Umberto Eco, *The Role of the Reader* (Bloomington: Indiana University Press); and Gerard Genette, *Palimpsestes: La littérature au second degré* (Paris: Seuil, 1982).
3. Michael Issacharoff, 'Labiche et l'intertextualité comique', *Cahiers de L'Association Internationale des Études Françaises*, no. 35, May 1983, p. 171. Our translation.
4. John McGrath, *A Good Night Out* (Methuen, 1981), p. 5.
5. Mel Gussow, *Conversations with Pinter* (Nick Hern, 1994), p. 25.
6. Harold Pinter, 'Writing for myself' in *Plays: Two* (Methuen, 1977), p. 11.
7. Harold Pinter, Speech on receiving the Hamburg Shakespeare Prize, 1970, quoted in Michael Scott (ed.), *The Birthday Party, The Caretaker, The Homecoming: A Casebook* (Macmillan, 1986), p. 9.
8. Kate Saunders, 'Pause for thought', *The Sunday Times*, 9 July 1995.
9. Gussow, op. cit., p. 106. Cf. Eckart Voigts-Virchow, 'Pinter still/again Pinteresque? Opacity and illumination in *Moonlight* (1993)', *Contemporary Drama in English: Centres and Margins*, vol. 2 (Trier: Wissenschafthcher Verlag), p. 121.
10. Gussow, op. cit., pp. 124–5.
11. *Moonlight*, pp. 75–6.
12. Gussow, op. cit., p. 95.
13. Benedict Nightingale's review of *Moonlight* in *The Times*, 8 September 1993.
14. Cf. Gussow, op. cit., pp. 100 and 124 , 151. *Time Out*, September 1993, pp. 15–22.
15. Maria Santacatterina, 'Il cittadino Harold Pinter', *Il Manifesto*, 5 May 1993. Cf. *Moonlight*, pp. 4–5.
16. Gianfranco Capitta and Roberto Canziani, *Harold Pinter: Un Ritratto* (Milan: Edizioni Anabasi, 1995), p. 176.
17. Richard Nelson and David Jones, *Making Plays: The Writer–Director Relationship in Theatre Today* (Faber, 1995), p. 52.
18. Quoted in Ronald Knowles, *The Birthday Party and The Caretaker: Text and Performance* (Macmillan, p. 62).
19. David Sexton, 'Life in the old dog yet', *Daily Telegraph*, 18 March 1995. Pinter's new persona has also reached more people through the mass media: he appeared on LWT's *London Stage '95* on 8 October 1995, and one of his short stories, 'Girls', was given the centre spread of *The Sunday Times'* book supplement on 1 October 1995).
20. *Moonlight*, p. 43.

8

'The Play's the Thing': The Metatheatre of Timberlake Wertenbaker

Christine Dymkowski

Timberlake Wertenbaker is one of the most exciting playwrights to have emerged in Britain in the past decade. Her most notable work is self-reflexive, interrogating the nature and function of theatre in individual and communal life; through devices such as doubling and mirroring, her plays engage in a dialectical relationship with their audiences about the experiences they are undergoing as they watch. This essay will explore the myriad ways in which Wertenbaker initiates and sustains this relationship in two of her plays, *Our Country's Good* and *The Love of the Nightingale*, both first staged in 1988.

Based on Thomas Keneally's novel *The Playmaker*, which was itself drawn from fact, *Our Country's Good* tells the story of the first (European) theatrical performance in Australia, the production on 4 June 1789 of George Farquhar's *The Recruiting Officer* by the convicts of Sydney Cove penal settlement[1]. Wertenbaker's play, directed by Max Stafford-Clark, opened at the Royal Court Theatre, London, on 10 September 1988, and played in tandem with Stafford-Clark's production of Farquhar's comedy, using the same cast.

Wertenbaker's play is explicitly concerned with 'the power and the value of theatre', which, she explains, was confirmed by her visit to Wormwood Scrubs Prison to see long-term inmates perform Howard Barker's *The Love of a Good Man*: the experience proved 'pivotal for the acting and writing of *Our Country's Good*'[2] and, in the Methuen Modern Play edition of the work, Wertenbaker reprints correspondence from three of these prisoners as eloquent testimony to the transformative potential of theatre. The epigraph to the play, an excerpt from R. Rosenthal and L. Jacobsen's *Pygmalion in the Classroom* that recounts how teachers' high but unfounded

expectations of certain children's academic performance had actually increased their intellectual ability, makes its message even
clearer: our personal selves are not givens but constructs, our characters and abilities shaped not only by inherent qualities but also
by social interaction. *Our Country's Good* sets out to show that theatre
can be one of the most powerful shaping forces we encounter.

The play begins with a seemingly hopeless situation: the trans-
portation of a group of starved, beaten and degraded convicts to
a penal colony sharply divided along ideological lines. The Royal
Marine officers garrisoned there, believing in innate criminality,
espouse the merits of flogging and hanging, while the liberal governor, Arthur Phillip, argues that more enlightened treatment may
change the convicts' 'old ways' (Act 1, Scene 3, p. 3). Their dispute
soon focuses on a single representative issue: whether the spectacle
of hanging is the convicts' 'favourite form of entertainment' because 'they've never been offered anything else'. Phillip is determined that they be exposed to the 'fine language [and] sentiment'
of 'real plays' (p. 4), and eventually Second Lieutenant Ralph Clark,
anxious for notice and promotion, agrees to direct the convicts in a
play, even though it is clear at this stage that he has neither any real
interest in theatre nor any true belief in the convicts' humanity.[3]

Although the officers' discussion locates theatre as a forum of
fine feeling and thinking, Wertenbaker in fact problematizes the
issue: she uses Farquhar's middle-class play to question the idea of
a class-based morality inherent in the Royal Marine view. While
reading the part of Justice Balance during auditions, Ralph *'laughs
a little'* at his comment that 'I was pleased with the death of my
father, because he left me an estate'; apparently growing uneasy, he
then explains that 'This is a comedy. They don't really mean it. It's
to make people laugh [...]' (Act 1, Scene 5, p. 14). The callous
desire for economic gain that allows an already comfortable gentleman to rejoice at the death of a parent because it brings him an
income of £1200 a year is reflected in the sense of humour that finds
the remark funny; such greed stands in stark contrast to that 'of
stealing from the colony's stores' for which three hungry men had
earlier been condemned to death (Act 1, Scene 3, pp. 2–4). The
contrast between the two types of selfishness, however, does not
excuse the latter: although motivated by genuine hunger (the play
makes clear that the whole colony is on short rations), the theft
represents pursuit of individual needs at the expense of the com-

mon good, the importance of which the play goes on to demonstrate powerfully.

The problem of a play's content is one to which Wertenbaker returns throughout *Our Country's Good*: she is careful to distinguish between the dramatic text *per se* and the collective experience of theatre-making and theatre-going. Through Dabby, she pokes fun at the predictability of dramatic form: 'I can't remember what they were called, but I always knew when [plays] were going to end badly' (Act 1, Scene 5, p. 13). Even unfamiliarity with a particular play is no bar to knowing its content:

> *Dabby*: [...] I want to play Mary's friend.
> *Ralph*: Do you know *The Recruiting Officer*, Bryant?
> *Dabby*: No, but in all those plays, there's always a friend.[4]

Similarly, when Governor Phillip argues, *pace* Justice Balance, that the convicts will benefit from 'speaking a refined, literate language and expressing sentiments of a delicacy they are not used to', Captain Tench is more concerned that Farquhar's plot will allow 'the convicts [to] laugh at officers' (Act 1, Scene 6, p. 21). Phillip's argument that 'The Greeks believed [...] it was a citizen's duty to watch a play' fails to convince Tench that the 'social virtues' necessary to perform this 'work' – 'attention, judgment, patience' – can be developed in the convicts (p. 22). Their debate introduces the idea that an audience should interrogate a play's content and the values it implies.

Although Wertenbaker is signposting the kind of attention she wants from her own audience, it is neither the content of *The Recruiting Officer* nor their response to it that transforms those involved in the production, but rather the actual process of staging it. Significantly, the change begins not in the prisoners, but in Ralph, who is surprised to find that in 'saying those well-balanced lines of Mr Farquhar, [one or two convicts] seemed to acquire a dignity, they seemed – they seemed to lose some of their corruption' (p. 22). As he begins to see his actors as people, he begins to treat them 'with [the] kindness' he had earlier thought impossible to extend to them (Act 1, Scene 4, p. 8).[5] The kindness is at first no more than simple courtesy in rehearsal, as shown in this exchange between the director and the aggressive Liz Morden, described by Phillip as 'one of the most difficult women in the colony [...] Lower than a slave, full of loathing, foul mouthed, desperate' (Act 2, Scene 2, p. 58):

> *Ralph*: [commenting on her delivery of a speech] That's a little better, Morden, but you needn't be quite so angry with her. Now go on Brenham.
> *Liz*: I haven't finished my speech!
> *Ralph*: You're right, Morden, please excuse me.
> *Liz*: *(embarrassed)* No, no, there's no need for that, Lieutenant. I only meant – I don't have to.
> *Ralph*: Please do.
>
> (Act 1, Scene 11, p. 49)

Provided through their common enterprise with the opportunity for human and equal interaction, Ralph and the convicts are slowly transformed.

Like Ralph's, the convicts' original involvement in the project is motivated by self-interest, with rehearsals providing an opportunity for escape or for finding favour, for self-assertion, for mockery of others, for physical aggression, for self-expression, for social acceptance, for safety.[6] Act 1, Scene 11 shows 'The First Rehearsal' as a *débâcle*, with name-calling, hissing and spitting, and refusal to submerge actual identity in the characters of the play: for example, Duckling Smith baulks at playing 'Liz Morden's maid' (p. 41). However, by the time of 'The Second Rehearsal' (Act 2, Scene 5), common activity has forged a collective spirit and identity, movingly illustrated when Major Ross and Captain Campbell persist in their humiliation of the actors despite Ralph's efforts to protect their dignity and 'modesty' (pp. 62–4). As the officers insist Mary lift her skirt higher to reveal the tattoo on her inner thigh, '*Sideway turns to Liz and starts acting, boldly, across the room, across everyone*' (p. 65). The line he begins with, 'What pleasures I may receive abroad are indeed uncertain; but this I am sure of, I shall meet with less cruelty among the most barbarous nations than I have found at home', poignantly comments on the convicts' situation at the same time it demonstrates the dignity the officers had sought to deny. Genuine community spirit is again evinced in the final scene, just before the performance is to begin: Liz comforts Duckling, whose lover has died, by suggesting 'Let's go over your lines. And if you forget them [in performance], touch my foot and I'll whisper them to you' (Act 2, Scene 11, p. 84).[7]

Just as the process of staging Wertenbaker's play-within-the-play transforms her characters, their relationships to one another, and the possibilities of their situation,[8] the metatheatrical aspects of *Our Country's Good* operate in similar ways for its own audience. The point that the play does not simply recreate historical events but treats contemporary concerns is explicitly made:

Dabby: Why can't we do a play about now?
Wisehammer: It doesn't matter when a play is set. It's better if it's set in the past, it's clearer.

(Act 2, Scene 7, p. 74)

Wertenbaker in fact makes evident the connection between events in eighteenth-century Australia and those of 1980s Britain by contemporizing the theatrical milieu of the play: for example, not only is Ralph the 'director' at a time when such a concept did not exist (Act 1, Scene 7, p. 24), but Liz responds to the offer of a part as a modern actor would, saying 'I'll look at it and let you know' (Act 1, Scene 5, p. 16). Similarly, when Ralph complains that Sideway's sobs are drowning out Plume's lines, Sideway anticipates Stanislavsky in explaining that he is 'still establishing [his] melancholy' (Act 1, Scene 11, p. 44).

Furthermore, many of the players' discussions about their theatrical venture with Farquhar relate directly to the modern audience's experience of *Our Country's Good*. Because 'Major Ross won't let any more prisoners off work' (Act 2, Scene 7, p. 73), Wisehammer has to double the part of Captain Brazen with that of Bullock, a decision to which he objects:

Wisehammer: It'll confuse the audience. They'll think Brazen is Bullock and Bullock Brazen.
Ralph: Nonsense, if the audience is paying attention, they'll know that Bullock is a country boy and Brazen a Captain.
Wisehammer: What if they aren't paying attention?
Ralph: People who can't pay attention should not go to the theatre.

Unsurprisingly, Ralph's line received one of the biggest laughs of the performance, as the audience was flattered at its own ability to cope with the doubling and even trebling of parts.[9] As Ralph notes, however, the playing of several parts by each actor in *Our Country's*

Good did more than 'display the full range of [her/his] abilities': it also 'challenged and trained' the audience's 'imagination' (p. 73), embodying as it did one of the play's central concerns, the linking of individual potential to social interaction. Thus, when Harry admits that he 'look[s] at the convicts and [. . .] think[s], one of those could be you, Harry Brewer, if you hadn't joined the navy when you did' (Act 1, Scene 4, p. 7), the point was powerfully reinforced by having the same actor, Jim Broadbent, play convict John Arscott. Indeed, all the officers' and convicts' parts were doubled with one another, creating a vivid stage reality of the different potentials inherent in each person. Moreover, the fact that the same cast appeared in Stafford-Clark's concurrent staging of *The Recruiting Officer*, playing the parts they had rehearsed in *Our Country's Good*, carried the idea of different potentials and possibilities into the other production: seeing both plays, in whichever order, added an extra layer to the audience's perception of actors playing a part. For example, one had a simultaneous awareness of Silvia in Farquhar's play as herself, as Mary Brenham the convict, and as Lesley Sharp the actor.

Doubling was also used to challenge prejudice of different kinds. Jude Akuwudike, a black actor playing not only an Aboriginal Australian and Black Caesar but also Captain Watkin Tench, commented in the persona of the latter that 'A savage is a savage because he behaves in a savage manner. To expect anything else is foolish. They can't even build a proper canoe' (Act 1, Scene 6, p. 19). The actor's own presence on stage effectively belied Tench's racist attitude and, at the same time, cut the word free from the stereotype embedded in that attitude: the idea of savagery defined through behaviour rather than race implicates not the Aborigines but the ruling white officers who can dispassionately discuss, let alone inflict, the vicious lashing that reveals 'the white of this animal's [Sideway's] bones' (Act 2, Scene 5, p. 64).

Similarly, Dabby's late desire to play Sergeant Kite instead of 'a silly milkmaid' (Act 2, Scene 7, p. 75) raises a problem of cross-gender casting for the play-within-the-play that the production of *Our Country's Good* had already handled successfully, with the women actors donning wigs and jackets over their convict rags to play some of the male officers. The issue raised goes beyond Dabby's assertion – proved by the audience's own experience – that such casting can work if people 'use their imagination and people with no imagination shouldn't go to the theatre' (p. 75): it also focuses attention on the circumscribed roles available to women not only in plays but also in reality.[10] Furthermore, the metatheatrical framework of the problem poses the question of why an audience would deem it inappropriate for Dabby Bryant to play Sergeant Kite in *The Recruiting Officer* – which it would – when it accepts Mossie Smith as both Dabby Bryant and Second Lieutenant William Faddy in *Our Country's Good*. The answer has in fact already been hinted at: when Dabby complains that she wants 'to see a play that shows life as we know it', thereby voicing some possibly conflicting attitudes of the audience of *Our Country's Good*, she unwittingly upholds the realistic convention that will frustrate her desire to play Kite. Wisehammer, on the other hand, could be describing Wertenbaker's own work when he says 'A play should make you understand something new' rather than tell you 'what you already know' (p. 74).

In its insistence on the need for imagination and in its demonstration of the value of community, *Our Country's Good* most acutely addresses the condition of 1980s Britain, a time during which the ruling Conservative government steadily dismantled the welfare state, destroyed the country's manufacturing base, disempowered the trade unions, and sold off public utilities, and whose leader, Margaret Thatcher, even declared that 'There's no such thing as society.' An ideology that elevates the idea of the free market and individual endeavour as the highest possible good, focusing on opportunities for the wealthy and powerful few without regard to the deprivations of the poor and powerless many, depends on a denial not only of collective life but also of imagination, exemplified in Ralph's response to Ketch Freeman's account of how he came to be transported:

> *Ketch*: [...] If only we hadn't left [Ireland], then I wouldn't have been there, then nothing would have happened, I wouldn't have become a coal heaver on Shadwell Dock and been there on the 23rd of May when we refused to unload because they were paying us so badly, Sir. I wasn't even near the sailor who got killed [...] they caught five at random, Sir, and I was among the five, [...] and when they said to me later you can hang or you can give the names, what was I to do, what would you have done, Sir?
> *Ralph*: I wouldn't have been in that situation, Freeman.
>
> (Act 1, Scene 9, p. 37)

It should be stressed, however, that *Our Country's Good* does not present the notion of theatre as a simplistic solution to personal and national problems. While it provides most of the convicts with pleasure and a sense of purpose, it does not satisfy Dabby 'Because it's only for one night' (Act 2, Scene 11, p. 85). Her plan to 'slip away' to freedom in the 'confusion' at the end of the play almost cancels the performance, with Mary threatening to tell Ralph about the scheme and Dabby refusing to act if she does. In the end, the collective 'good' – the performance – prevails, keeping Mary silent and allowing Dabby her chance, an uneasy compromise that in fact affirms the symbiotic relationship between individual and communal life.

That idea is also encoded in the title of Wertenbaker's own play, a phrase drawn from Wisehammer's prologue to *The Recruiting Officer* that provocatively identifies the convicts as 'True patriots all', who 'left our country for our country's good' (Act 2, Scene 11, p. 89). But the indirect celebration of the convicts' new Australian identity does not ignore the cost to the country's indigenous people, a cost emphasized by the brief but contrapuntal appearances of a lone Aborigine throughout the play. In addition, the otherwise sensitive Wisehammer comments that 'Here, no one has more of a right than anyone else to call you a foreigner' (p. 85), while Sideway's response to the news that the Aborigines are coming 'around the camp because they're dying' of smallpox (p. 83) is as heartless as the officers' attitudes to the convicts: 'I hope they won't upset the audience.' Both of these statements represent the obverse side of communal identity, the out-group, and Sideway's could just as easily refer to the beggars lining the pavements of London's theatre district over which consciousness-heightened playgoers will have to step at the end of *Our Country's Good*. As Phillip recognizes, one of the most important aspects of theatre is that by 'watching [something] together, for a few hours we will no longer be despised prisoners and hated gaolers' (Act 1, Scene 6, p. 21), but his vision is limited in scope: although he hopes that the convicts involved in putting on the play may be changed by the experience, he sees no opportunity for the *Recruiting Officer*'s audience to change their society for more than the duration of the performance. Wertenbaker's own play goes beyond his vision of forging a temporary collective identity, its metatheatrical dimensions creating a collaborative enterprise between actors and audience, one which provokes a conscious engagement with the relationship between fiction and reality, theatre and life, and demands that we carry the concerns of one into the world of the other. In so doing, *Our Country's Good* stresses the need for an inclusive idea of community not just in the fiction of the play and the experience of performance but in society at large. *The Love of the Nightingale*,[11] which was directed by Garry Hynes and premiered by the Royal Shakespeare Company at The Other Place, Stratford, on 28 October 1988, is a retelling of the myth of Philomela and Tereus, which also explores the idea of theatre, both ancient and modern, and its relevance to individual and political life. Its metatheatrical devices – the staging of *Hippolytus* as a play-within-the-play, the rough puppet-theatre of Philomele, and the use of two choruses, one female and one male, both in *Hippolytus* and in the play proper – engage the audience in a dialectical relationship with the action on stage. This relationship is engendered in the first instance by a juxtaposition of action and choric comment that requires the audience to analyse its own laughter.[12]

Much of the humour of Scene 5, set in 'The theatre in Athens' (sd, p. 8) during a performance of the tragedy *Hippolytus*, is self-reflexive, turning on definitions of comedy and tragedy. Philomele and her mother, arriving late, miss Aphrodite's opening speech, but King Pandion reassures his daughter that 'She only told us it was going to end badly, but we already know that. It's a tragedy' (p. 9). Similarly, when Tereus is later shocked by Phaedra's falling in love with 'Her own stepson', Pandion's response is phlegmatic: 'That's what makes it a tragedy. When you love the right person it's a comedy' (p. 10). Those in Wertenbaker's audience who know the outcome of the myth of Philomele and Tereus as well as the Athenian court knows the story of Phaedra and Hippolytus are in a position analogous to that of the on-stage audience. However, where foreknowledge makes the Athenian audience certain of its expected responses to *Hippolytus*, foreknowledge in Wertenbaker's audience makes it unsure of its amused responses to the characters of *The Love of the Nightingale*: it is difficult to reconcile present laughter with knowledge of Philomele's fate. Definitions of comedy and tragedy and the questions they generate problematize the nature of the play the audience is watching, as it watches.

The problematizing of Wertenbaker's play is enhanced by her treatment of the Greek one: although *Hippolytus* is offered as entertainment, its audience sees a further potential. Pandion hopes that it will 'help [him] come to a decision' about whether to send Philomele to her sister in Thrace,[13] while Tereus is initially resistant to the play, disturbed that it seems to 'condone vice' (p. 10). As his unsophisticated, but not unreasonable, response to a contemporary play clashes with the audience's own appraisal of a classical text, the meaning and function of both *Hippolytus* and of *The Love of the Nightingale* are interrogated: if the audience cannot be sure of the meaning of the Greek play, how can it be sure of the meaning of the present one? How should it interpret what it sees? The Queen gives a hint, applicable both to the play and to the play-within-the play, about how to ascertain meaning: 'Listen to the chorus. The playwright always speaks through the chorus' (p. 11).

This self-reflexive message provokes laughter, but gives no certain clarity, since the chorus of *Hippolytus* generates different meanings for its contemporary audience. Tereus seizes for self-justification on what he perceives to be the play's argument – that destructive passion cannot be resisted – and hatches his plan to violate Philomele.[14] Pandion, on the other hand, lights upon another line spoken by the Chorus and decides that Philomele should not leave Athens;[15] he is persuaded by Philomele, however, that she is 'not Hippolytus' and 'Tereus isn't Phaedra'. The correspondence between 'life' and art – that is, between the fictional action and the play-within-the play – is denied at the same time that Wertenbaker's own audience recognizes it.

Having established this correspondence, Wertenbaker encourages her audience to make further connections between the world of the play and the world the audience itself inhabits. In Scene 8, the members of the Male Chorus trace the meaning of the word 'myth', asking how it came to be transformed from 'public speech' and 'counsel, command' to 'unlikely story'. In so doing, they suggest another way to look at the play, but warn that it is too easy to understand its content as 'about men and women [. . .] a myth for our times': 'You will be beside the myth. If you must think of anything, think of countries, silence, but we cannot rephrase it for you. If we could, why would we trouble to show you the myth?' (p. 19).[16]

The rest of the play reverses the process the chorus describes, turning a 'remote tale' back into 'public speech'. When Philomele loses her tongue, her attendant Niobe pities her, noting that 'the one alive who cannot speak, that one has truly lost all power' (Scene 16, p. 36). But Philomele in fact regains her 'voice' in Scene 18, when she stages a play using three life-size dolls, representing her, Tereus, and Procne, both to recount her story and to reclaim her lost identity (p. 40). Just as Wertenbaker has played with her audience, encouraging its laughter only to question it, so Philomele's mime-play allows its audience to laugh at its unintentionally '*gross and comic*' re-enactment of her rape before engaging their understanding and '*very silent*' response to the depiction of her mutilation (sds, p. 40). Neither the play nor this puppet-play-within-the-play simply 'tells' its audience what it is about and how they should respond, as passivity does not allow for true engagement and comprehension: each involves the audience in the creation of meaning, one by the absence of words and the other by the refusal to be explicit about its content.

By giving Philomele back her voice through the medium of theatre, Wertenbaker also implies that theatre can give voice to others who are silenced, both on the personal and individual level and on the wider political and international one. Indeed, by suggesting rather than stating her theme, she invites the audience to collaborate with the play not just in determining meaning but also in listening to the silent and in making present the absent, albeit only internally in each individual audience member.[17] Such collaboration happens most clearly when the choruses engage directly with the audience,[18] inviting it to supply its own meaning to the myth, as in Scene 8 discussed above and again in Scene 20, when the Female Chorus voices the necessity of dialogue:[19]

Iris: To some questions there are no answers. [...]
June: Why do countries make war?
Helen: Why are races exterminated?
Hero: Why do white people cut off the words of blacks? [...]
Helen: Why are little girls raped and murdered in the car parks of dark cities?
Iris: What makes the torturer smile?
Hero: We can ask. Words will grope and probably not find. But if you silence the question.
Iris: Imprison the mind that asks.
Echo: Cut out its tongue.
Hero: You will have this.[20]
June: We show you a myth.
Echo: Image. Echo.

(pp. 45–6)

The choric comment positions the audience to fill out the 'echo' of the play with its own specific images, dependent on time, place and experience: the genocide of Pol Pot in Cambodia or the 'ethnic cleansing' in former Yugoslavia, the official apartheid of the old South Africa or the unofficial apartheid of the West's inner cities, the latest local brutality.

Perhaps most importantly, the kind of dialogue the chorus insists on is not declamatory but interrogative: the asking and answering of questions demands genuine interaction and hopes for mutual understanding. Consequently, the play's final scene shows the metamorphosis of Philomele and Procne into the nightingale and swallow of legend as a positive transformation, necessary rather than escapist (Scene 21, pp. 48–9). On this new plane, the nightingale and her erstwhile victim Itys can break the spiral of violence threatened by the play's events and engage in a dialogue – consisting mostly of questions and answers – in which they seek to understand each other. As the play demonstrates, such interaction is essential to growth and movement, to transforming an unending cycle of violence and death into the possibility of life and hope.

As demonstrated, each of the two plays discussed here is intensely self-reflexive, calling attention to itself as theatre and thereby provoking its audience to consider what theatre means, how it functions, and how it relates to the society the audience inhabits.[21] Paradoxically, in turning this kind of mirror onto itself, each play impels its audience to engage dynamically with political and social realities, thereby returning the word 'theatre' to its radical meaning as a place of 'seeing', but in a metaphorical rather than a literal sense. In so doing, Timberlake Wertenbaker also recreates the Greek ideal of theatre as a forum where the 'social virtues' Governor Phillip so eloquently espouses in *Our Country's Good* can be encouraged, developed and exercised.

Notes

1. Thomas Keneally, *The Playmaker* (London: Hodder & Stoughton, 1987), p. vii.
2. Timberlake Wertenbaker, Preface to *Our Country's Good* (London: Methuen, 1991), unpaginated. All further references are to this edition and occur in the body of the text.
3. See Act 1, Scene 4, in which Ralph discusses his desire for promotion with Harry Brewer and asks him to tell Phillip 'how much I like the theatre' (p. 9); Harry's surprise at this news suggests Ralph's self-interest rather than real interest. In discussing *The Tragedy of Lady*

Jane Grey, the only play he seems to know, Ralph also questions 'how [. . .] a whore [could] play Lady Jane' (p. 9).

4. Even though Ralph corrects her that Silvia 'doesn't have a friend. She has a cousin. But they don't like each other', Dabby is right in surmising that in such a play 'a girl has to talk to someone' (p. 13) and that there will be a character fulfilling that function in *The Recruiting Officer*. It was clear in performance that Ralph, rattled by Dabby's demand for the part, made the technical correction both to put her in her place and to bolster his authority.

5. In fact, he eventually falls in love with Mary Brenham, who reciprocates his feeling; they negotiate their relationship through the medium of rehearsing their parts as Ralph and Silvia. See Act 2, Scene 7, pp. 69–71, and Act 2, Scene 9, pp. 78–9.

6. For example, Robert Sideway wants to recreate the pleasure of his London theatre-going (Act 1, Scene 5, p. 12); Dabby and Liz nearly throttle each other when Dabby taunts Liz with being unable to read (Act 1, Scene 8, p. 33); Ketch Freeman hopes to abolish the stigma of serving as hangman (Act 1, Scene 9); John Wisehammer can indulge his appetite for words and pursue his interest in Mary Brenham (Act 1, Scene 10); John Arscott attempts an escape instead of attending rehearsal (Act 1, Scene 11, p. 51); Black Caesar, having participated in the same escape attempt, pretends to have been at rehearsal and then insists on being given a part to substantiate his alibi (p. 51).

7. Liz's own remarkable transformation is portrayed in the preceding scene. Under sentence of death for her (unproven) part in the conspiracy to steal from the colony's food store, Liz has refused to speak in her own defense 'Because it wouldn't have mattered' (Act 2, Scene 10, p. 82). She finally admits she 'didn't steal the food' when pressed by Ralph, Captain Collins and Phillip (respectively) to 'speak'. 'For the good of the colony.' 'And of the play'. She breaks her silence not only because of their appeal to the collective good but also because of her own growing awareness that her speaking matters to at least some of the ruling group. Having done so and been believed, she finds a new voice:

Phillip: [. . .] Liz, I hope you are good in your part.
Ralph: She will be, Your Excellency, I promise that.
Liz: Your Excellency, I will endeavour to speak Mr Farquhar's lines with the elegance and clarity their own worth commands.

The credible dignity with which she delivered the line provided one of the most electrifying moments of the production.

8. For example, Wisehammer abandons his wish to return to England when his sentence has expired, since as a Jew he was always an outsider there; instead he decides to stay in Australia and become its 'first famous writer' (Act 2, Scene 11, p. 85). Similarly, Sideway declares he will 'start a theatre company' when he is released, and Liz and Ketch indicate they will join it (p. 86).

9. The play's 22 parts (5 female and 17 male) were played by 10 actors (4 women and 6 men).

10. When Mary had earlier insisted that to act a part one has 'to be' it, Dabby had objected there was 'No way I'm being Rose, she's an idiot' (Act 1, Scene 8, p. 31); later she objects to taking Liz's part of Melinda, if necessary, as 'All she does is marry Sideway, that's not interesting' (Act 2, Scene 7, p. 76).

11. Timberlake Wertenbaker, *The Love of the Nightingale* and *The Grace of Mary Traverse* (London: Faber & Faber, 1989). All further references are to this edition and occur in the body of the text.

12. The opening scene of the play invites us to laugh at a stylized depiction of war as a game of schoolboy insults, but audience response is then suddenly wrong-footed by intervention from the Male Chorus and its change of tone, questioning the treatment of war as entertainment; please see my 'Questioning Comedy in Daniels, Wertenbaker, and Churchill', in *Contemporary Drama in English: New Forms of Comedy*, ed. Bernhard Reitz (Trier: Wissenschaftlicher Verlag, 1994), pp. 34–5, for a fuller discussion of this point. Some of the present essay draws on my earlier analysis, although there my focus is on the use of comedy rather than on metatheatre.

13. He says, 'I find plays help me think. You catch a phrase, recognize a character' (p. 9).

14. Tereus's 'Ah!' after a choric speech emphasizing passivity in face of 'the bitter poison of desire' (p. 11) suggests its effect on him. Similarly, his temptations and his decision to give in to them are presented subtextually:

> *Philomele*: [...] I want to feel everything there is to feel. Don't you?
> *Tereus*: No!
> *King Pandion*: Tereus, what's the matter?
> *Tereus*: Nothing. The heat.
>
> (p. 11)

At the end of the scene, Tereus, who had earlier deferred to Pandion about whether Philomele should journey to Thrace (see pp. 8–9), is decisive about leaving with her 'Tomorrow' (p. 13).

15. Pandion focuses on a choric comment that regrets the hero was sent 'far away, out of your father's lands to meet with such disaster from the sea-god's wave' (p. 12).

16. Niobe reiterates this idea in the context of the play's fiction, stating that 'Countries are like women' as she describes the destruction of her island-home (Scene 13, p. 31).

17. In *Our Country's Good* Wertenbaker explicitly makes the absent present by including the Aborigine, reminding the audience of an oppression it would otherwise have been able to ignore, while in *The Love of the Nightingale* she positions the audience to fill in such blanks by itself.

18. In the RSC production, unless the lines demanded that they interact with each other, the members of the play's two choruses addressed the audience directly.

19. The lines of the Female Chorus quoted below imply the need to

listen to silence as well as to words and, since the play itself shows that non-verbal enactment may have as much power as language, 'dialogue' here does not simply mean speech; rather it implies an engagement with what is outside oneself.

20. Hero's 'this' refers to Philomele's murder of Itys in the following scene – in other words, an endless cycle of revenge and retribution.

21. Wertenbaker's latest play, *The Break of Day*, which was first performed at the Leicester Haymarket on 26 October 1995, was written for Max Stafford-Clark's new company, Out of Joint, as a companion piece to his production of Chekhov's *The Three Sisters*; as with the coupling of *The Recruiting Officer* and *Our Country's Good*, it was written to use the same cast. The metatheatrical dimension of *The Break of Day* differs from that of the two plays discussed in this essay: rather than actually staging theatre, it uses Chekhov's play as a reference point in its consideration of the nature of work, the hope for the future, and the meaning of motherhood at the end of the twentieth century. By presenting the plays in tandem, the two productions allow them to engage in a dialogue with each other: for example, Catherine Russell's Masha disintegrates when Nigel Terry's Vershinin leaves her at the end of *The Three Sisters*, suggesting she has lost her only chance of fulfilment; however, in *The Break of Day*, Russell's Tess becomes increasingly desperate as she sees motherhood as her only hope of fulfilment, causing her ultimately to reject her husband Robert, also played by Terry (see *The Break of Day* (London: Faber & Faber, 1995), Act 2, pp. 70–4, 77, 90). The implicit juxtaposition of the two characters engages the audience in a consideration of the notion of progress in woman's cultural and social position this century.

Bibliography

Dymkowski, Christine, 'Questioning Comedy in Daniels, Wertenbaker, and Churchill', in: *Contemporary Drama in English: New Forms of Comedy*, ed. Bernhard Reitz (Trier: Wissenschaftlicher Verlag, 1994), pp. 33–44.
Keneally, Thomas, *The Playmaker* (London: Hodder & Stoughton, 1987).
Wertenbaker, Timberlake, *Our Country's Good* (London: Methuen, 1991).
——, *The Break of Day* (London: Faber & Faber, 1995).
——, *The Love of the Nightingale* and *The Grace of Mary Traverse* (London: Faber & Faber, 1989).

9

Tom Stoppard's Metadrama: The Haunting Repetition
Nicole Boireau

Steering a bold course away from naturalistic representational conventions and resolutely opting for the fictional and the literary, Tom Stoppard has developed his own idiosyncratic brand of metadrama. Following René Magritte's comment that the apple represented on the canvas 'is not an apple' but its image, Stoppard's plays never fail to advertise that whatever is represented on stage looks like theatre and *is* first and foremost theatre.

Stoppard's exploration of the nature of drama and theatre through drama and theatre encompasses a wide spectrum of literary tactics, which cut across the clear-cut boundaries of parody and pastiche. *Rosencrantz and Guildenstern Are Dead* (1967), *The Real Inspector Hound* (1968), *Travesties* (1974) and *The Real Thing* (1982) contain the classical device of the play 'within'. *Dogg's Hamlet, Cahoot's Macbeth* (1979) are playful adaptations, whereas such later plays as *Hapgood* (1988), *Arcadia* (1993) and *Indian Ink* (1995) function as metaphors of the art of playwriting. Stoppard plays his favourite game of ping-pong[1] with layers of fictionality, deftly juggling with postmodern practices, therefore carefully avoiding fixed meanings and rigid categories.

Poised between seriousness and frivolity, the play's the thing that repeats literary history in repeating itself and, at the same time, dramatizes the principle of iteration inherent in *mimesis*. In conveying a sense of *déjà vu*, the self-conscious, self-reflexive, dynamic force at work in Stoppard's plays appears as the *primum mobile* of the creative act: ultimate reality. Theatricality is its metaphor. In this lies the revelatory power of Stoppard's prismatic metadrama, whose mechanisms deserve to be examined.

THE SECOND TIME AS FICTION

Stoppard's versatile intertextual modes have been extensively analysed by numerous critics.[2] It seems therefore hardly necessary to recall that Shakespeare is the inspiring force of *Rosencrantz and Guildenstern Are Dead*, of *Dogg's Hamlet, Cahoot's Macbeth*, that Oscar Wilde's *The Importance of Being Earnest* is the unmistakable hypotext of *Travesties*, and that extracts of *'Tis Pity She's a Whore* are inserted in *The Real Thing*, whose title and theme have been borrowed from Henry James. Stoppard's plays always assert their textual origin. Excerpts from the original plays can be simply quoted, sometimes with major changes, or they can also be performed on stage, where they assume the status of the 'inner play,' and are made visible and recognizable, closely bound up, structurally and thematically, with the outer play (or frame play).[3]

However recognizable the 'play within' may be initially in some of the constructions, its contours are soon blurred, as inner play and outer play tend to lose their autonomous status and to merge into a new compound. Inner play and outer play absorb each other, thus demonstrating their fictional nature. The dynamic is particularly visible in *The Real Inspector Hound*, where the final play is the actual continuation of the whodunit, the original inner play the two critics are attending. In *Rosencrantz and Guildenstern Are Dead*, dramatic necessity derives from the pattern of inevitability set by Shakespeare's *Hamlet* and acknowledged by Guildenstern: 'Each move is dictated by the previous one – that is the meaning of order' (p. 42). The model, or the play supposed to be 'within,' freezes its meaning and controls the dramatic construction of the outer play. The same device operates in *Travesties*, a dizzying composite of *The Importance of Being Earnest* and *Ulysses*, which conjures up different layers of fictionality, each one masquerading as the other. The dramatic structure of *Travesties* consists of inscribed plots, each one mirroring the other. The main story is the playful adaptation of Wilde's well-known plot amusingly summed up in Joyce's sartorial plot: 'You enter in a debonair garden party outfit – beribboned boater, gaily striped blazer, parti-coloured shoes, trousers of your own choice' (p. 52), itself then compressed into the spy-plot, announced later through the authorial voice of the stage directions: 'CARR *enters, very debonair in his boater and blazer, etc.* CARR *has come to the library as a "spy"'* (p. 70). The mirroring process, or 'mise en abyme', is unequivocally full scale here, in this Chinese nest of plots within Carr's experience of Wilde's play. The compulsive repetition of the trick, un-writing and re-writing the model *ad infinitum* has become the major dramatic action of *Travesties*, the outer play.

The Real Thing also thematizes the art of playwriting and raises the question of the 'real thing'. The play is made of three plays, 'The House of Cards,' *'Tis Pity She's a Whore*, and Brodie's scenario re-written by Henry, all drawing on the lives of the characters that belong to the outer play (or first level of fictionality). In *The Real Thing*, the inner plays are juxtaposed rather than interlocked as they are in *Travesties*. Apart from *'Tis Pity She's a Whore*, a recognizable literary model, the other 'inner' plays are barely distinguishable from the outer one, in both dramatic and theatrical terms. No demarcation line is perceptible between the fictional levels alternating in front of the spectator's eyes.

The first scene of *The Real Thing*[4] appears as a witty domestic comedy of middle-class manners, seasoned with adultery between two sophisticated intellectuals, Max and Charlotte. The scene conveys the absolute conviction of being only the straightforward revelation of a (common enough) marital infidelity. The second scene immediately undermines that certainty by making it clear that the first scene was only the rehearsal of Henry's latest play, 'The House of Cards'. Thus retrospectively invested with fictitious status, the credibility of the first scene collapses like the house of cards Henry is building. Yet the 'reality' status of the second scene is by no means unequivocal itself; on the contrary, its ambiguity deepens as 'Max' and 'Charlotte', the characters of the first scene and of Henry's play (the inner play), retain their pseudofictitious names when re-entering the outer play. 'Max' and 'Charlotte' remain in character, though in different frames, at all times. Stoppard repeats the trick twice, in scenes six and ten, adding further levels of fictionality. In these two scenes, the 'play within' performed on stage dramatizes the action of reading and turns out to be Henry and Brodie's jointly written scenario in the process of being read out. Dramatic action is thus devolved to the repetition of a trick that denies the very existence of a pseudoreality level. The clear referential system established by the classical use of the play-within-the-play is shattered in the process, obliterating the traditional illusion/reality debate and redirecting the action into the act of writing. Stoppard's plays are made of plays that are both within and without, never letting us forget that what we are watching is fiction, preferably written twice over.

Eager to overemphasize the fictional nature of the model and its double, Stoppard goes for repetitive dramatic situations which carry a high level of improbability. The obvious example is the coin-tossing scene of *Rosencrantz and Guidenstern Are Dead*, with Ros turning 'heads' 85 times in a row. The detective play cum farce, of which *The Real Inspector Hound* is the archetypal example, is a genre twice removed from any form that can lay claim to a touch of plausibility. The farce that grows out of the initial whodunit requires firm structuring and careful handling to be in any way effective, and both genres thrive on the repetition of improbable patterns. Here again design dictates action. The Agatha Christie model, complete with the corpse lying in the middle of the stage before the play starts, controls *The Real Inspector Hound* and reappears in *Jumpers*, the metaphysical thriller. Both plays subvert the detective story genre, upstaging the riddle proper to the benefit of rhetoric. Once again, significant action derives from the making of fiction.

Whereas the early plays are based on the re-enactment of the literary heritage, the later ones introduce the biographical genre, an ambiguous literary discourse, partly historical and partly fictional, which has to establish a credibility contract with the reader/spectator to attain its goal. In *Arcadia* and *Indian Ink*, where biographies turn out to be pure fantasy, suspension of disbelief is achieved as truthfulness is made irrelevant. The truth of the tale is in the telling, not in the tale itself. Fake literary history, made up as the play goes along, with Byron being kept on the margins of the dramatic world, paradoxically gives the family drama of *Arcadia* its credibility. Likewise, the fictitious story of the poet Flora Crewe in *Indian Ink* serves the exploration of the actual multicultural myth. The skilful authorial hand preserves the autonomy of the play as self-referential literary entity, furthering the exploration of fiction through fiction and disclosing the working of the ropes at the same time.

The characters lending themselves to Stoppardian juggling also affirm their status as essentially textual. Henry Carr the narrator is at the same time Old Carr, young Algernon, a menial consular clerk masquerading as the Consul, and James Joyce in the process of writing *Ulysses*. Stoppard's *dramatis personae* do not claim to be human beings endowed with levels of subjectivity. They are not characters looking for an author, nor are they actors in search of a role, as the role is already pre-defined by the model. Minor characters in Shakespeare's original, Ros and Guil come to the fore in Stoppard's play to act out their own death. They disappear in the

final tableau, overtaken by their inevitable fate, as events act themselves out in an oracular fashion. They participate in the cathartic
sense of pity and fear contained in the tragic model and re-enacted
by its repetition. Repetition brings the certainty that the second
time Shakespeare's play comes around, it comes as fiction with
major alterations but also as tragedy. Gilles Deleuze reminds us
that tragedy and comedy are both an effect of repetition, itself a
tragic necessity (Deleuze, 1968, p. 364). If tragedy comes with repetition, so does comedy. *Rosencrantz and Guildenstern Are Dead* is described as 'thematically tragic and theatrically comic' (Homan, 1989,
p. 119). In the Stoppardian universe, repetition of the literary heritage is bound to carry ambivalent overtones.

The compulsive repetition of literary patterns, one of the modes
of Stoppard's metadrama, generates its own inner necessity and
points up the ultimate autonomy of art. Drama in performance
goes a step further when it comes to highlighting the seams of the
disguise.

REPEATING THE PERFORMANCE

If repeatability is a condition of action, it is also a prerequisite of
performance, which operates within a structure of spectatorship,
the 'trinity' of playwright, actor and spectator, which is central to
Rosencrantz and Guildenstern Are Dead (Homan, 1989, p. 108) and to
Travesties. Being is saying is performing, the ontological truth of the
Player:

> *Guil*:   Well [. . .] aren't you going to change into your costume?
> *Player*:   I never change out of it, sir.
> *Guil*:   Always in character.
> *Player*:   That's it.

(p. 24)

As performing entities, Ros and Guil are sometimes difficult to
identify, like the confusing interchangeable doubles running riot
in *Hapgood* and forcing the spectator to fight a losing battle working out who is who on the stage. Indeed, there is no space for
fallacious realistic characterization in Stoppard's dramatic world. If
the truth lies in the making of fiction,[5] it also derives from the act
of performing.

Travesties is the epitome of the play committed to its own per-formance, re-echoing and repeating itself like an old record. Per-formance is both its theme and structure, as the play re-enacts Henry Carr's participation in Joyce's production of *The Importance of Being Earnest*. It simultaneously performs and therefore deconstructs the dynamics of performance through its layers of role-playing. Re-petitive performance in *Travesties* signals representational codes as deceptive. It undermines surface realism, uncovering the simulacrum of realistic imitation which appears as nothing more than a mask or a mediation. Stoppard puts down the 'time slips' of Carr's erratic wanderings to his defective memory, which the repetitive structure of the play is supposed to 'represent.' Stoppard thus pretends to pay lip-service to surface realism: *'the effect of these time slips is not meant to be bewildering'* (p. 27), while concurrently undermining it in the structure of the play. Repeating the act of performing subverts the naturalistic conventions of representation. In denying their le-gitimacy, performance becomes a discourse (a text?) in its own right, thus enacting what postmodern terms have adequately described as the 'meeting of the performance/text double' (Vanden Heuvel, p. 14). Any claim to a representation of the world is wiped out to the benefit of self-referential performance, whether verbal or visual. Compulsive verbal repetition strips the mechanism of *mimesis* to its naked core. Such is the metaphorical function of the striptease act in *Travesties*, where Cecily mimetically sheds layers of potential ideologies in the same way as the dramatist sheds layers of fake representational practices. While pretending to submit to the imi-tative order, Stoppard discreetly sabotages it.

The 'circular self-reference' of the performance aspect of Stop-pard's plays (Brassell, p. 262) could also apply to the playful hand-ling of language, fictionalized and self-dramatized to the point of becoming an abstract reflection of itself. The performative function of language,[6] has been the object of many illuminating demonstra-tions by J. L. Austin, Jacques Derrida (1972) and Shoshana Felman among others who, in the wake of Nietzsche, have brought out the force of words over meaning. Stoppard exploits the equivocal and arbitrary relationship between signifier and signified to the full in order to over-emphasize the performative function of dramatic lan-guage. On the stage, a speech-act can be repeated *ad infinitum*, as it is not operative outside its theatrical context. In Stoppard's plays words are acts, and verbal exchanges create self-contained situa-tions. As action is verbal and feeds on itself, the dialogues often carry more cumulative than dramatic power. *Dogg's Hamlet*,[7] is the ultimate example of a language that generates its own rationale within the conventions of the stage context. The Lewis Carroll verbal situation is recognizable in the coded language of the play: 'Scabs, slobs, yobs, yids, spicks, wops [. . .]' (p. 28). Although it only occupies 15 minutes of the spectator's time, *Dogg's Hamlet* makes an important statement on the essential self-referentiality of dramatic language.

In *Arcadia* Thomasina cultivates the art of asking pointed questions: 'Septimus, what is carnal embrace?' (p. 1); Hannah sees rhetoric as 'performance art' (p. 65), even as 'aerobics' (p. 65). Bernard and Hannah, engaged in a battle of wits, vie with each other rhetorically. Lady Croom also proves in complete control of the verbal (and theatrical) situation: 'I have had experience of being betrayed before the ink is dry, but to be betrayed before the pen is even dipped, and with the village noticeboard, what am I to think of such a performance?' (p. 72). In *Arcadia*, where the former historical period is only signalled by a few references to Byron and to the landscaping of parks, language seems immeasurably free, almost transparently self-referential, conveying no fixed meaning but floating in a privileged state of grace. Self-contained Stoppardian language acquires physicality and performs its self-perpetuating laws. Linguistic playfulness demonstrates the power of dramatic language as an autonomous system.

In achieving a high degree of stylization in his theatricalization of language, Stoppard does more than produce a textbook of applied pragmatics, he also shows that *trompe-l'oeil* effects can be verbal as well as visual. Poised between Stoppardian seriousness and frivolity, wit also operates within the actor/spectator structure as a *mise-en-scène* of language. Wit is the mask that signals itself as a mask generating other masks. But 'the mask is the face' says J. W. Cooke (Zeifman, p. 200) echoing Oscar Wilde's 'The Truth of Masks'. Like Cecily's striptease routine, wit strips language of its naturalistic trammels and creates theatrical distance. Stoppard's metadramatic approach uses language in performance as a privileged tool to do away with all mediations (or travesties).

Stoppardian theatrical discourse is also designed to topple certainties. *Hapgood* and *Arcadia* foreground the scientific relativisim that has upstaged Newtonian certainties and questioned the epistemological heritage of the Enlightenment since the turn of the century. The cryptic dialogues of *Hapgood*, which fit the Lecarré situation, also deal with universals such as light being at once both waves and particles. Treated as a theme in *Hapgood* and *Arcadia*, Einstein's theory of relativity informs the dramatic construction and verbal exchanges of the plays. 'Well, maybe there is anti-matter as well as matter; anti-atoms made of anti-particles.' says Kerner, the spyphysicist in *Hapgood* (p. 72), rationally stating the viability of contradictions and impossibilities in all areas of experience. This is true also at the theatrical level. The dual time and space structure of *Arcadia* and *Indian Ink* theatricalizes the reversible time of physicists. Dramatic time is out of joint, moving back and forth, from present to past and vice versa. Waves and particles hop about in chance encounters that can be only predicted within certain limits. The same laws of necessity and randomness also apply to the sonnet scene in *Travesties*, where the sonnet cut into a myriad pieces comes out of Tristan Tzara's hat as another fully-fledged poem: 'I offer you a Shakespeare sonnet, but it is no longer his. It comes from the wellspring where my atoms are uniquely organised, and my signature is written in the hand of chance' (p. 53). Determinism and chance operate in the realm of performance just as much as they govern creativity in the making of fiction.

As initiated in *Travesties*, both literary and scientific discourses merge centre stage in *Arcadia*. *Tabula rasa* is made of the 'Grand Narrative' whose validity Stoppard questions by theatricalizing the artificiality of coded discourse. Dramatic meta-discourse is a travesty, which Stoppard exposes and satirizes with Moon and Birdboot, the two drama critics pompously holding forth in *The Real Inspector Hound*: 'The groundwork has been well and truly laid, and the author has taken the trouble to learn from the masters of the genre' (p. 35) says Birdboot, mimicking academic practice. Drama in performance carries its own subversive potential and does not need the travesty of fraudulent discourse to prove its social and moral necessity. *Cahoot's Macbeth* derives its meaning from its associations with two forbidden Czechoslovakian actors.[8] Stoppard's deft recontextualization of the original carries much emotional power. The interplay between the outside drama – the drama of reality – and the drama contained in Shakespeare's original confer on Stoppard's play its moral purport. To be adequately perceived, painful reality needs powerful drama, initiated by a great poet and taken up by a skilful playwright. In *Travesties*, the major artefacts of Western culture provide the only adequate objective correlatives to match the chaos of the Great War. When repeating the performance, drama wears the masks of both comedy and tragedy while voicing its own comment on its inherent validity. The haunting repetition of fiction in performance introduces new perspectives on the visible and makes the straitjacket of ideological discourse unnecessary.

THE VISIBLE AND ITS DOUBLE

The deceptive metaphor of the theatre as mirror is blatantly theatricalized in *The Real Inspector Hound*, where a huge mirror used as a backdrop reflects the two critics and part of the auditorium. The mirror metaphor is exposed while the very possibility of a straightforward mirroring process is immediately undermined by the dramatic structure of the play, which distorts all attempts at linear representation. In his plays Stoppard introduces a more subtle metadramatic practice in which an in-built sense of perspective shows that *mimesis* is more about creation than slavish imitation.

The word and the gaze are two sides of the same act of perception. This Aristotelian principle also underlies Stoppard's metadrama. The visible is what we go by, what we hold on to, like the different fictional levels of *The Real Thing*, which recall in a more sophisticated way the structure of *The Real Inspector Hound*. In all the plays, no level is endowed with more inherent credibility than the other. Inseparable from a situation of observation, the spectator's gaze is the *raison d'être* of the theatrical experience. 'The act of observing determines the reality' claims Kerner, the spy-physicist in *Hapgood* (p. 12), echoing Henry in *The Real Thing*: 'There is nothing real there separate from our perception of them' (p. 53), thus denying the existence of a transcendent truth. Highly subjective, observation is fallible, and the reality it determines can go wrong. Such is the tragedy at the heart of *Artist Descending a Staircase*,[9] whose dramatic impact derives from Sophie failing to recognize the man who loved her (the real thing?) on the photograph, owing to her defective eyesight. Kerner's comment also applies to the sense of perspective and to the pictorial associations dramatized in *Arcadia* and *Indian Ink*, where changes to the layout of Sidley Park and the making of a painting are the organizing forces of the fables. *Arcadia* recalls Poussin's celebrated masterpiece in its classical re-ordering of the landscape. *Indian Ink*, as the re-write of a radio play,[10] also marks Stoppard's distinctive return to a visual mode of representation.

The visual is inseparable from a sense of distance, the primeval necessity of pictorial and theatrical representation. The aesthetic of distance (V-Effekt) that governs Stoppard's drama is sited within the self-contained and abstract universe created in the stage directions and turned, like language in performance, into a self-referential entity. What applies to fictional structures and to language also applies to the treatment of space. Self-referential space in Stoppard's plays gives a strong sense of hyperrealism, the very mark of *trompe-l'oeil*, which advertizes its fake perspective and points to itself as a copy in the making. Stoppard paradoxically creates reality effects by de-realizing the visible. The sense of physical and metaphorical perspective obtained in the plays is that of an Italian style theatre, where the picture is permanently framed and the frame is as visible as the contents.[11] Classical perspective, fixed since the Renaissance,[12] sustains the gaze down the oblique lines converging in the vanishing point. Stoppard's idea of perspective is a *trompe-l'oeil* construct set in perpetual motion, endlessly shifting orbits and centres.[13] His taste for design in dramaturgical constructions (to think only of the geometrical structure of *Artist Descending a Staircase*), added to his repeated use of pictorial associations, creates a contrived, yet necessary, sense of order. If perspective can be defined as 'an ordering of the visual phenomenon' (Panofsky, 1991, p. 71) Stoppard's dramaturgical and theatrical perspective metaphorically suggests a reordering of experience. Stage space encompasses the subjective and the objective.

The visible and the invisible, the one and the other, the twin and its double, is the unsettling repetitive mystery at the vanishing point of Stoppard's sense of perspective. Peggy Phelan sees *Hapgood* as a meditation on Shakespeare's comedies. In the play, Stoppard takes up the metaphor of the double in the twentieth-century context of espionage. The predictable capriciousness of lovers, common to both Shakespeare and Stoppard, falls within the pattern of determinism and freedom represented by the particle and wave image. As the mathematical translation of the previous plays, *Hapgood* demultiplies into double, triple or quadruple figures to a maddening extent. The longing for the complementary particle (for unity?) is one of the invisible forces of *Hapgood*, *Arcadia* and *Indian Ink*. The immense success and joyous power of *Arcadia* can probably be explained by its holistic vision. Metaphorized perspectival metadrama reveals a totalizing image of reality beyond the creaking machinery of the visible.

Arcadia and *Hapgood* can also be grasped as the ultimate meta-phorical ciphers of their own theatricality, although neither play seems to fall within the classical metadramatic description.[14] Those plays are uncannily invested with a freshness of vision related to Stoppard's avoidance of copying the world to better theatricalize cognitive faculties. *Arcadia* dramatizes a happy meeting-point between pure language and pure thought, thus falling, again, within the Aristotelian framework.[15] Apart from being the focus of the action in *Travesties*, *Hapgood* and *Arcadia*, cognitive activities are also on the alert, exploring knowledge and generating it. *Arcadia* metaphorically performs the art of inductive scientific thought, and in doing so it echoes *Travesties*.[16] Sidley Park is the unattainable Eden where the essential is found, the essential language of signs, of love and of erroneous literary discourses; it is also the place where scientific discoveries can be made. In *Hapgood* and *Arcadia*, the diegetic world of nature and the mimetic world of the stage both carry the abstract quality of an algebraic formula. Valentine gives a graphic representation of iteration through ciphers: 'What she's doing is, every time she works out a value for y, she's using *that* as her next value for x. And so on. Like a feedback. She's feeding the solution back into the equation, and then solving it again. Iteration, you see' (p. 44). Iteration is produced by an endless movement of particles. Postmodern re-interpretive practices are given full recognition in Stoppard's playful (yet complex) handling of mathematical signs. Valentine's definition fits both the inductive method of scientific observation, and the act of articulating signs, that is to say perceiving, reading and writing, the very mechanism of dramatic creation. Iteration is the *primum mobile* of the creative act. The paradigmatic relatedness between scientific discourse and theatricality gives Stoppard's later plays their metaphorical dimension. The play that is recognized as play becomes a metaphor for the process of saying, seeing and being, the cornerstone of the dramatic experience.

By its very existence, each literary product asserts its reality and marks its absolute difference from the original.[17] The illusory sense of order that seems to be established by in-built perspective is simultaneously disrupted in the repetitive process. Stoppard's metadrama seems to have removed the filter on the lens in order to capture the essential principle of being. If the key-word in Oscar Wilde's title is 'being' (Rosset, 1979, p. 12), Heidegger would advise us to cross it out to better understand it. This Stoppard does with Henry Carr, who is caught up in the dual process of being and not being, acting out and un-writing Wilde's play in the same never-ending movement.

Stoppard's sense of history lets itself be seen and heard but, hologram-like, cannot really be grasped. The past lends itself to Stoppardian 'bricolage'. It can be performed and made visible. Past and present coincide spatially in *Travesties*, *Arcadia* and *Indian Ink*. Henry Carr, the archetypal clown of *Travesties*, is haunted by the Great War. In *Arcadia* a different sort of historical drama is enacted within the drama. A chance meeting between a bright young girl and Fermat's marginalia creates a vision of history. In *Hapgood* and *Arcadia* fake Le Carré and fake literary history dramatize the essential forces of the universe. The past is re-ordered and obliterated in the same sweeping movement. Stoppard seems to fit in the twentieth-century debate on the 'de-definition of art,' in which the artist 'disdains to deal in anything but essences.' (Rosenberg, 1983, p. 13) This flirtation with 'essences' possibly accounts for what can be recognized and has been criticized as Stoppard's elusive sense of history.

The historical forces that have shaped the century are diluted in the neutral zone of Stoppardian theatricality, where no space is provided for clear-cut ideologies to expand. Although the cultural issue is not fully developed in *Indian Ink*, Stoppard makes it clear that some kind of harmony is achieved between the Indian painter's observation of Flora Crewe and his knowledge of Eastern and Western pictorial traditions. The ordering of experience that underlies perspective conveys a sense of unity. The sense of historical perspective that emerges from Stoppard's metaphorized metadrama foreshadows a necessary reunification of sensibility. The unity that underlies fragmentation calls for a return to the basic tenets of romanticism. Invisible forces lurk behind the visible world, taking the form of a belief in a unified Eurocentric culture.

Repetition carries emotional overtones intimately bound up with the drive for knowledge. The 'still centre' (the vanishing point) is made all the more poignant as it remains invisible, and a distant echo from T.S. Eliot. The love story behind *Hapgood* is the essential link in the chain that justifies the puzzle. The reported death of witty Thomasina immediately after the waltz scene at the end of *Arcadia*, is also a cathartic moment of emotion for the spectator. Immediate emotional commitment to a cause or to a work of art is necessary for the cognitive faculties to come into play, demonstrates Antonio Damasio questioning Descartes' mechanistic division between reason and emotion. The perception of emotion is the non-cartesian credo that emerges from a study of Stoppard's meta-drama.[18] An avatar of the Grand Narrative, rationality is likewise a *trompe-l'oeil* construction that only exists in the mind of the would-be thinker. Duality, another manifestation of ready-made rational systems, is obliterated in all the plays. Indeed, breaking the Cartesian order and pointing up the necessity to recognize the chaos in the middle is Carr's mission in *Travesties*. We need Henry Carr compulsively remembering his soiled tweed Savile Row trousers, for chaos to be re-created and confronted. Carr's frivolity is necessary to measure the seriousness of the situation, seriousness and frivolity exchanging their masks at breakneck speed and 'affirming the morality inherent in human actions.' (Delaney, 1990, p. 126)

Like the past, chaos repeats itself unless it is well remembered and fully digested, or so Freud tells us. In repeating itself like an old record, each time with a major change, *Travesties* echoes all the traumas of the century, which is made of the previous eras and contains them all. But Stoppard's haunting metadramatic repetition carries no absurdist overtones. Instead, it brings out the full significance of the metaphor of theatre as memory.[19] *Travesties* and the later plays juggle with the multi-storeyed (and highly organized) fabric of human memory whose power can only be matched by unlimited dramatic creativity. Drama within and about drama tolerates no boundary, whether theatrical or ideological. Reinterpretation of the theatre by itself follows the compulsion to reinterpret the past and search for the essential still centre, where the world makes and unmakes itself in the rumblings of history.

Metadramatic repetition is conducive to *anagnorisis*, a heightened response to experience, a cathartic moment of recognition identified as the change from ignorance to knowledge (Rosenberg, 1982, p. 176), an exalted level of consciousness, 'a discovery in which we see, not our past lives, but the total cultural form of our present life' (Frye, 1973, p. 346). Awareness of the repetitive pattern leads the spectator from heightened experience to self-knowledge, and in a word, to the revelation of the theatre as ritual. The play's the thing in which the anxiety of repetition acts itself out.

CONCLUSION

Stoppard's trans-historical melting-pot defines a dramatic world made of mirrors and false perspectives. It is a fictional ideology-free zone which has long been held in high suspicion by correct intellectuals. Yet, to have a censorious view of Stoppard's glittering theatricality has ceased to be *de rigueur*.[20] The intellectual determined to criticize Stoppard's metadrama on the basis of his puns and games, however well-meaning, is bound to get bogged down in a quagmire of irrelevance. Indeed, trying to locate Stoppard on one side of a fence is a self-defeating enterprise in itself, as the very idea of a boundary – whether theatrical, ideological or metaphysical – is precisely what the haunting repetition of his complex metadrama sets out to challenge. Questioning the frames of thought that underlie the making of values is Stoppard's distinctive (and distinguished) hallmark. Joyous relativity in Stoppard's drama on drama clears the way for the world to be perceived anew.

Notes

1. Stoppard's own comment on *Jumpers* and *Travesties* (Hayman, 1978, p. 12).
2. See Cohn (1991), Zeifman (1993), Brassell (1985), Brugière (1983).
3. For a thorough examination of their fluctuating status, see the chapter by Ruby Cohn (1991) 'Theatre framing theatre,' in *Retreats from Realism in Recent English Drama*.
4. See analysis by Hersh Zeifman (1993) of the first scene of *The Real Thing*.
5. In his chapter on Poe's 'La lettre volée' in *La carte postale*, Derrida (1980) demonstrates that fiction tells the truth (p. 495).
6. Assertions sever all links with outside reality and are meaningful within the context provided by the stage.
7. *Dogg's Hamlet* is based on Wittgenstein's *Philosophical Investigations*. 'The appeal to me consisted in the possibility of writing a play which had to teach the audience the language the play was written in', says Stoppard in the Preface to the play (1980, p. 8).
8. Pavel Kohout (to whom the play is dedicated) and Pavel Landovsky.
9. A radio play adapted for television.
10. The radio play entitled *In the Native State* leaves more to the imagination and possibly carries more emotional power than *Indian Ink*.
11. It is important to note that Stoppard never breaks through the fourth wall. Nor does he play games with the audience as Saunders does in his early plays.
12. See Erwin Panofsky's illuminating demonstrations.
13. I develop that particular point in 'Marginalizing the Centre: the Case of Tom Stoppard'.
14. Surprisingly enough, Paul Delaney describes scene 6 of *Hapgood* as a 'play within a play' (p. 134).

15. According to Aristotle's *Poetics* 'all that is produced by words has to do with thinking' (1980, chs 19, 56 a 36, p. 101 [my translation]).
16. In his eulogistic *Encounter* article, Clive James points out the presence of the quantum physics metaphor in *Travesties*.
17. Deleuze is the obvious reference here.
18. Helen Reinelt-Keyssar-Franke had brought out the emotion of Stoppard's drama in 1975.
19. See Frances Yates's book.
20. In a *Times Literary Supplement* article David Edgar comments: 'Stoppard's *Arcadia* and *Indian Ink* both borrow the double-time scale literary investigation format so popular in the contemporary novel, as does my own play *Pentecost* (in essence a political thriller encased in a historical whodunit).' Edgar's surprising need to measure himself against Stoppard's yardstick is worth mentioning.

Bibliography

Aristote, *Poétique* (Paris: Seuil, 1980).

Boireau, Nicole, 'Marginalizing the Centre: The Case of Tom Stoppard', in: Bernhard Reitz (ed), *Centres and Margins* (Trier: Wissenschaftlicher Verlag, 1995), pp. 99–108.

Brassell, Tim, *Tom Stoppard: An Assessment* (London: Macmillan, 1985).

Brugière, Bernard, 'De la parodie à une esthétique de la duplication: etude de *Travesties* de Tom Stoppard', in: Georges Bas (ed), *Études Anglaises*, Cahiers et Documents 6 (Paris: Didier Erudition, 1983), pp. 141–54.

Cohn, Ruby, *Retreats from Realism in Recent English Drama* (Cambridge University Press, 1991).

Cooke, John William, 'The Optical Allusion: Perception and Form in Stoppard's *Travesties*', in: Zeifmann and Zimmerman (eds), *Contemporary British Drama* (London: Macmillan, 1993), pp. 199–216.

Damasio, Antonio, *L'erreur de Descartes: La raison des émotions* (Paris: Odile Jacob, 1995).

Delaney, Paul, *Tom Stoppard: The Moral Vision of the Major Plays* (London: Macmillan, 1990).

Deleuze, Gilles, *Différence et répétition* (Paris: PUF, 1968).

Derrida, Jacques, *Marges de la philosophie* (Paris: Seuil, 1972).

——, *La carte postale de Socrate à Freud et au-delà* (Paris: Aubier-Flammarion, 1980).

Edgar, David. 'Back to Narrative: Popular Influence on Playwrights of the 1990s'. *The Times Literary Supplement*, 28 April 1995, p. 7.

Frye, Northrop, *Anatomy of Criticism* (Princeton University Press, 1973).

Felman, Shoshana, *Le scandale du corps parlant* (Paris: Seuil, 1980).

Hayman, Ronald, *Tom Stoppard* (London: Heinemann, 1978).

Homan, Sidney, *The Audience as Actor and Character: The Modern Theater of Beckett, Brecht, Genet, Ionesco, Pinter, Stoppard and Williams* (London & Toronto: Associated University Press, 1989).

James, Clive. 'Count Zero splits the Infinite', *Encounter*, 45, 1975, pp. 68–76.

Panofsky, Erwin, *Meaning in the Visual Arts* (London: Penguin Books, 1983).
—— , *Perspective as Symbolic Form* (New York: Zone Books, 1991).
Phelan, Peggy, *Unmarked: The Politics of Performance* (London: Routledge, 1993).
Reinelt-Keyssar-Franke, Helen, 'The Strategy of *Rosencrantz and Guildenstern Are Dead'*, *Educational Theatre Journal*, 27, 1975, pp. 85–97.
Rosenberg, Harold, *The Tradition of the New* (Chicago & London: Phoenix Edition, 1982).
—— , *The De-definition of Art* (Chicago Press, 1983).
Rosset, Clément, *Le réel et son double: Essai sur l'illusion* (Paris: Gallimard, 1976).
—— , *L'objet singulier* (Paris: Editions de Minuit, 1979).
Stoppard, Tom, *Rosencrantz and Guildenstern Are Dead* (London: Faber & Faber, 1967).
—— , *The Real Inspector Hound* (London: Faber & Faber, 1970).
—— , *Jumpers* (London: Faber & Faber, 1972).
—— , *Travesties* (London: Faber & Faber, 1975).
—— , *Dogg's Hamlet, Cahoot's Macbeth* (London: Faber & Faber, 1980).
—— , *The Real Thing* (London: Faber & Faber, 1983).
—— , *Hapgood* (London: Faber & Faber, 1988).
—— , *In the Native State* (London: Faber & Faber, 1991).
—— , *Arcadia* (London: Faber & Faber, 1993).
—— , *Indian Ink* (London: Faber & Faber, 1995).
Vanden Heuvel, Michael, *Performing Drama / Dramatizing Performance: Alternative Theater and the Dramatic Text* (Ann Arbor: the University of Michigan Press, 1991).
Wilde, Oscar, 'The Truth of Masks', *The Complete Works of Oscar Wilde* (London: Collins, 1988).
Yates, Frances, *The Art of Memory* (London: Routledge, 1992).
Zeifman, Hersh, 'Comedy of Ambush: Tom Stoppard's *The Real Thing'* in: Zeifman Hersh and Zimmerman, Cynthia (eds), *Contemporary British Drama* (London: Macmillan, 1993), pp. 217–31.

10

Hauntings:
Ghosts and the Limits of
Realism in *Cloud Nine* and
Fen by Caryl Churchill
Ann Wilson

Caryl Churchill's plays are characterized by their stunning theatricality which the playwright marshals to critique social relations.[1]
Her sense of theatricality, aside from forging a theatrical style which
accommodates a left-wing politic, often seems to be a reconsidera-
tion of conventional notions of theatricality. In the case of *Cloud
Nine* and *Fen*, two plays which have strong realist elements, the
appearance of ghosts demands that the audience reconsider theatrical realism with particular attention to the implications of its ideological investment in patriarchy.

To begin, I want to remind readers that Churchill is, as Sheila
Rabillard notes, a playwright who is acutely aware of the relation
between theory and practice. Rabillard (1994) notes that:

> in her early works, she [Churchill] took inspiration from the theo-
> ries of R. D. Laing (*The Hospital at the Time of Revolution*), and
> Michel Foucault (*Softcops*). Speaking of one of the dramas that
> made her name, she remarked that 'Fanon's *Black Faces, White
> Masks* was one of the things, (along with Genet) that led to Joshua,
> the black servant being played by a white in *Cloud Nine*.
>
> (p. 62)

Indeed, Churchill's sense of the relation between theory and practice
is wittily established in an exchange been Lin and Victoria in *Cloud
Nine* when the two women, with Victoria's brother Edward, gather
late one night in a London park. In the darkness, the three drunk-
enly try to summon the 'Goddess of many names' (1985, p. 308). In

the midst of chanting an invocation, Victoria launches into a lecture on matriarchy which Lin resists, responding, 'Don't turn it into a lecture, Vicky, it's meant to be an orgy' (p. 309). Replies Victoria, 'It never hurts to understand the theoretical background. You can't separate fucking and economics' (p. 309).

Although in this chapter, I am concerned neither with fucking nor with economics, I want to use Victoria's comment as a point of departure and suggest that it is a fair assumption that a playwright of Churchill's intellectual calibre is, as her experimentations with theatricality suggest, aware of the theoretical stakes of dramatic form. As if to disrupt the realism of the second act of *Cloud Nine* and of *Fen*, Churchill has ghosts appear. The problem which I want to explore in this essay is the significance of the appearances of ghosts within contexts which adhere, on other counts, to notions of theatrical realism. My position is that Churchill understands that theatre depends on a privileging of the visual and drama depends on some sense of a correspondence to the 'real' or 'actual'. Both *Cloud Nine* and *Fen* suggest that for Churchill, conventional modes of theatrical realism are ideologically over-determined, tending to capitulate to patriarchal values.

Historically, theatrical realism depends on the assumption that reality can be mimetically reproduced on the stage and can be understood fully, or mastered, by the audience. Given that representation is symbolic, and so within representation orders over-determined by patriarchy, the challenge facing a feminist playwright, like Churchill, is how the representational apparati of theatre can be exposed to indicate the degree to which they are invested in ideologies which oppress women. Ghosts, according to Freud, mark the repressed ('Gravida', 1959, p. 38). By having ghosts appear in *Cloud Nine* and *Fen*, Churchill signals the illusion of theatrical realism fully representing the 'real,' because ghosts, both the sign and effect of the repressed, exceed the conventions of theatrical realism.

The first act of *Cloud Nine* suggests Churchill's consciousness of the operation of theatrical languages to produce meaning. She disrupts the notion of correspondence[2] by having particular characters played by actors whose gender and race is at obvious odds with that of these characters: a man plays a woman, a woman plays a male homosexual youth and a white man plays a black man. Through this casting, Churchill creates a veritable primer for the ways in which woman, homosexuality and race are constructed within patriarchy. In the introduction to the play, published in *Churchill*

– *Plays: One*, Churchill (1985) writes that she returned to a theme touched upon in the workshop:

> the parallel between colonial and sexual oppression, which Genet calls 'the colonial or feminine mentality of interiorised repression'. So the first act of *Cloud Nine* takes place in Victorian Africa, where Clive, the white man, imposes his ideals on his family and the natives.
>
> (p. 243)

The opening of the play establishes Clive's patriarchal perspective. With the Union Jack fluttering in the background, Clive and his family sing the praises of England and Empire, followed by Clive presenting those assembled to the audience. 'This is my family', he tells the audience. 'Though far from home/We serve the Queen wherever we may roam/I am a father to the natives here, And father to my family so dear' (p. 251). He then presents his wife, Betty, who is *'played by a man'* saying, 'My wife is all I dreamt a wife should be, /And everything she is she owes to me' (p. 251). With that as her cue, Betty steps forward and identifies herself in relation to Clive:

> I live for Clive. The whole aim of my life
> Is to be what he looks for in a wife,
> I am man's creation as you see,
> And what men want is what I want to be.
>
> (p. 251)

Given that Betty is being played by a man, the line 'I am man's creation as you see' is a witty meta-theatrical comment, pointing to Betty's failure to appear as woman. As Marc Silverstein (1994) comments:

> Betty's (dis)appearance before the audience reminds us that while women appear within the ideological theatre that stages sexual difference, they have been cast in roles determined by the image-repertoire of masculine fantasy. Woman as Symptom; Woman as Fetish; Woman as Lack; Woman as Object of Desire; Woman as Exotic Other, Woman as, in Clive's words 'irrational, demanding, inconsistent, treacherous lustful' (p. 282) – these are only some of the significations inscribed on the text of the female body,

significations which foreclose the representational options through
which the body could 'accede to its own specific symbolization.'

(p. 10)

Silverstein continues that 'If Betty, played by a male actor, lacks a
body that can "accede to its own specific symbolization", Victoria
lacks *any* body' (p. 11). Victoria, Clive's daughter, in the first act of
Cloud Nine, is represented by a doll, as if to suggest that to a female
child within patriarchy is to be a toy; or, alternately, to be something akin to a ventriloquist's dummy who has no agency but speaks
the words of the (male) manipulator.

That Churchill, in the first act of *Cloud Nine* mounts a powerful
and stinging critique of patriarchy is uncontested by critics. Her
critique extends beyond the construction of woman – who is recognized only in relation to man and whose desires are unrecognized
– to the insistence that patriarchy, as articulated in European cultures, depends on notions of racial supremacy. To be white, as Clive
suggests in his opening speech, is to position one's self as 'a father
of the natives', as if indigenous populations are children who are
without parental figures and so look to the colonizers as those who
will lead them to maturation. Within conventional notions of realism, the second act of *Cloud Nine* might seem problematic. Whereas
the first act is set 'in a British colony in Africa in Victorian times.
Act Two takes place in London in 1979. But for the characters it is
only twenty five years later' (p. 248). The point which Churchill is
making is simple enough: the chronological passage of time does
not have a commensurate impact on the lives of the characters who
experience change at a slower rate. As Karl Toepfer (1991) suggests:

> some characters re-appear as themselves in the 'liberated' Lon-
> don of the 1970s, and because for the most part they do not seem
> happier than they were in the previous century, the play wittily
> dramatizes the perception that the modern bodies contain values
> and sentiments from a past which has been repudiated. We are
> not free of the past because we are not free that our bodies be-
> long to an old force external to them, namely language, the ab-
> stract apparatus by which ideology and desire encode difference
> with the most enduring consequences.

(p. 127)

The contrasting constructions of time in *Cloud Nine* (between chronol-
ogy and the experience of time) is, as Janelle Reinelt (1987) suggests,

a Brechtian alienation effect so that the 'realism' of the second act must be read 'from a distance similar to the way the 'past' is seen, that is, historically' (p. 87). Toepfer (1991) and Reinelt both point to the stylistic contrast between the two acts as signalling the need to historicize the present with the same rigour which we apply to the past. These critiques invite the questions: why does Churchill revert to realism? Why not choose another theatrical form? An answer would entertain some sense that in *staging* patriarchal ideology, Churchill is commenting not only on patriarchy but also on its implications for her medium, drama.

Thematically, this is signalled by Betty, in Act Two, being in the process of divorcing Clive who is not seen in the act. Significantly, Clive, the figure of patriarchy in act one is not dead; in other words, patriarchy still figures in the lives of the characters as an ideology with which they must negotiate in order to reformulate their current social roles. That the characters, with the exception of Lin's daughter Cathy, are played by actors whose genders correspond to those of the characters, serves as an indication that divorcing patriarchy has brought the social roles assigned into a closer fit with the characters than was the case in Act One. However optimistic this lessening of the gap between the social role and character may be, its theatrical result is realism, a form which is not ideologically neutral but brings a particular history and ideology to bear.

Realism, characteristically set within households, tends to focus on the way in which people stage themselves within the domestic sphere before members of their family or other intimates. Set within the confines of the domestic, tremendous emphasis falls on the individual and her psychology, often eclipsing a sense of human subjectivity as determined by the society's production of roles which the individual must perform. In theatrical realism, individual characters may not be conscious of the degree to which their choices are governed by socially produced roles; realism implies that if the characters had that consciousness, they would be free to make other choices. The focus, then, is on the individual and the choices made by that individual. What is elided in realism is the recognition that the option of choices which the individual perceives is overdetermined by the dominant ideologies of society. Human consciousness is socially produced and therefore the options which individuals understand – even when those options are dissident – occur as a response to, and hence within, the dominant ideology.

Churchill's use of the Brechtian-like devices of alienation in Act

One, notably by having characters portrayed by actors whose gender and race are at odds with those of the characters, instructively reminds the audience that the roles which individuals play are stagings. Act Two, with its more realistic style, to some degree undermines this initial claim by implying that in the 1970s, the social roles assigned to individuals are closer to their bodies: men play men and women play women. The perhaps problematic implication of Act Two for the audience is one of historical progress, that role and character are more closely aligned than in the preceding century, that by divorcing patriarchy, society comes closer to allowing people options in terms of social roles which more 'naturally' fit the determinations of gender and sexuality than did those of the preceding century.

My brief discussion of realism suggests the ideological implications of realism which privilege notions of individualism. There are several signals in the second act of *Cloud Nine* that whatever optimism Churchill may have, she isn't naive enough to believe that progress is anything other than a problematic concept. First, the chronological passage of time, a hundred years, is only experienced by the characters as 25 years: the 1970s and the emergence of the liberated woman rather curiously seems a rehearsal of the emergence (in the late nineteenth and early twentieth centuries) of the New Woman seeking independence from male domination, as we see in realist dramas like Ibsen's *A Doll's House* or *Hedda Gabler*. In some senses, the struggles faced by Victoria in Act Two are strikingly similar to those faced by Nora in *A Doll's House* and by Hedda in *Hedda Gabler*. Further, Churchill does not adapt realism completely in Act Two: as if to allow her staging to incorporate same disjunction in time experienced by the characters, the portrayal of Lin's daughter Cathy by an adult man seems a stylistic carry-over from the first act. In so doing, Churchill erodes any sense that she, as the author, has a privileged insight not enjoyed by her characters: as the characters in Act Two carry their histories from the nineteenth century into the 1970s, so Churchill, playwright, brings stylistic devices from Act One into Act Two, as if her plight as a dramatist is akin to that of her characters. This serves as a qualifier that she may not perceive her own dramaturgical practices in the same emancipatory light as do her supporters.

In this context, the setting of Act Two in a park within London has particular significance in relation to Churchill's own sense of dramaturgy. In one sense, setting the scene within a park is a modest emendation of the conventions of realism which normally locate the action within the domestic sphere of the home. I would suggest, however, that the significance of setting the scene in a park returns us to Churchill's sense of the problematic nature of her medium, drama. This park is within an urban location, a setting which invokes a controlled (or perhaps given the presence of Edward as the gardener, a cultivated) sense of nature. The park, then, is a construct which alludes to nature before the civilizing force of man; but, because it is an allusion, marks itself as an effect of the social, a nostalgic invocation of the natural. From this perspective, the setting can be seen as an analogue to theatrical realism which corresponds to the actual world, reproducing it on stage. But realism involves a process of selection as Maupassant (1902) suggests in the Preface to *Pierre et Jean*:

> The realist, if he is an artist, will endeavour not to show us the commonplace photograph of life, but to give us a presentment of it which shall be more complete, more striking, more cogent than reality itself. To tell everything is out of the question; it would require at least a volume for each day to enumerate the endless, insignificant incidents which crowd our existence. A choice must be made – and this is the first blow to the theory [of realism as] 'the whole truth.'
>
> (p. 1)

Even those playwrights whose work, like Ibsen's, are categorized as exemplifying realism fail to meet fully the terms of conventional definitions of realism as art which corresponds to the 'actual' world because there is always a gap between the world and the representation of it.

Realist strategies, in all artistic media, always exceed the terms of, and consequently, undercut their own projects. Given the inherent instability of realism as a category, resulting in a range of forms of realism from, as Damian Grant (1970) suggests, 'critical realism' to 'visionary realism' (p. 1), we need to question whether an audience in the late 1970s would query Churchill's apparent undermining of realism in Act Two of *Cloud Nine* with an alienation effect like having Cathy played by a man. While this might initially seem jarring, I suspect that it is important to entertain the possibility that it might become a theatrical convention subsumed within the dominant style of realism. Given the possibility that the audience might

accept the cross-gendering casting as a device, the radical political
implications are apparent mainly to critics. The same sort of arguments can be made about the other cues in the act which disrupt
realism, with the exception of the appearance of the ghost of Lin's
brother.

The appearance of the ghost exceeds the conventions of both the
Brechtian and realist styles of the play. Both these styles depend on
an investment in materiality. The Brechtian techniques of Act One
in *Cloud Nine* suggest that social relations which produce the discourses of gender, sexuality and race can be made apparent, or
staged, for the audience to see. The conceit of theatrical realism is
that the world can be reproduced mimetically onstage; in other
words, that world can be made perceptible to the spectator. And
indeed, given that theatre relies on materiality – the body of the
actor staging the drama before the bodies which comprise the audience – both modes are particularly suited to the theatre. The
appearances of ghosts onstage in *Cloud Nine* and in *Fen* – the appearance of the dead to the living, of the immaterial body before
the material – challenges the theatrical assumptions of both Brechtian
dramaturgy and 'classic' realism. Indeed, the appearance of a ghost
onstage challenges the nature of theatre which is a place for seeing;
for when a ghost appears onstage, what does the audience see?

In theatre, which depends on the presence of the bodies of the
living, the appearance of a ghost reminds the audience of the limits
of representation. The actor's portrayal of someone who is dead
foregrounds the gap between the sign and referent. Given this gap,
the question arises: what does a ghost on stage represent? Freud, in
his reading of Jensen's *Gradiva*, suggests that when the protagonist
of the story, Norbert Hanold, sees the ghost of a woman, through
a complex linguistic translation, he is seeing the figure of an unresolved adolescent love, Zoe, whose surname (Bertang) has linguistic derivations, including 'Gravida' (1959, pp. 37–8). Writes Freud,
'But, lo and behold! that very name now turns out to have been a
derivative – indeed a translation – of the repressed surname of a
girl he had loved in the childhood which he was supposed to have
forgotten' (p. 38).

What is significant in Freud's formulation is its sense of the appearance of a ghost as related to the repressed which are impulses
that are inadmissible into consciousness ('Resistance', p. 296). Ghosts
are repressed impulses moving into consciousness which are perceived as fleeting appearances by the intangible figures of the dead;

as such, ghosts are not simply the effect of repression but serve as a metaphor for the impulses buried in the unconscious which are manifest briefly to the conscious mind through the mediation of figurative language. That a ghost is both the sign and effect of repression makes it difficult to establish the meaning of a ghost's appearance.

Thematically, in both *Cloud Nine* and *Fen*, ghosts are figures who surge into consciousness as phantasms of a past which the contemporary characters, adhering to notions of historical progress, believe themselves to be beyond. In *Cloud Nine*, Bill appears as a figure who reminds the audience of the colonialism of Act One which was maintained by particular constructions of masculinity, including the construction of male desire. In the contemporary England, notions of Empire are devalued and with it, possibilities for particular forms of male heroism. In Act One, Clive has sex with Mrs Saunders in the name of protecting the matrimonial property of her deceased husband and Harry, whose homosexuality is outside acceptable social mores within England and so explores the uncharted (for Europeans) territories of Africa (ostensibly in the name of Empire); in contrast to Clive and Harry, Bill cannot ascribe a political dimension to his desire. The relation between masculine desire, Empire and heroism is so debased by the late 1970s that Bill, the British soldier serving in Northern Ireland, speaks of desire only in personal terms, without once suggesting the implications of the military presence in Ireland as the last vestiges of England's imperial glory. Almost as if to indicate the tawdriness of the imperialism in the 1970s, Bill speaks of his desire only in terms which are linguistically limited to variants of 'fuck' (as in, 'No I have come for a fuck. That was the worst thing in the fucking army. Never fucking let out. Can't fucking talk to Irish girls. Fucking bored out of my fucking head. [. . .] I got so I fucking wanted to kill someone and I got fucking killed myself and I want a fuck' [Churchill, 1985, pp. 310–11].) Bill's desire to be manly and kill someone becomes a deadly inversion that results in his being killed, perhaps a political allegory for the risk of England maintaining its armies in the six counties of Ireland. By including the ghost of Bill, Churchill seems to be suggesting that England has repressed the connection between the patriarchal masculinity of the nineteenth-century Empire and England's political relation to Ireland in the late 1970s. She seems to suggest that we are like Lin whose perspective on the world focuses largely on individuals and their personal relationships. When

Lin sees her brother, she says 'I miss you. Bill. Bill' (p. 311), a response which expresses only her personal loss.

Her response, arising from a sense of individualism, is compatible with the values of 'classic' realism. The appearance of the ghost, as the last vestiges of Imperialism which haunt the contemporary Britain, suggests that the sense of history as a progressive, linear development may be the result of repressing those aspects of change which don't fit the model: if you believe that England a hundred years later has progressed as a society, you may not want to entertain the notion that a 100 years is experienced as only 25 years by the characters and the New Woman, as a social effect of contemporary ideologies, is set to stage her entrance, for the second time.

In many ways, *Fen* seems an exploration of the implications of dramatic form which extends logically from *Cloud Nine*. This production, like *Cloud Nine*, was a result of the collaborative practices of Joint Stock (see Ritchie.) The company went to the Fens of England, interviewed a range of people living there and, through workshops, created scenarios which Churchill fashioned into a script. The resulting playscript has the feel of a documentary, as if it selectively records aspects of the lives of the people – most notably women given that the cast calls for five women and a man. The episodic structure which cuts between the experiences of the various women is a Brechtian device drawn from cinema. *Fen* rather boldly assumes that its audience is conversant in the cinematic effects of editing, perhaps to the degree that the audience no longer finds them alienating but accept that they are an aspect of (documentary) film which ostensibly records accurately its subject matter. Despite the potential of film to record, the content of the play's initial 'frames' or scenes render problematic any impulse which the audience might have to suture the vignettes into a 'classically' realist narrative.

Fen begins with '*a* BOY *from the last century, barefoot and in rags* [. . .] *alone in a field, in a fog, scaring crows*' (Churchill, 1990, p. 147). The use of fog as a scenographic device gives the boy a ghostly presence. The scene is followed by the Japanese businessman, Mr Takai, presenting a history of the Fens, read through the filter of international capital: the Fens now are owned by multinational corporations. Mr Takai reads this ownership as the logical progression of history, beginning in 1630 with 'rich lords' who 'planned to drain fen, change swamp into grazing land, far thinking, brave investors' (p. 147). He notes that 'Fen people wanted to keep fishes

and eels to live on, no vision' (p. 147). Despite the protests of the
workers, the capitalists had their way. As Mr Takai notes:

> We now among many illustrious landowners, Esso, Gallagher,
> Imperial Tobacco, Equitable Life, all love this excellent earth. How
> beautiful English countryside. I think it is too foggy to take pic-
> tures. Now I find teashop, warm fire, old countryman to tell tales.
>   (p. 147)

The final moment of Mr Takai's comments ('too foggy to take
pictures') depends on the inter-relation between capital, the wealth
which it generates and the resulting leisure for tourism. Mr Takai's
presence on the landscape is the consequence of capitalism which
shapes how he sees the land. He relishes the beauty of the landscape which seems curiously devoid of people, as if he simply
doesn't notice them. The way in which Mr Takai sees involves a
particular blindness (or repression) so that what he sees is compatible with an economic articulation of patriarchy, capitalism.

The juxtaposition of the first two scenes of *Fen* is important in
establishing the tension within the play between impoverished lives
of workers and capitalism. Mr Takai offers a reading of history,
filtered through capitalism, which understands the aspirations of
workers as outdated: history, within Mr Takai's purview is progressive (and hence compatible with the ideologies of 'classic' realism in which narrative unfolds progressively.) Further, Churchill
signals that this sense of history as progressive is complicit with
capitalism and its effects, including Mr Takai's sense that the Fens
accord visual pleasure which can be recorded by a camera which,
like realism, is associated with a faithful rendering of reality. Mr
Takai's perspective of life on the Fens is clearly at odds with the
experience of the boy from the nineteenth century (toiling in isolation and abject poverty) and the depiction of the contemporary Fen
people whose lives seem not terribly dissimilar from those of fore-
bears. Progress, it would seem, is a luxury of the wealthy whose
economic gains seem to depend on their repressing, like Mr Takai,
the lives of the workers whom he seems to have banished from the
landscape.

What is striking about *Fen* is the degree of isolation which is
experienced by the various characters. The characters, while severely oppressed by life on the Fens and often conscious of the
oppression, cannot take the final step and imagine another life. The

inability to imagine is a consequence of the community's powerful mechanisms of regulation, including self-regulation. The community's regulation registers on three distinct levels: a failure to imagine life other than the one being lived; the regulation of dissident voices and the repression of historical consciousness. The consequence of this regulation is violence which pervades the community and frequently erupts as self-abuse.

Val and her lover, Frank, are examples of the first mode of regulation. She is just about to leave the community and approaches her lover to suggest that he, she and her children should move to London to start a new life (pp. 151–2). The opening of the scene has Frank on his tractor, envisioning his confrontation with his boss, Mr Tewson. In this monologue, Frank anticipates the ways in which Tewson will counter the objections to the demands for higher wages by assuming that the employer will present labour relations in terms of the family.

> But I remember when your dad worked for my dad and you and your brother played in the yard. Your poor old brother, eh Frank? It was great when we got him into that home when your mom died. We're like family. We'd both put up with a lot living this good old life here.
> I hate you, you old bugger.
> FRANK *hits* MR TEWSON, *that is he hits himself across the face.*
>
> (p. 151)

Frank has a limited degree of analysis which allows him to perceive that the invocation of the family to describe social relations of labour is a form of regulation which denies political agency because love within the family is imagined to have its origins in the pre-social, to be disinterested and beyond analysis. Frank seems on the brink of an alternate analysis in which he sees himself as worker in relation to the employer and hence, in terms of capital. Brought to the brink of a potentially emancipatory analysis, he can't take the final step and identify himself as worker, within a historic context of the centuries of exploitation of workers on the Fens, and so turns his anger on himself. When Val approaches him, ready to leave the confinement of life on the Fens and move to the wider social sphere of life in London, Frank resists. They kiss, a gesture which is a capitulation to feeling which resists political analysis. Val decides to return to life on the Fens: 'I suppose I go home now. Unpack' (p. 152).

Val's ambivalent decision to return home causes her no end of despair. She moves in with Frank, leaving her children in the care of her mother and their father and, in the process, becomes alienated from her family and is forced to endure her mother's harsh criticism, 'What you after? Happiness? Got it have you? Bluebird of happiness? Got it have you? Bluebird?' (p. 159). Happiness evades Val who returns home and then leaves again, turning in desperation to the church which promises community, only to find that it casts those whom it perceives as wayward as having succumbed to the temptation of sin (pp. 174–6). Finally Val sees her only option as death and asks Frank to kill her, a request with which he complies (p. 187).

Social regulation, evident in the church's demand that those who do not adhere to its codes identify themselves as sinners, is shown in an earlier scene depicting girls from the community approaching a single woman, Nell, as she works in her garden. Nell's ostracizing by the community registers in the girl's claim that Nell is a 'morphodite' which they understand as someone who is 'a man and a woman both at once' and then as 'witch' who 'eats little children' (p. 155). As if Nell's difference from community norms cannot be contained simply by labelling her, one of the girls, Becky, takes a hoe and begins to poke at Nell (p. 157). In this scene, like many others in *Fen*, differences which might disrupt the community – whether Frank imagining that he will confront Tewson, or Val wanting to leave to begin a new life, or Nell's refusing to adhere to conventional sexual codes – are regulated with a horrifying (and in the case of Frank and Val, self-inflicted) violence. Whereas *Cloud Nine's* second act offers an optimistic perspective that the constraints of codes of sexuality and gender, two of patriarchy's most powerful articulations of regulation, might be transformed thereby allowing the oppressed to be emancipated, the message of *Fen* seems bleak. It is as if Churchill acknowledges that the catalyst for change in the second act of *Cloud Nine* is an effect of theatre. Whereas the characters in Act Two begin the scene with a level of consciousness which facilitates change, the characters in *Fen* approach that moment, but patriarchal ideology pervades all aspects of their lives (including, for some, the dissatisfaction which brings them close to change and then transforms the sense of change into self-loathing) that emancipatory options seem impossible. In some sense, *Cloud Nine's* utopian view that patriarchy can be dismantled is tempered by a realization in *Fen* of the degree to which change may be dream, articulated within the theatre, but having little real effect beyond the performance space.

In *Fen*, the appearances of ghosts – from the boy at the beginning of the play, to the woman who appears to Tewson, telling him that she is starving and that 'you bloody farmers could not live if it was not for the poor, tis them that keep you bloody rascals alive [. . .]' (p. 163) to Val's appearance at the end of the play as a ghost who names the oppression of various people, ending finally with a recognition of Becky's tormented childhood because she is abused by her stepmother (pp. 188–9) – mark the return of repressed histories (both social and personal) which have been displaced from the history of the community. The appearance of ghosts in *Fen* is thematically similar to the appearance of the ghost in *Cloud Nine* because in both plays, ghosts are the return of voices displaced from history because the recognition of these experiences would disrupt the claim of history as progress. The question remains, what do these ghosts signal in terms of Churchill's sense of theatrical practice?

Curiously, repression involves a form of violence, a suppression from consciousness of events which are part of the identity of an individual or history of a community. Repression is also, following the work of Lacan, a key aspect to the acquisition of language. I do not want to belabour an explication of psychoanalytic theory's explanation of language acquisition, except to remind readers that:

> *Oedipus Rex*, dramatizing as it does *the primal scene* of *desire*, in effect takes place on the *other scene* of *language*. 'The unconscious', says Lacan, 'is the discourse of the other.' *Oedipus Rex* could be viewed as nothing other than a spectacular dramatization, a calculated pedagogical demonstration, of this formula. For Oedipus' unconscious is quite literally embodied by the discourse of the Other – of the oracle [. . .]
>
> The Oedipal question is thus at the centre of each practical psychoanalysis, not necessarily as a question addressing the analysand's desire for his parents, but as a question addressing the analysand's misapprehension, misrecognition [*méconnaissance*] of his own history.
>
> (Felman, 1983, p. 1025)

Several elements of Felmans' formulation are key to questions of Churchill's sense of theatricality. A history, whether personal or collective, are linguistic constructs, characterized by repression which is marked in the text by misrecognition. Churchill theatricalizes this premise by the appearance of ghosts whose voices haunt the theatrical scene, a reminder that the repressed is in a constant interplay with that which is known consciously. Thematically, ghosts appear in *Cloud Nine* and *Fen* as history which has been repressed from consciousness. But, Churchill, as a playwright whose medium, drama, depends on the repression associated with the language, moves her audience beyond the thematics to consider issues of dramatic form. If both *Cloud Nine* and *Fen* signals the audience through the appearances of ghosts to be attentive to the ways in which theatrical realism elides certain aspects of history which the form cannot accommodate, then a thornier, and indeed, tautological problem remains: can representation ever be free of the over-determination of patriarchy? Does representation depend on repression? Churchill's emendation of the conventions of realism through her use of ghosts instructively critiques the ways in which realism is bound to patriarchal ideology and its complex array of social technologies, including capitalism and codes of gender, sexuality, and race. Churchill, through her use of ghosts, sounds a warning to her audience that representation depends on repression. Thematically, she alerts us to the misrecognition of history-as-progress which results from repression. But, if representation depends on repression, she as a playwright, and I, as a critic, cannot begin to address the most troubling of questions: what have her theatre and my critique repressed? What voices have we silenced in our very different processes of writing? Churchill's work provides a useful cue to look to the social as dependent on repression, to ask: in her theatre (and indeed in my own critique of her work), what has writing silenced? What appears only as hauntings on the scene of representation?

Notes

1. Writers who have commented on the Brechtian elements of Churchill's work include: Diamond (1988), Kritzer (1991), Merill (1988), Randall (1988) and Reinelt (1987).
2. Correspondence in the theatre includes the actor and his or her body corresponding character; the vocal production and physical movements of the actor seeming 'natural'; the costumes of the characters corresponding to what the audience believe those characters, if they were actual, would wear; the set corresponding to what the audience recognizes could be a location in the actual world.

Bibliography

Churchill, Caryl, *Cloud Nine*. *Plays: One – Owners, Traps, Light Shining in Buckinghamshire, Cloud Nine* (London: Methuen, 1985), pp. 241–320.

——, *Fen, Plays: Two – Softcops, Top Girls, Fen, Serious Money* (London: Methuen, 1990), pp. 142–92.

Diamond, Elin, 'Closing No Gaps: Aphra Behn, Caryl Churchill, and Empire', *Caryl Churchill: A Casebook*, Phyllis R. Randall (ed.) (New York: Garland Publishing, 1988), pp. 161–74.

Felman, Shoshana, 'Beyond Oedipus: The Specimen Story of Psychoanalysis', *Lacan and Narration*, Robert Con Davis (ed.) (Baltimore and London: Johns Hopkins University Press, 1983), pp. 1021–53.

Freud, Sigmund, 'Jensen's "Gravida"', *Jensen's 'Gravida' and Other Works. The Standard Edition of the Complete Psychological Works of Sigmund Freud*, vol. IX (1906–8, James Strachey with Anna Freud, Alix Strachey and Alan Tyson (trans) [London: Hogarth Press, 1959], pp. 3–95).

——, *Introductory Lectures on Psychoanalysis*, James Strachey (trans. and ed.) (New York: W. W. Norton, 1966), pp. 286–302.

Grant, Damien, *Realism* (London: Methuen, 1970).

Kritzer, Amelia Howe, *The Plays of Caryl Churchill: Theatre of Empowerment* (New York: St. Martin's Press, 1991).

Maupassant, Guy de, 'Of "The Novel"', Introduction to *Pierre and Jean*, Clara Bell (trans) (New York: D. Appleton, 1902), pp. xii–lxiii.

Merill, Lisa, 'Monsters and Heroines: Caryl Churchill's Women', *Caryl Churchill: A Casebook*, Phyllis R. Randall (ed.) (New York: Garland Publishing, 1988), pp. 71–89.

Rabillard, Sheila, 'Fen and the Production of Feminist Ecotheater', *Theater* vol. 25, no. 1, spring/summer 1994, pp. 62–7.

Randall, Phyllis R., 'Beginnings: Churchill's Early Radio and Stage Plays', *Caryl Churchill: A Casebook*, Phyllis R. Randall (ed.) (New York: Garland Publishing, 1988), pp. 3–23.

Reinelt, Janelle, 'Caryl Churchill: Socialist Feminism and Brechtian Dramaturgy', *After Brecht: British Epic Theater* (Ann Arbor: University of Michigan Press, 1994), pp. 81–107.

Ritchie, Rob (ed.), *The Joint Stock Book: The Making of a Theatre Collective* (London: Methuen, 1987).

Silverstein, Marc, ' "Make Us the Women We Can't Be": *Cloud Nine* and the Female Imaginary', *Journal of Dramatic Theory and Criticism*, summer 1994, pp. 7–22.

Toepfer, Karl, 'From Imitation to Quotation', *Journal of Dramatic Theory and Criticism*, spring 1991, pp. 121–36.

Part III
Enlightening Interplays

11

Watching for Dolphins by John McGrath: The Single Voicing of a Multiple Voice Performance

Jean-Pierre Simard

Given a public airing at the University of Edinburgh in August 1991 with Elizabeth MacLennan, *Watching for Dolphins* by John McGrath was produced at the Tricycle Theatre in London in November 1991, and invited in March 1992 at the Comédie de Saint-Etienne in France. It draws new prospects as the playwright and his wife entrust their reflections to the memories of an activist, a single female character, turning into a Bed and Breakfast owner in North Wales.

The political and sociological changes in Britain and the world have altered the ethical relations among individuals. Reynalda seeks a new ideological and social adequacy matching a truthfulness to life-negated commitments which had been gradually reached. Strength can be said to be drawn from the pathetic indulgence of that woman in her past, since 'when the theatre comes closest to reflecting a truth in society, it now reflects more the wish for change than the conviction that this change can be brought about in a certain way', as Peter Brook wrote.[1]

J. McGrath patiently explored every side of popular theatre with periods when his social and cultural ethics echoed the people's, then with adverse ones, when the very idea of collective, or even of belonging to a common society were blurred. In the present monologue, the individual example means to partake of our common history.

Watching for Dolphins, an intimate play, incorporates every characteristic of an epic. Beyond social classes, it reflects an orphan

171

generation hoping for a new humanism to be discerned in the dolphin parable. It scans the far side of the popular forms the playwright favours. His ethics are potentially universal in today's unsteadied community. Baz Kershaw[2] clearly situates the state of fragmentation and uncertainty of societies, particularly British, in the 1990s:

> November 9, 1989, was a major watershed in post-war world history. Around the globe millions watched their television screens to see the Berlin Wall at last begin to come down. [...] (It) signaled the start of an all-pervasive transformation of the world order. [...] Maybe it [Brecht's ghost] was hanging back, puffing on a ruminative cigar, wondering what kind of protest the new political order might demand. [...] Despite the good news, in Britain, ten years of Thatcherism seemed to have created a chronically unstable socio-political order.[3]

SINGULARITY AS A MEDIATION

The playwright names his characters and grants them a place and a moment to act. Choosing a monologue, J. McGrath has privileged an intimacy in which other characters embodying the values he holds for negative are created and performed by Reynalda with a mirroring effect. The audience is confronted with a single voicing. If the playwright respects the basic rule in drama not to talk about oneself but to have someone else do it, a subjectivity close to his suppresses other hidings. The gap however permits him to devise emblematic fictitious situations and actions in which many a spectator will find an echo to those they have experienced. Trifling with *me*, I perform on *you*. My ethical and social rather than psychological anxieties are yours. This double mirroring effect examplifies the new modes of complex performance in which drama meditates on the artificiality of its conventions within their very frame. It is subjected to the critical eye of audiences who, with the playwright, attend the social denial of their common truths. The title and Reynalda's thoughts in her long central monologue on the evolution of the world since 1980, with no funny cooking interruption and no reference to her imaginary guests,[4] assert the everlasting hopes found in the dolphin parable:

I went on a boat to Cyprus once, from Marseilles. As we rounded Sicily, there appeared a school of dolphins, playing with us, roving freely through the warm seas, frisking like kittens, having fun, moving as one, smiling at this big black fish with the twisting tail. Then, just as suddenly, they went away. I spent the rest of the voyage standing at the rail, hoping to catch another glimpse.

I feel like that now. Every night I read the newspapers, watch my telly, phone my friends – 'just to keep in touch'. But I stand here now, at the rail, at 52, watching for dolphins. I scan the sea, but it's polluted, empty. But they are there. They will come.[5]

The power of the message lies in the sustained metaphor, which is a true allegory, according to Roland Barthes's definition of mythical writing. J. McGrath's allegory, in his personal mythical quest, thus partakes of an ancient collective hope he revises, which is roughly tried in current stormy human developments. The definition P. Brook gives of Jean Genet's drama could rightly fit J. McGrath's: 'His images are private, yet national, and he comes closest to discovering myths.'[6] That statement confirms R. Barthes's demonstration in *Mythologies*[7] where myths, and therefore mythical writing, are necessary for mankind and societies to proceed.

INTERCULTURAL MEDIATIONS

The emotional strength of the play lies in its having the constitutive myths of socialism questioned by a shattered person when society, in which individualism has triumphed, blurs them. J. McGrath wishes to contribute aesthetically to a reflection on progressive humanist hopes so as to weigh positively on their survival. The audiences share his views especially when including members of the 1968 generations, a time of assured left-wing ideologies. Music acts in the telling as a reflection rather than an interval, as the character illustrates and humorously stresses her emotions, doubts and beliefs. 'Where have all the garlics gone', she sings while savagely carving into the leg of lamb she's about to roast. The audiences remember the antinuclear peace movements of the 1970s. She also alternates piano playing and asides when evoking Mikis Theodorakis, a model of rectitude and faithfulness whose now emprisoned, now free life, remained true to beliefs presently considered as obsolete or even criminal:

And gallant little England was fighting wicked Adolf Hitler [. . .]
And when I was five, we won the war, and we danced in the
streets [. . .] and Mikis Theodorakis, the young Greek composer,
got out of the Nazi prison.
(she plays Theodorakis' piece)
    By the time I was ten, they were bad, these communists [. . .]
but my father who had fought all his life for Freedom for the Colo-
nies said at least the Reds believed in the self-determination of
nations, so I joined the Young Communists. But, when I was 16,
the Hungarians were a bit over-determined and the Russians in-
vaded them and said who the government should be, and father
sadly had to admit that all that was precisely what he'd been
fighting against all his life. He found he had a lot more free
evenings, and I took up tennis.
    And Theodorakis was a Communist so he was put back in pri-
son by the Greeks – But he didn't give up [. . .]
(plays more Theodorakis: Z theme.)[8]

The biting humour concerning the over-determination of Hungary,
or the bitter one about the new leisure of activists is noticeable. To
refuse an unpleasant now, the character finds refuge in infantilism.
The distancing effect achieved by the playwright is powerfully
strong. Short co-ordinated sentences and selected words make realities all the more unfair. Reynalda comes forward as a little girl
true to her assured fatherly model. A direct metacommunication
with the audiences implicated in the discourse on the *I* of the playwright clearly operates. When naively confiding in them, Reynalda
embodies new forms for intimate narration. The *I* of the character
is supposed not to think about her standing as a speaker, but produces the fragilized wording of the perturbed artist seeking an
answer to the present upheavals. A coded dramatization of the
tragedy of history, to which the character, the audience, the actress
and the playwright are confronted, is at work. This double game
relies on the metaphoric in the intertextual illustrations, of which
the music pieces are the richest examples. The playwright discreetly
stresses the constant shift from epic to postmodern forms. The
evocation of the 1956 Hungarian sufferings echoes a former metatheatrical musical sign. When, bored with ironing, Reynalda 'plays
a disturbing piece of Bartok' and says 'Poor Bartok! Fancy being a
Hungarian in 1939?',[9] the parallelism is significant. As he questions
our late past, J. McGrath suddenly revives a recurrent theme in British political plays.

However, M. Theodorakis' counter-example confirms J. McGrath's positive views on communism, especially when including a denunciation of arbitrariness. The wording is stressed by the diegetic dimension of the piece the actress plays. When hearing the extract from Z audiences don't need any comment. It illustrates the connotative richness of J. McGrath's play. The strength of its message is an attempt at catharsis, in the Aristotelian sense. If a purification for the audience through a performance, it is one for the playwright too. It is a release of emotions meant to externalize the memories of former traumatizing events. It is, however, different too, for those events belonging to the field of politics have never been repressed. Besides, using Aristotelian definitions seems daring for a theatre which claims to be epic, a theatre in which, beyond pleasure, reasoning and analysing are called for. The effect that is sought is definitely not empathy. The affective tearing is strong, though. Like J. McGrath's early plays, this one somehow accepts such analysis. The example of M. Theodorakis will occur again both as a musical metaphor and an explicit reference in the monologue. Associated with the dolphin parable, it allows an optimistic reading of the play, even though the character says:

> Socialism. And the very word socialism has become a foul word, anathema, another scar on history, like Nazism and the holocaust. We have become in the eyes of the world, the very horror that we had set out to drive off the face of the earth. [...] And whether it is true or a brilliant archipelago of lies, we are defeated by it. For the moment. And it is best to admit it.[10]

Beyond Reynalda's, the words are obviously E. MacLennan's own. Her existential doubting confers the character with a fragility audiences can approve of, so currently used as they are to plays in which psychological disarray replaces the sharing of social popular realities. Such privacy will comfort them too, while they will be seduced by the performance of drama on drama with such diverse mimed characters as the German Justice and his wife, the American company Vice-President, the headmistress, the National Front parents or the TV crew.

Watching for Dolphins is both an outcry and an analytical metaphor in a cartesian sense as well as freudian. The play grounds its intimate fervour on the objective artistic and ideological observations it underlines. It thus allows the social *I* of the character, and behind it, the *I* of the playwright and that of the actress to be expressed. The intertextuality is not simply referential. It structures the telling in its making. The piano and the performed works are almost characters, nurturing the character's thinking, while expressing her subconscious through emotionally played musical metaphors. The pieces have been selected by the playwright, but seem spontaneous. Apparently born of a saying, they partake of the thorough ideological and aesthetic discourse, and prompt their combined evolution. The direct asserted addressee of the musical rendering, and inevitably, interpreting, in a psychological sense, is the spectator.

Consequently, the metatheatrical performing of models, fictitious mimed characters and the narrating of childhood memories blur and reveal the anxiety emerging from the current destabilization. The seducing description of Reynalda in the initial stage directions reflects the prominence of the playwright, as the genitor of both the character and her ever present model father. The regressive transference is now double. J. McGrath also wants her to be a liberated feminist. When she sets up house with an immigrant, she soon discharges him in the name of Women's liberation. She supports, along with that of all minorities, the disputed freedom of the homosexuals while asserting she's not one. The social frustration of a person bruised by every oppression equally applies to men and women.

It is clear that J. McGrath adjusts his former aesthetic knowledge. He particularly perfects his sharp reflection on stereotyped characters on stage to suggest a personal vision of their epic functions.

ON J. MCGRATH'S APPROACH AND USE OF THEATRE STEREOTYPES

A stereotyped character is usually considered as a dehumanization to prompt ideological propaganda. It is true of the rapidly designed conventional sterotypes in agitprop theatre in which fixed social emblems are found such as the silk-hat company manager or the honest worker in overalls. It is, paradoxically, also true with naturalist plays in which a lack of inventiveness and observation of the diversity of individuals when psychologically sketching the characters out turns them into simplistic stereotypes of a different kind. Alternately, J. McGrath does not model his emblematic characters on the rethorical types currently found in symbolic drama, such as the warrior, the poet or the heroic youth. An extrapolation of such emblems is found in the German expressionistic theatre with the worker, the unemployed, the representative of the people leading to the Russian Socialist Hero, often a meritorious tractorist. Nevertheless, J. McGrath became convinced that 'there does come a moment when one must, to tell the truth, use a different form of writing from the naturalist or "realist" ideal of fully rounded character drawing'.[11]

Reynalda is a particularly achieved instance of stereotypes complex enough to surpass former models and build up some of their contradictions. Her fits of depression or enthusiasm unveil her revolutionary feminist energy combined with her affection for her model father. Identifying elements could lead to a psychoanalytical reading. If the partner piano binds her musical culture to her questioning, the interpretation iconically betrays her anxiety and mood. The central character allows the playwright to keep a critical distance with the query a constant identification might obliterate. The characters she stages contribute to such stylization. Judge Shenker embodies justice subjected to political power. The delegate of an American company is a model capitalist. Both belong to ancient marxist types. Their utter reduction is a metaphor of the ideological simplification Reynalda, the playwright and audiences used to be satisfied with. Their sudden inanity is unsteadying, while the caricature echoing accepted models informs each spectator of the sayings of their genitors, the playwright, initially, then the actress. The hetero- or homogeneous structure of each given audience will bring a different approving or sceptical social validation. Theatre thus becomes, through the sharing, the place for a confrontation of theories with realities and acquired experience. Social groups and individuals experience the merging of history with their own stories. The play ends when the first fictional 'real' visitors definitely inscribe Reynalda and her discourse within the necessity of compromising. The ultimate stage direction, immediately before 'Black out. End' indicates: 'Noise and light outside of a car stopping. The door bell rings. She knows what it means.'[12]

Humour also contributes to building a complex image of Reynalda. J. McGrath makes use of the accumulated aesthetic knowledge of clownlike performing forms, in circuses or music halls, he has built through meeting popular audiences. Both his sets of conferences at Cambridge crucially help to theorize that.[13] A clownesque reading of the various elements building the theatricality of this play can be made in addition to its questioning being offered. It adds a new intertextual metaphoric dimension. Reynalda's look on society and the new world order is that of 'the funny man'.

Awkwardly taking pains, she breaks a pot of geranium or lets her cake burn in the oven. A long series of domestic catastrophes obviously echo the world of the circus, and the names she invents for her spoilt dishes contribute to a complex performing of the contradictory appearance and reality of a woman who claims to survive as a B&B owner. Like a clown, she exposes herself, while, alone in the ring, the acting character has every ability to play the piano or create and perform the parts of the partners of her sayings. The B&B owner, her Headmistress, the National Front parents or the journalist are formerly encountered characters. The social stereotypes are fictitious. Everyone breaks in and vanishes through short duets with Reynalda who manipulates them. Aren't miming and referential music the only universal tools in clown art?

The clown performs a single character, his own self. It is often characterized by a fresh look, a somewhat naive childish candour. Reynalda's candour is naive when evoking her childhood or teen years. Like the clown, she rebels against injustice and authorities. She is a Charlie Chaplin. Moving and expertly designed, she is a fallen angel. Like the clown, the questions she addresses to us make her a bearer of hopes in a world where every man lives so secluded as to forget interdependence. Unwillingly solitary, she evokes the schools of dolphins sticking together which she saw, while standing at the rail aboard a ship bound for Greece. Out of work since her eviction as a teacher, she is ready, in order to survive, to greet the first visitors to her hermitage. She hesitates to the last second to merchandize the social intercourse she longs for. Like Ionesco or the clown, she wonders about the necessity to create such a bruising world. Like Footit,[14] she stresses the social function of laughter. She is J. McGrath's brilliantly complex tool to explore the gap between experienced and transposed reality.

Choosing popular forms when representing the triviality of laughable day-to-day realities, J. McGrath valorizes an art based on a modesty to facts, which is too little known a form of intelligence. The performing arts are now constantly riding the edge of mixed genres. By privileging clowning art to throw up the many degrees of laughter, he suggests a definition of the status of the playwright, the actor, the character and the spectator. By entrusting that task to a female character, J. McGrath transgresses an interdict. Female clowns are rare, unless they hide as transvestites behind the 'funny man', for no female clown character exists in the circus. Being herself, the female clown witness of the social drama in *Watching for Dolphins* challenges audiences on ethical stakes they cannot ignore. Similarly, the religious parable of the hermit in winter is opposed to her function as a tourism trader in the temple when spring comes. Paying guests do come precisely when she murders the imaginary fiction of her symbolic ones. A fatal irony annihilates the strength of her monastic pledge and grants the ideological introspection with further emotional fortitude.

BETWEEN EPIC AND POSTMODERN, TRIFLING WITH CONVENTIONS

Beyond a complex use of stereotypes, J. McGrath turns to a critical integration of prevailing postmodern cultural proceedings. The active intertextual inclusion of such songs as Joan Baez's or 'Bandiera Rosa', 'the Internationale', and 'When Spring Smiles' induces a revolutionary culture to be acknowledged if not shared by the audience whereas the pieces of music borrowed from Mozart, Beethoven, Bartók, Scott Joplin, Theodorakis or Shostakovitch function as direct metaphoric prominences generating further reflections. Both kinds of illustrative pieces contribute to establish Reynalda as an atypical hostess. Cultivated and a good musician, she obviously represents the actress's own cultural identity. The latter contributed to the choice of the works she wanted to play, and thus influenced the development of the confidence. Reynalda is also an activist. Her farcical disorderly domestic actions precisely insert a running caricature of the business she is compelled to accept by adverse social conditions. Such a view is confirmed by her own words. She narrates a past incident. Asked to deliver a conference in Sheffield, she rebels against her B&B owner when leaving the next morning. A coarse sexual provocative evocation is associated with death and echoes a reference to *Giselle*. While Reynalda is in the toilet, the lady comes into her room to collect her one set of bedsheets to wash them 'for the next victims'. In the apparent present time of her own fictional existence, Reynalda has just regretted the slow drying in wet Welsh air of her own freshly washed sets of sheets. The rebel turns into a provocative stereotype while this remembered burlesque episode teaches her how to be efficient:

Fortunately, I had my spray-cans with me, I managed to get
Auschwitz in pretty big letters all over the front wall before she
spied me at it – I was on my Kawasaki and half-way to Leicester before she could get my number [. . .] and that's why I'm
having two set. Cotton.[15]

The connotative reference also evokes the German judge, who happens to be in charge of the case of a female friend of Reynalda's
involved in the Baader Meinhof group. It announces a further episode too. The motorbike flight echoes the threatening characters in
the scenario the playwright makes her imagine. This richly complex
set of multiple drama on drama performances[16] allows J. McGrath
to be explicitly ironical with the postmodern performing manner-
isms while proving he can expertly use them too. Reynalda stages
a television crew who have come to interview her after her dis-
missal as a teacher. The imaginary director suggests a fictionalized
scenario of her story. The gap between the two levels of performance is bitingly critical of television using metatheatrical inserted
levels in docu-dramas. Under American influence, the symbolic
distortion of truth leads to scandalous peeping, when this genre
originally belonged to the documentary, then realistic tradition of
British cinema and was primarily meant to give a fair or committed
rendering of social issues. That pretended view on the character
prominently doubles Reynalda's direct image as perceived by audiences in her surrounding linear confession. J. McGrath actually
introduces a double mirroring effect, as the suggested character in
the film is watching a film on television when the crew is frighten-
ingly heard arriving. In the latter film with the very same synopsis,
a lone woman is attacked by hooligans coming on powerful, noisy
motorbikes. For a brief suspended moment, the spectators do not
know which is the story and who is telling it. Narrating and performing these mirroring fictional memories, Reynalda grants her
own fictional existence with a stronger convincing truth. Still, distancing effects soon allow the audience to share the playwright's
double point on present historical and cultural realities and the
media manoeuvres which contribute to blur their meaning through
such a complex narrativity. The recurrent recollection of the filming
technicalities clearly helps the spectators with the 'CUT' indications
and the double taking of Reynalda's testimony to satisfy the quality
of the sound recording. A metatheatrical artificiality is created in
which performing becomes a distanced object. It is strongly effective,

as it introduces the direct narration by Reynalda of her actual eviction under National Front parents pressure, which then logically enough ends into her miming her German and American guests she had welcomed almost at the beginning of the play as a coherent philosophical metaphor.

Later in her monologue, the relation of a journey to Japan, as a committed journalist, in the same position to events as the one who interviewed her just before, functions with several levels too. Authentic historical facts are ascribed to Reynalda by the playwright. They act as an intertext in which audiences read their own reflections when watching the news. The threatening armed activism of students fighting alongside farmers who protest against the building of a new airport is paralleled with the brutal strength of the police. However, the peeping complacency of television channels showing the confrontation live generates despair in Reynalda, and obviously in the playwright too. She consequently questions the sincerity of both sides in action and wonders if that could not be a mere cathartic show for decaying societies, justified by some necessary television exhibitionism. Reality is described and analysed by a fictional character as an artificiality produced by society in order to survive. As the ultimate witnesses, the audience will decide between the mirrored reflections in that relation which part of reality they are ready to accept, which artificiality they will refuse.

Herbert Blau[17] has recently questioned the most contemporary interpretation of various expressions under many forms of ideology in theatrical performance. He makes an estimate of the present states of writing, of performing and of relating to audiences. He draws from the term postmodern a phenomenology of the polysemic intercultural performance in most of the contemporary productions. Brecht is constantly called for as the necessary initiator of the move from the modern age to the new one. The dialectic dimension of his reflection allows the birth of the concept of 'the imminence of a not yet' as the complementary pole to the social gestus, 'that moment of historicization' which is the sign of already shared experiences.[18]

Doesn't such a suggestion meet hopes at stake behind J. McGrath's double aesthetic change in his most recent plays to preserve apparently obsolete certainties in a world characterized by its atomization? The core of those hopes rests on an ideological introspection leading, in the present play, to the uncertain prospects of a near future limited to wishful thinking. The character's temporary inability to throw light upon her hopes make it an open play.

CONCLUSION

Watching for Dolphins represents an outcome in which the thematic contents and their aesthetic expression merge to meet both the playwright's own style and the collective writing of British alternative theatre. R. Barthes's terminology is purposely being used here, as he names the collective style of a literary trend with the word 'writing'. With all its complex variety and aesthetic or ideological specificities, the alternative trend can be assimilated to a vast school, or theatrical movement at least. The word style rather points out the autarkic specific ways of each writer and digs into their intimate mythologies. J. McGrath precisely meets both standards while he also definitely belongs to the narrow group of major contemporary British playwrights. His choice to privilege popular audiences led to this extremely personal and universal, as well as strikingly powerful, play.

This text loaded with so much personal implication reflects J. McGrath's present art of writing, thus echoing his early plays, while inheriting the manners carved out of his vast rooted social experience with popular writing. Analysts had noticed such a deep personal involvment in his early writing. It then did not question the value of his ideological beliefs. His plays revealed his hesitations when confronted to outer oppositions from a seducing but estranging cultural establishment in which he was reaching fame and success. The modest examination of *Watching for Dolphins* allows to survey the notion of drama on drama or beyond, as it suggests, the laying of multiple forms of performance within an intimist monologue. A key multireferential framework is created to allow popular audiences to share the queries of the playwright both with compassion and reflection. If the reflexive intimacy of the confession is a philosophical questioning on the confused end of a century, this self-introspection by the playwright is carefully kept at a distance through a female mouthpiece who apparently guarantees a stronger loyalty to commitments. Every member of the community is thus offered a similar ideological examination which entitles the analyst to acknowledge the strong survival of a critical drama presently trying to adapt and evaluate the means at its disposal to pursue, while confiding in its audiences, an aesthetized reflection on the ethical moves in the contemporary world. Meanwhile, it keeps asserting the importance of history and collective memory as key components of today's cultural knowledge, however loaded with complexity and uncertainties it may be.

Notes

1. Peter Brook, *The Empty Space* (London: Penguin, 1990), p. 94.
2. Baz Kershaw, *The Politics of Performance* (New York & London: Routledge, 1992).
3. Ibid., pp. 206–7.
4. John McGrath, *Watching for Dolphins*, unpublished manuscript, pp. 18–23.
5. Ibid., p. 20.
6. *The Empty Space*, p. 94.
7. R. Barthes, *Mythologies* (Paris: Ed. du Seuil, 1957).
8. *Watching for Dolphins*, p. 13.
9. Ibid., p. 7.
10. Ibid., p. 19.
11. John McGrath, *Some Uses of Stereotype*, unpublished manuscript, p. 2.
12. *Watching for Dolphins*, p. 25.
13. Both sets have been published as books by Methuen (London), *A Good Night Out*, 1981 and *The Bone Won't Break*, 1990.
14. Foottit, a famous clown, led a thorough reflexion on performance and the status of the artist, stating, for instance : 'We are caricatures of the audience in which every attendant considers every neighbour and recognizes them in the picture drawn by the artist. But if everyone realized I mirror their own faces and absurdities, they would pick up a gun and kill Meeee.' Quoted by Robert Beauvais 'Les Excentriques', pp. 56–8, p. 56, *Clowns et Farceurs*, Jacques Fabbri & André Sallès (eds), (J. P. Simard (trans) Paris Bordas, 1982).
15. *Watching for Dolphins*, p. 3.
16. Ibid., pp. 8–12.
17. In Herbert Blau's book *To All Appearances, the Imminence of a Not Yet* (New York & London: Routledge, 1992).
18. Ibid., p. 56.

12

Devising Drama on Drama: The Community and Theatre Traditions
Anne Fuchs

The fictitious worlds of theatre like those of the novel or of any other representational art are modelled on those of the real world[1] and, to a greater or lesser degree, according to the rules and modes of previous forms of theatre performance. Devised theatre as opposed to authorial theatre involves the creation of a fiction based on the differing experiences of the real world by those concerned in the devising; and they are influenced in this and in their choice of mode by the various forms of theatre with which each is familiar. As often as not devised theatre has a link with a particular community and may be created to further the cause of women, gays, ethnic groups, political groups, or environmentalists. The question may, however, be asked whether the literary and performance modes which devised work chooses as a model or at least uses in some way as reference have a particular relationship with the community involved. Although other devised work may be the result of a group of actors or 'devisors' coming together on an equal footing and, it can be presumed (although not taken for granted), making equal contributions to the choice of a theatrical paradigm, the three examples we propose to consider all have the added factor of a facilitator or scriptor (perhaps already an established playwright) intervening and, it may be thought, making final decisions.

That the copyright should have been taken out for *Heartlanders* in 1989 by the three dramatists Stephen Bill, Anne Devlin and David Edgar even though acknowledgments are subsequently made in the cast list to 'Community play co-ordinators' and 'workshops',[2] indicates a proprietorial mastery over the dramatic text which is undeniable. *Fen*, on the other hand, although its original and subsequent copyrights are always attributed to Caryl Churchill,[3] already has a mention of publication 'by Methuen London in association with Joint Stock Theatre Group'. In her general introduction to *Plays: Two*[4] Caryl Churchill very much assigns to herself the role of scriptor: 'It's a play where I have a particularly lively sense of how much it owes to other people, those who talked to us of course, the actors and Les Waters [the director of *Fen*], and it will always be inseparable in my mind from Annie Smart's set of a field in a room.' The third work under consideration attributes far less credit to individual authors than the other two: the copyright for *Lear's Daughters*[5] in 1987 was taken out by the Women's Theatre Group, *from an idea by Elaine Feinstein* (our italics). According to the published edition, this play was entirely devised by the five actresses, the director and stage manager.

The fictitious worlds created by these three productions are first and foremost linked by direct or indirect reference to a historical twentieth-century setting. In the case of *Fen* and *Heartlanders* there are specific allusions to situations clearly delineated by time and space: *Fen* talks about land problems in the contemporary setting of the Fens, *Heartlanders* is about contemporary Birmingham, the city in the heart of England and its varied population. The codes used in these two plays are immediately recognizable by a twentieth-century audience as far as language, behaviour, ideologies and epistemic references are concerned. The title *Lear's Daughters*, on the other hand, introduces an immediate intertextual reference to another dramatic text so strong that it might almost exclude twentieth-century cultural codes. At first sight this seems the case with setting and fable indicating no obvious twentieth-century reference. Is this a purely intertextual composition? It is a question to which we shall return, but we can already perceive that the ideological code of feminism *Lear's Daughters* has in common with *Fen* and much other twentieth-century devised drama constitutes in itself a non-negligible social reference.

Before proceeding further it is necessary to define the way in which we intend to use this term 'intertextuality' invented by Bakhtin but since then adapted to many different purposes. In fact two uses of the term seem relevant here: sources of fictitious worlds which an audience might recognize as texts because their status has always been that of fiction, or others which in a play like *Fen* are recognized as texts within the dramatic text because their 'reality' has been framed by a 'telling' process such as a letter or story passed from generation to generation. The other use we shall make of 'intertextuality' is that more directly of 'drama on drama' or drama inspired by other specifically dramatic texts; even this, however, will be enlarged to include the concept of 'theatre on theatre' with modes of representation imitating previous modes.

With regard to the first case of intertextuality, all three plays have very obvious 'framed' material which the audience will already be familiar with or easily pick out as such. Without entering into all the details, the most striking examples may be said to contribute to the construction of the fictional world without having the status of actants or playing a major role in the fable. The discotheque and its DJ, the National Exhibition Centre with its computer sales women, the maternity hospital and its dance class for pregnant women, all contribute with their framing devices to reminding a Birmingham audience of *Heartlanders* of the frames they encounter within the reality of their daily lives. It must not be forgotten that the play was devised for a specific audience to celebrate Birmingham's centenary. Finding and losing others, finding and losing one's own identity are the two main threads of the search or quest that the characters are engaged in. The beginning of the play with its context of arrival and departure at the Digbeth bus station is an iconic representation of the constant intermingling of populations in the big industrial city which still welcomes English country, Welsh, Irish, Afro-Caribbean and new Indian immigrants. The ritualistic timetable of arrival and departure might in itself be considered as a framing device, but far more significant and incidentally more extraordinary in the sense that it goes beyond the everyday experience of the spectator, is the named Indian ritual of the last scene in the play. Culminating the search for the other and the quest for identity, Diwalli is transformed into Christmas; the Hindu circle, shrine and music change into a Christian procession for Christmas with the singing of the Coventry [sic] Carol. The birth of the 'poor youngling'[6] who must be protected symbolizes a little too patently the birth of the new Heartlander whose identity will entail a cultural mingling of race and religion. City of adoption or city of birth, the final image of Birmingham is that of a double or even treble frame: the spectator watching the play whose characters watch a procession and then the stage directions inform us the final quartet of characters, 'a successful businesswoman, an elderly Welshman, a young woman he picked up in a bus station, her three-day old child', 'become aware that they are the centre of attention, of the procession and the audience'.

It says much for the skill of the facilitators or scriptors that all these framing or 'framed' sequences within *Heartlanders* are drawn from the spectators' real life experience, but experience which is particularly appropriate as if it already contains a spectacular element. The same is not true of the framed sequences of *Fen* which may be acknowledged by the public as fictional texts embedded within the dramatic text or not, as the case may be. The characters who act as audience within the play are essentially listeners. This preference for listening over watching a framed spectacle is indicated in the first scene of the play where the Japanese businessman, whose company has bought up part of the Fens, arrives onstage with his camera and decides: 'I think it is too foggy to take pictures. Now I find teashop, warm fire, old countryman to tell tales.'[7] Although dramatic and spectacular elements are not lacking in the play with ghosts from the past returning as witnesses and a murder taking place on stage, the material which Caryl Churchill and the Joint Stock Company collected for the play in the region is used in direct telling by one character to another or as part of the fable without the frame-within-a-frame technique. Sequences which might have been given an audience within the play are, in what is a more Brechtian technique, addressed purely to the spectator: Scene Five for instance is composed of one stage direction: 'Val and Frank dance together. Old-fashioned, formal, romantic, happy.'[8] At the end of Scene Seven after the young girls have done everything they can to annoy Nell who is hoeing her garden, there is a Brecht-like reaction to the girls' future which appears to be reflected in Nell's working conditions with what is called the 'Girls' Song', where the latter all aspire to be teachers, hairdressers or nurses, never to leave the village, but also to have children and get married. In the present state of affairs these aspirations, as the girls realize, are entirely contradictory as the only work available in the village for men or women is that of farm-labourer. The other song situated at the end of the play also concerns unfulfilled aspirations and is addressed once more directly to the theatre audience.[9] It is also foregrounded by the preceding scene of horror and despair.

Three important sequences in *Fen* are taken from some kind of written text in real life. As Caryl Churchill tells us herself in the introduction,[10] 'The murder story of Frank and Val was taken from a newspaper cutting and the murder story of the man in the coffin from the unpublished memoirs of farm worker Charles Hansford. Most of what the ghost says is taken from a threatening letter written at the time of the Littleport riots.' The newspaper cutting has been completely transformed into a dramatic sequence at the climax of the play; the murder is integrated into the fable as a direct consequence of the personal and social problems of Val and Frank and integrated into the fantastic mode which prevails when the ghost of Val immediately returns to haunt the stage as have ghosts of the past in other sequences. A boy from the nineteenth century scaring off the crows in a field had been used as a kind of prologue to the play and a nineteenth-century woman in Scene Nine uses the diatribe of the threatening letter when as a ghost she arraigns Tewson the landowner for not improving the lot of the farm workers. The only framed sequence embedded within the play is that of the story of the man in the coffin; this is presented in the text of the play as the telling of a story by one character, Nell, to a group of other characters. This is an obvious framing as it is heterodiegetical. Less obvious are occasions when characters recount episodes from their own past life: how Margaret was saved by Jesus and how Ivy the 90-year-old grandmother lived in the past.

The telling device in *Lear's Daughters* is instrumental in creating the fictitious world but at the same time is itself connected with, or suggestive of, other framed fictions. The device is often introduced or made explicit by the character of the Fool, a kind of Brechtian barker or music-hall compère. At the end of scene one he announces: 'Three princesses, living in a castle, listening to fairy-tales in the nursery'[11] and, in Scene Nine, he asks the Nurse to 'tell me a story'.[12] The first case of the 'fairy-tale' is the tale of the birth of Lear's three daughters which appears, thus framed, to be a reference to a fantastic fairy-tale world in general, while the second case is a far more explicit reference to an already famous tale, that of the Pied Piper of Hamelin. In Scenes Seven and Ten when Regan insists on the Nurse 'telling' them the truth about when the sisters were small and how their Mother the Queen had died, the Nurse gives the 'telling' a biblical frame: 'Once, Lear had not been there, and then suddenly he was. It rained for forty days and forty nights before he came home and when he did, the sun came out. The King walked over the water to meet us.'[13] The Nurse later admits 'It was a story. You were all upset. It was for comfort.'[14] This very direct allusion to the Bible and its 'comforting' properties at once casts Lear in the role of God and at the same time reflects upon the absence of 'truth'[15] in the biblical stories.

Apart from 'telling', *Lear's Daughters* abounds in framing devices on a popular and to a large extent children's register: limericks, children's games such as blind man's bluff, riddles and nursery rhymes appear throughout the play often introduced by the Fool. Particular importance is given to 'Sing a song of sixpence'; the Fool makes it clear that he is 'singing' for money and there are various allusions to the King in his 'counting-house' and the Queen 'in the parlour eating bread and honey'. Introducing references to these popular frames has the effect of making sure the audience will recognize the cultural codes which relate back to their childhood and induce a sense of security which might otherwise have been lacking: as the psychologist Daniel Berlyne pointed out to De Marinis[16] maximum novelty is not always the way to maximize theatrical success. *Lear's Daughters*, which was certainly directed towards a popular albeit feminist audience given its innovative form, could not afford to do without some points of reference which all could appreciate. Two other popular framing devices have a more topical bent; the position of Lear as 'King' and what this represents for his family in a contemporary setting is indicated by the description of his return 'triumphant from a sporting tournament':[17] 'The title "King" demeans his status – he is a demi-god. He has competed against the best and won. His countrymen weep with pride, and disbelief'; secondly, the ritual of the contemporary marriage ceremony is highly satirized in the last but one scene of the play where Goneril and Regan are 'Two brides waiting to be swept off their feet.'[18]

Of the three plays under consideration, the only one which is a drama inspired directly by another textual drama is of course *Lear's Daughters*; balancing this, and perhaps as a result, its devisors have also made the greatest effort towards innovative form, allowing themselves a complete departure from the realistic setting and psychology of the personae both of *Fen* and *Heartlanders*. The initial premise for this departure is the surmise that every spectator must be familiar with at least the basic story of Shakespeare's *King Lear*. The play is therefore structured around an already well-known family myth concerning the relationship between a father and his three daughters. The emphasis, however, is now placed on the point of view of the other(s); instead of relating the fable from the point of view of the father, we are given the origins of the fable from the point of view of the daughters. Scene One is entitled 'The beginning' (both of the play and of the fable) and at the end of *Lear's Daughters* the Fool throws the power-symbol of the crown in the air with the words 'An ending. A beginning.' It is indeed the end of the origins of the fable and what may be considered as a beginning to Shakespeare's play with the struggle for power between the three sisters and those who surround them. The psychology of Shakespeare's three sisters is explained from their births right up to the situation in which they find themselves in *King Lear* both by their social and emotional environment. Particularly important is the absence of the Queen or mother-figure in *King Lear* which signifies the absence of a feminine role-model for Regan and Goneril and the peculiar bonding between Lear and Cordelia with the latter being unconsciously forced into replacing the wife.

Lear's Daughters are born with high hopes and portents of their greatness. In their early childhood the Queen is still present but plays the same role in the life of her daughters as does Lady Capulet in that of Juliet. The devisors have borrowed from the same play the second servant-mother, the Nurse, or Nanny as she is called in the modern play. She too has a sexual and social life of her own and a special relationship with the Fool. The three girls feel the lack of their mother when she is still alive and after her death: what is the truth about their mother, why did she die? Their 'paid' mother, the Nurse, is no real substitute and their obsession with their father, whom as little girls they try to please, turns sour when they realize that after having killed their mother with repeated rape (or marital duties?) he is now turning his attention to them. Regan becomes pregnant, Goneril refuses his insistence that his eldest daughters should stay at home after their marriages, and Cordelia still fascinated by her father has nevertheless a gift and keen attraction for words and their meaning which she is not prepared to betray. *Lear's Daughters* ends and *King Lear* begins.

This explicit drama on drama is also iconically represented through the formal structure of the play which has many segments of metadrama. At the end of the second scene the Fool narrates the arrival at the Palace of the Nanny or Nurse; after her arrival, he carries on the narrative mode with the Nurse speaking her own words followed by the Fool's own commentary: 'She said: [. . .] "Will you be stopping long?" I asked.'[19] This results in the destruction of the deictic here and now while retaining the mimetic effect. In the following scene the Fool acts the role of the Fool playing the Queen; he subsequently plays Lear and discusses playing the fool for money. At the beginning of Scene Ten,[20] he sums up the play as 'Scene One, Fool introduces the play. Good (reads. Keeps paper).

Scene Two, Nanny and the princesses [...]' and so on, until he
gets to 'Scene Thirteen, Fool talks about Investment.' This last idea
excites him considerably and he literally lays a 'nest egg' which
turns into a 'fool doll'. The soliloquy ends with a return to the sisters; 'Investment. Three princesses all grown older, thinking about
their father and counting the cost.' It is as if in *Lear's Daughters* we
are told of the 'investment' or 'input' which will create the situation of *King Lear*.

Although in the other texts of *Fen* and *Heartlanders* there is less
distinction to be made between intertextuality as meaning the play
directly inspired by one other dramatic text, and intertextuality as
a mode of representation referring back to previous theatrical modes,
we should like to suggest that each verbal text may owe more than
a mere similarity of theme to preceding performance texts. The obvious reference for *Heartlanders* is one of the scriptors' own works,
also described as a 'community play' and also commissioned to
celebrate an English town; it seems to us that the very title *Entertaining Strangers* might equally have been used by David Edgar for
Heartlanders. *Entertaining Strangers* was in fact written and performed
for the town of Dorchester 'in a church established by one of the
central characters, within a stone's throw of a brewery founded by
the other'. Its setting is a nineteenth-century 'English country town
in the process of transformation from an essentially rural to an
urban society'. The main protagonists represent opposite poles in
human relationships: the business woman who can only love her
own family and the Victorian vicar she suspects of 'having more
time for the needs of utter strangers than for those they know'. The
latter, as Edgar himself puts it, 'cannot apply this lesson to relations
with his own son'.[21] Coming to terms with the 'other' whether a
member of one's own family or group, or a member of another
social caste in a changing society but also within a setting of changing moral and religious values seems to be the underlying theme
for both of Edgar's plays; one can only think that *Entertaining Strangers* from 1985 must have strongly influenced *Heartlanders*.

It is once again David Edgar that we should like to quote but this
time as a theorist explaining in at least two different articles the
origins of the type of community theatre we are speaking of. According to Edgar the Eighties (when all three plays were created) is
a period in which political ideas in the theatre are deeply resented
and his explanation as to how radical ideas may be presented at
this time in a form which has been cross-fertilized by two recent

theatre traditions seems particularly relevant to both *Fen* and *Lear's Daughters*:

> What seems to me most important is the way that, hand in hand
> with alternative cabaret, performance art has influenced the new
> feminist theatre (and indeed vice versa) to create a style of pres-
> entation of radical ideas which owes little to the increasingly
> arid forms of cartoon agitprop, but is by contrast wacky and in-
> dividual and lively and provides at least the basis, perhaps at
> last, for a synthesis between the literary, cerebral, intellectually
> rigorous but visually dry work of the university-educated politi-
> cal playwrights of the 1960s and 1970s, and the visually stunning
> but intellectually thin experiments of the performance artists in
> and from the art schools.[22]

It is obvious that *Fen* and *Lear's Daughters* are good examples of the
'new feminist theatre' which Edgar is alluding to with characters
more highly individualized in *Fen* than in *Lear's Daughters*. The
latter may be seen rather as a collage of music-hall, nursery-rhyme
and fairly-tale forms with characters who are types such as Fool,
nurse, ogre-king and princesses involved in the reverse side of fairy-
tale situations. The music-hall patter of the fool also gives the play
a contemporary popular flavour which we have tried to show is
present in *Fen* and *Heartlanders* often through embedded framing
devices.

Where we might differ from Edgar is when he suggests that in
the 1960s and 1970s 'University-educated political playwrights' produced only 'visually dry work'; in another article he gives as an
example of this 'polemical', 'didactic' and 'Brechtian' work (not yet
having been cross-fertilized by the 'surreal', 'symbolic' and absurd)
the very company whose first play, it seems to us, constitutes what
one might almost qualify as the *ur*-play for the new community
theatre works of the 1980s. *The Cheviot, The Stag and the Black, Black
Oil* began its tour of the Highlands in April 1973 and was the first
of a series of productions by the 7:84 (which means 7 per cent of the
population of Great Britain owns 84 per cent of the capital wealth)
Theatre Company. Although the socialist didactic bent of the play
is in no doubt, it 'was conceived in the form of the traditional
Highland ceilhid'.[23] That is, a radical message is conveyed not only
through some highly intellectual form whether it be agitprop or
imitating the methods of Brecht but also by adopting a form which

the members of the audience in a particular time and space are already attuned to. John McGrath, Writer/Director, as he is termed in the credits of *The Cheviot* says that 'it seemed obvious [to him] that the form should be a popular and traditional one'.[24] But what is 'popular and traditional' in the Great Britain of the Eighties (or even more so today)?

It is here that we may begin to investigate our last point trying to find what is specific in the use of 'drama on drama' in the devised play as compared to this metadramatic mode or technique in other plays. It would appear from these fully or partly devised plays from the eighties that what may link them together is a bond with a particular community. This bond is in each case multiple but in different ways. *Heartlanders* associates the community of Birmingham in the actual production of the play (Birmingham Repertory Theatre and the Theatre of the Unemployed) and the setting and fable are the here and now of its first audience (autumn 1989); the scriptors themselves were all based in the City; the project and funding of the play were to celebrate the City's centenary. Contrary to what happens in *The Cheviot*, the emphasis is not on the past being a lesson for the present with the emphasis on secular tradition in a particular setting, but on the possibilities of the present bringing together, creating and celebrating a new community with all the difficulties this may represent for outworn values of the past.

Heartlanders gives the point of view of various ethnic and social groupings in the new Birmingham and can achieve this through the process of devising with workshop contributions from Indian, Irish, Welsh and West Indian participants as well as the born and bred 'brummies'. It is a play about a melting-pot which no doubt the founding fathers of the City would have had difficulty in recognizing as 'their' community. If *Fen*, as *The Cheviot*, looks back in part to the past to draw its lessons (and incidentally often drawing the same lesson about the changing ownership of land with landlords just as oppressive, whether members of the native aristocracy or foreign multinationals), the play scripted by Caryl Churchill does not necessarily have a community link with its audience. The Joint Stock Theatre Group researched the play in the Fens of Eastern England with a village workshop but from then onwards it is the Theatre Group and Caryl Churchill who interpret this community to audiences with no direct links with the village in question. The community link between stage and audience is rather that of the theme of the contemporary woman's point of view, showing the solidarity but also the dissensions within the women's community and family units and more essentially underlining the hardships of a countrywoman's working life.

The feminist theme of *Lear's Daughters* is far more explicit: the published play is part of a series, much-mocked for its main title: *Herstory* which is qualified by *'plays by women for women'*. The women's community spirit or point of view is highly exclusive in that when Cordelia asks the Fool: 'Are you a man or a woman?',[25] the latter replies: 'Depends who's asking.' The only specifically male character is of course Lear himself whose role will be played by the androgynous fool. The daughters' story is therefore a version to complement His story or that of Lear told by Shakespeare (not to say by an idiot!); in *King Lear*, the 'unnatural' behaviour of his daughters is already a given fact and for centuries this behaviour has been put down to greed, ambition, lust. In the twentieth century an attempt has been made to explore the reasons which may account for Goneril and Regan's rejections of their father and Cordelia's reluctance to acknowledge her love. In this play 'for women', the emphasis is on both the oppressive men/women relationship, the social relations involving second mothers or 'nannies' bringing up the children living in a world apart from reality and also on the high expectations of social standing enforced upon the children from birth. This is very much a man's world with masculine values. How far this analysis will be shared by an audience is another matter. The community input with the popular framing of nursery rhymes and fairy stories will appeal to the subconscious of men and women alike, but the message itself is likely to be received more favourably by the women's audience to which it is directed.[26]

Devised drama, as would be expected, constructs on the whole a less individual fictitious world than other plays, expressing community projects and themes with the help of framed rituals and other framed devices belonging to a common general cultural code. This does not, however, imply that this sort of drama, particularly when scripted by experienced playwrights, will ignore dramatic themes and functions already explored elsewhere; as we have tried to show, it is branching out into a byway where it may make use of more specific community ideals but also of spoken and written tradition to address an already limited audience. There may be a danger in leaving the broad highway of universal tradition. But is it not better to be sure of a limited popular audience rather than have no popular audience at all?

Notes

1. See Keir Elam, *The Semiotics of Theatre and Drama* (London & New York: Routledge reprint, 1988 [1980 Methuen]), p. 98.
2. S. Bill, A. Devlin, D. Edgar, *Heartlanders* (London: Nick Hern, 1989).
3. On the front cover of the (London, Methuen 1983) edition of Churchill, *Plays: Two* (which includes *Fen*) it should be noted that there is inscribed at the bottom 'Introduced by the Author.'
4. Op. cit., p. ix.
5. *Herstory: Plays by Women for Women* (Sheffield Academic Press, 1991). Vol. 1 includes *Lear's Daughters*, pp. 19–69.
6. The first and the last stanzas of the Coventry Carol include this expression.
7. Op. cit., p. 147.
8. Op. cit., p. 153.
9. Op. cit., p. 145. Production note: 'May sings, ie she stands as if singing and we hear what she would have liked to sing. So something amazing and beautiful – she wouldn't sing unless she could sing like that. In the original production it was a short piece of opera on tape.'
10. Op. cit., p. ix.
11. *Lear's Daughters*, op. cit., p. 24.
12. Ibid., p. 47.
13. Ibid., p. 41.
14. Ibid., p. 54.
15. Ibid., p. 55. Regan accuses the Nurse of lying about the death of their mother: 'Tell me the truth. Tel me the truth. Tell me the truth.'
16. See note 26, p. 111.
17. *Lear's Daughters*, op. cit., p. 33.
18. Ibid., p. 62.
19. Ibid., p. 26.
20. Ibid., p. 51.
21. Introduction, *Plays: Two* (London: Methuen, 1990), p. xii.
22. David Edgar, *The Second Time as Farce: Reflections on the Drama of Mean Times* (London: Lawrence & Wishart, 1988), p. 175.
23. John McGrath, *The Cheviot, The Stag and the Black, Black Oil* (London: Methuen, 1994 [1974]), p. 77.
24. Ibid., p. 77.
25. *Herstory*, op. cit., p. 32.
26. See Marco de Marinis, 'Dramaturgy of the Spectator', *The Drama Review*, vol. 51, no. 2 (T. 114), 1987, pp. 100–14.

13

Representing Gender/ Representing Self: A Reflection on Role Playing in Performance Theory and Practice
Lizbeth Goodman

Waiting on the queue (or in my own lingo, 'on line') at the book-shop of the National Theatre in one of the first weeks of the new year 1996, I glanced up and caught the eye of the man in front of me. It was a familiar face: Tom Stoppard's. The visage was immediately recognizable, and the associated impulse to act was unconscious and instantaneous. I smiled and opened my mouth, about to say Hello (or in my lingo, 'Hi'). By the strange split-second timing that separates the role-playing of everyday life from that of theatre, something stopped me from speaking (or reacting), just in time. It wasn't that I wanted to be unfriendly; it was, rather, the sudden realization that he did not know me, would not recognize my face as I did his. So, I met Tom Stoppard, but he did not meet me. We both went off to see some 'real' theatre.

Theatre and everyday life are distinct, but not completely different. Images and ideas, representations and reflections, rebound in and out of both. What we each catch on the rebound is what interests me, and that is determined in part by who we are (where we come from, where we've been, where we want to go) and by the form in which we engage most frequently with representations of 'life' in art. Some prefer sculpture, music, film, gymnastics, fly fishing . . . I prefer theatre. Many do.

Theatre involves transferring the lived experience of playwrights, directors, designers and actors, through the various creative fields and senses in which they work (words, ideas, images, colours,

196

sounds, movement), into some frame for a story or event (or non-story, or non-event), all contributing to what is called, in most circles, 'the play'. But what is this thing, really? Is Tom Stoppard's *Rosencrantz and Guildenstern Are Dead* (not the one he wrote and probably still remembers writing, but the one he sees as a more or less finished product, just waiting for the final ingredient of audience reaction, when he sits in the audience of the Cottesloe Theatre in January, 1996) for instance, any different from the one I see, apart from the fact that he has a better seat? More to the point, is my view of the play influenced by my view of Stoppard, not necessarily in a literal sense, as I see him in the audience (or in the bookshop), but figuratively, as I might see him through a lens of reputation or expectation: Stoppard as experimental playwright, Stoppard as great writer, etc.? To some extent, anyone's view of any play (from any seat in the house) will be reflected through the cultural valuing placed on a writer, her or his kind of work, and the general valuing of theatre as an art form in its contemporary context.

So, how does all this change when we look through the lens of gender difference? Theatre reflects and resonates possibilities for experimentation with gender roles in and through two related creative processes: transferring ideas from the author's lived experience, through creative imagination to the fictionalized forms of theatre, and also transferring the content and political/artistic intent of plays to and from other media: television, video, fiction, audio performance, published play scripts. In all these double transfers, a double consciousness is embedded in the process of theatre; to reach an audience, the theatre 'text' becomes a public event mediated by a range of technological and social considerations, manipulating the (gendered) bodies of authors, readers, viewers, and listeners, and also manipulating a larger public consciousness of the social function or 'role' of theatre.

With 'feminist theatre', and indeed other 'bodies' of specifically politically oriented theatre, the forms of double consciousness inherent to theatre in general are rendered more persistent, more polemical, more apparent. With feminist theatre in particular, the double consciousness inherent to the playing of gender roles is brought to bear on the double consciousness of political theatre, 'readable' in and through performance.

Here, I shall offer a reflection on the notion of role play in relation to feminist theatre work which is forced to re-examine its own 'role' in culture, when faced with the realities (and symbolic implications, and practical historical consequences) of multimedia adaptation. Of course, this is a self-reflexive exercise, as the most worthwhile analysis looks beneath the surface or 'theatre product', whether play script or performance, to the process of making theatre. That 'behind the scenes look' necessitates a practical connection to the work in progress. For me, this means that my examples will be limited to plays in which I have been involved in some capacity, in the transfer of media, and in the documentation and subsequent analysis of that transfer. Due in part to the personal/political stake declared in the process of feminist performance and analysis in general, this particular analysis begins at the far side of 'drama', when the play script has already been transformed into a live performance. What is at stake, then, is a complex of processes involved in the transfer from medium to medium, potential audience to actual audience.

Gender and its connections to role playing will be highlighted in this analysis, at several levels: in the feminist politics which inform my choice of approach, and my choice of plays and practitioners, and also my choice of issues, images and ideas which seem central to my gendered and otherwise 'positioned' place within this discourse: both back stage and in the audience, and also at home with a video monitor and remote control, and with a computer screen capable of running performance on screen (several times removed from 'live performance', and yet still somehow 'interactive'). This provides quite a lot of material for view, review and reflection.

The 'role-playing' of feminist theatres, in theory and in practice, can be explored with reference to any number of performance traditions. Live Art and Performance Art, Installation, Site Specific Work, and Multi-Media Performance are all ripe for this kind of analysis. In the interests of space, however, I shall touch on these more interdisciplinary forms only in passing, only as they can be seen to inform discussion of 'feminist theatre'. Already, though, we run into a linguistic problem; even for readers who share a common knowledge of the English language, the term 'feminist theatre' – like most such political/artistic shorthand terms – needs some clarification. This term in particular has been defined, and can be endlessly redefined, in a multiplicity of ways.[1] For the purposes of this argument at least, the term 'feminist theatre' can be used simply to refer to feminist performance work which exists, at some point in time, as a printed script intended for live performance before an audience in a shared space.

We can consider three specific examples: Caryl Churchill's well-known 1982 play *Top Girls*, Sarah Daniels's 1995 stage adaptation of Pat Barker's novel *Blow Your House Down*, and as a counter-example, the 1991 American play *Small Domestic Acts* by Joan Lipkin, whose stage play will reach the UK and Europe, if at all, only in printed and audio form, but probably not in any visual performance, either live or mediated. Each of these three examples can in some sense be labelled 'contemporary feminist plays', though they differ considerably in style, format, content and intent.

REPRESENTING GENDER/REPRESENTING SELF

Whether we begin our study by looking at contemporary feminist theatre, or at 'classics' revisited and revamped, we engage immediately with a set of conflicting ideas about the value of live theatre in the age of new technology. Even a major company such as the RSC needs to rely, more and more, on packaging of 'classics' in terms of their appeal to modern audiences, including parties of schoolchildren and young adults. Family values may be emphasized in a production of *Romeo and Juliet*, or the romance of the play may be inflected through multiracial casting, employed in a practical way to expand an audience base in a particular area. For publicity officers of theatres reviving the classics, the job of making old plays palatable is often seen as directly proportional to the degree of sexual intrigue contained in a given play: if not in the title, then in the imagery the title suggests. So sex is a selling point even for Shakespeare. But this use of sexy images and iconography to get 'bums on seats' in England's (and North America's) surviving mainstream and subsidized theatres is a very different game from that played by contemporary women writers and directors. For contemporary feminist theatre, sex is not just a selling point but an integral issue, a part of the conflict of being a woman (and possibly also lesbian or bisexual, black, working class, non-'English') writer in what remains a largely male-dominated (heteropatriarchal, white, middle-class, 'English') field. Sex, sexuality, gender, race and class are all mixed up in the process of writing, of translating personal, lived experience of gender relations in the modern world to the stage, for interactive performance with an audience composed largely of women.

So, theories of sexuality and gendered role play inform the making of feminist theatre, and the transfer of that theatre to other media, in real as well as symbolic ways. In any transfer which involves the visual, it is likely that some visual shorthand system will be developed. For instance, certain images, object, colours, fabrics, shapes may be repeated, like the visual equivalent of textual repetition: a sight-oriented alliteration. The same kinds of techniques can be adapted for audio performances, when sound effects and modulations of tone and volume interact with actual speech/text to create a layered performance text. Visual shorthand is familiar to most of us from advertising in the modern world, and given the contemporary need to 'market' theatre events with similar styles of advertising, it is useful to compare the images and techniques of billboards and the 'boards' of old. Of course, certain themes lend themselves most readily to visual shorthand systems (or 'semiotic' signposting): political issues to do with gender and class are often 'sign-posted' in this way; think of the white garb of the suffragists, and the red ribbon of contemporary AIDS culture, both of which have direct and compelling connections to the field of theatrical representation. Elsewhere, I have analysed what I call the 'accidental semiotics' of some contemporary theatrical imagery, developing in the modern interplay of advertising and theatrical politics, as well as in political theatre.[2] But the most intriguing body of new work which can be 'read' through this kind of multimedia, multicontextual cultural sign-posting system is women's theatre, and specifically political feminist theatre(s).

While there is not space to acknowledge all the women whose working practices and theories inform the discussion which will follow, it is important to note that these ideas have grown organically out of the rewarding experience of working for the past ten years in various capacities in feminist theatre practice, as well as from a more traditional 'academic' background. Writing, producing and directing plays, leading comedy workshops and rehearsals, fund-raising and marketing and advertising for small scale and large scale women's theatre ventures has led me to adopt a practical approach to even the most theoretical material: if the people making the theatre can't, or can't be bothered to, follow the argument, because of its form, rather than its content, then the argument is not very useful to the theatre. In the hope that academic writing about theatre may not only be useful to the theatre but may also help to keep the theatre alive in these days of rapid replacement by other media, my recent work has involved transferring theatre to video, television, audio, radio and also CD-ROM. All this work has not taken me away from the theatre, but has rather strengthened the case for feminist theatre as an art form which requires the living, breathing atmosphere of live performance, but which can also be captured, in part, and for some good reasons (practical and theoretical) in other media. These other media, I will argue, do not destroy the essence of live theatre, but rather bring it to new audiences, who may in turn be encouraged to attend the theatre.

In the discussion which follows, there is not space to discuss the roots of the argument on offer, so I shall take a few sentences to give proper credits here. Ideas developed here have been drawn from a number of collaborative practical experiences, three of which deserve mention: Research Theatre International in Canada, where the 'Embodying Myth Embodying Women Project' has begun to explore Native American (body) language, oral traditions and theatres in comparison to the representations made by women in many cultures; The Magdalena Project (based in Wales, discussed below), which functions as the largest active international network of women making theatre in many forms and many languages; and The Divina Project (based in Torino, Italy), which has offered valuable opportunities to meet and collaborate with some of the world's leading women film-makers, theatre writers, directors, performers, critics and academics.[3] The experience of interacting with such a wide range of directors, writers and performers who agree on almost nothing has been alternately frustrating and exciting, but always challenging. Many women now work in non-narrative, non-textual forms of theatre, where the visual and the aural and the symbolic interact where once text or 'script' might have held sway.

As it takes more space to discuss work which cannot be referred to in print, the body of this piece will consider a range of questions in relation to printed plays, including: what is the relationship between 'theatre' and 'performing self' in everyday life?; in what ways does feminist theory inform theatre practice?; in what ways does performance theory inform consideration of women's roles in everyday life?; and to what extent can the terminology of theory obscure the aims of theatre practice, particularly when words are translated for and within different performance and audience dynamics?

Such questions cannot be satisfactorily and categorically answered, but can be constructively addressed in examples of work which crosses borders between the domains of performance theory, feminist theory, and theatre practice. The discussion which follows will consider the intersections and divergences of these domains, or territories, at the crossroads between theory and practice. It will consider the notion of 'double thinks' in society and in (meta)theatre, exploring the role playing of self in society and on stage, especially in work by writers conversant at some level with both feminist theory and performance theory. Caryl Churchill is one such playwright.

TOP GIRLS: FROM THE STAGE TO TV AND BACK AGAIN

Churchill is widely hailed as 'Britain's leading socialist feminist playwright', though she is not eager to embrace this or any other shorthand set of labels for herself or her work. The body of her plays, taken as a whole, does undoubtedly have a feminist impact on contemporary audiences, even if that is not the playwright's intent. But of course, the work is revered for many reasons, not least for Churchill's remarkable skill with language. With *Top Girls*, she introduced the technique of overlapping dialogue – previously experimented with in a lesser known play, *Three More Sleepless Nights* (1980) – and found that the technique worked particularly well for the representation of naturalistic dinner-party conversation. She then transposed the naturalistic conversation into a surreal context: a raucous dinner party at which female figures from myth, history, art and literature all gather to celebrate the success, in 'real' financial terms, of one modern woman, Marlene. The rest of the play is set in 1980s Thatcherite Britain, where Marlene and her sister Joyce are depicted at far ends of the class system and the political spectrum. *Top Girls* has already begun to be 'canonized', in part because it is 'historical' in the sense that it is identifiable as a play of the 1980s, and at the same time, it stands up to contemporary scrutiny in the sense that the dilemmas faced by the female characters are very much a part of the social fabric for women at the turn of the twenty-first century.

The first production of *Top Girls* was staged in 1982, directed by Max Stafford-Clark, at the Royal Court Theatre.[4] The revival of the play in 1992 was also directed by Stafford-Clark, with some of the same actors. In between these two major stage productions, Stafford-Clark directed the play for television. In fact, the television production functioned as the 'rehearsal' for the stage revival. The most permanent visual record of the play is the television production, now captured on video.

How do the concerns about gender and performance raised above inform and interact with a play which has undergone such considerable transformation? What follows is an abbreviated version of the 'inside story' of the recording of the play for video, analysed in terms of gender and role playing as mediated by and through contemporary cultural possibilities, technologies, and bodies politic.[5]

In 1994, the idea of teaching Caryl Churchill's play *Top Girls* to thousands of students, not 'live' but through 'distance teaching' in textbook and video form, was first discussed. A small team of academics and BBC producers (Mags Noble, Tony Coe and myself) debated the pros and cons of staging and recording our own production. The main 'pros' would have been: (1) we would be able to document the process of adapting the play from the page to the stage, and (2) we would then be able to document the process of adapting the text for video by considering the method of framing the play with camera angles and possibly the addition of special effects or elaborate sets. While these were worthy objectives, the benefits did not outweigh the considerable cost and time implications of mounting our own production(s) both for stage and video. We opted to use the 1992 television production, taking its many strengths with its few weaknesses. Our two main objectives were achieved in large part, though in order to make the play accessible on television, a number of changes had been made to the text; for instance, the first scene in the Top Girls Employment Agency was moved to the beginning of the play.[6]

In order to make the television production accessible on video, we had to introduce a few more changes. We added a workshop discussion at the beginning to introduce key themes and highlight the impact of the transition of media, and we added a set of interviews with the playwright, director, actors and academics. Early discussions affected the way we approached the process of transferring the play to video. For instance, we considered the practical implications of the video controls: 'pause', 'fast forward' 'rewind', and 'mute' options, which allow us each to control and interact, to some limited extent, with the performance in progress. More interesting, though, is the larger story of the 'behind the scenes' negotiation of performance with framing material, text with context and elements of process.

For example, when we considered staging our own version, we thought first of using a huge studio space, with three windows in the background to symbolize the division of experience between the different sets of the play (the restaurant, the office, Joyce's house). The windows would also have a reflective quality which would fracture light and create a sense of a shared space with the audience, who would be reflected in those windows (functioning at one level as mirrors). This use of the set would have been rich in semiotic significance, and would have offered valuable visual cross-references to the same images and symbols in other play texts ripe for gender-oriented readings, such as two early plays by men (Ibsen's *A Doll's House* and Shakespeare's *As You Like It*) which have been reinterpreted for modern audiences on video and CD-ROM, with particular attention paid to gender issues within the work; or such as an early 'feminist' play (Aphra Behn's *The Rover*), which has been modernized for contemporary audiences through slick marketing and stylish video adaptation.[7] Each of these videos contains, in some measure, sex and violence or the threat of violence, and each features one or more strong female character(s) fighting against the story from within. Each offers a metaphor of the mirror, in which the heroine(s) see themselves and also see possibilities for self-liberation, expression and expansion through subverting expected gender roles. Such themes offer intriguing visual possibilities for the stage, but these are not always easy to capture effectively on video.

With *Top Girls*, the mechanics of filming with mirrors were too complicated. On the one hand, the idea of the many characters reflected around the dinner party was so rich that we hesitated to give it up; on the other hand, we knew we would never capture it effectively on camera. What we needed was a stage idea that would transfer to video. Next we thought of setting the play 'in the round', with the audience on all sides. We thought of this as one way of bringing the audience into the dinner-party scene, so that noisy symphony of overlapping voices might have an 'extrascenic' dimension as well. This also seemed a good way to get around the problem of positioning the actors, since an 'in the round' format would mean that the actors could really sit around the table, facing each other, and all sections of the audience would be able to see some of their faces. This setting might have worked well for the dinner-party scene, but it would have posed problems for the rest of the play. We decided that even if we were to stage our own production, an 'in the round format' would not quite work.

In the recorded version for television, however, the cameras intervene in the playing space, creating the visual impression that the dinner-party scene is effectively set 'in the round'. The 'in the round' effect was created by a bit of technical 'cheating': a hole was cut in the centre of the table, and the camera was positioned there, and directed to pan around in all directions, capturing the faces of all the actors looking at each other. In the televised version, the 'in the round' shots are interspersed with shots taken from outside the circle of the table, so that we sometimes see the actors from behind. By combining shots and perspectives in this way, the scene takes on a 'realistic' quality in terms of the way the characters sit and interact with each other, even though the characters themselves and their fantastic appearance in the modern day scene are 'unrealistic', even surreal.[8]

What does the medium do to the presentation of gender? In this case, the female characters' 'performances of self' can clearly be seen as gender-related roles, carefully designed to develop with the years. The Marlene of the 1982 stage production was presented as very much a product of her times, believing in the possibility of successfully becoming a superwoman, even if at the expense of a personal and family life. Only ten years later, the promises of the Superwoman myth were gone, the glossy image of Thatcher as leader had begun to tarnish; the Marlene of the 1992 production is a product of this period, nervously defending her rights to self-promotion, but with a hint of hysteria about her. How much of this reading is imposed by my politics and position, and how much by my relationship to British culture, are fair questions. In any reading or viewing of the play, however, it is apparent to the audience, if not to the characters within the play, that the conflict which Marlene faced is neither unique, nor rare, nor outdated. The conflict of professional career and mothering, the conflict of a rising middle-class status and originating working-class status, the conflict of allegiance to self or to family, all still face women today, although the myth of achievement is implied by the term 'post-feminist', and images of successful 'new women' in functional new families smile down at us from advertisements. We all know the other stories, and can see the cracks in the façade. We know Marlene, even if she does not know us.

Feminist theory can be seen to inform theatre practice in both the 1982 and the 1992 stage productions of the play, and to a lesser extent also in the television production (which is not less politically motivated, but which loses the 'bite' in the flattening effect of the camera). Some of the political feminist impact is added on the video, quite deliberately, in the brief contextualizing 'video seminar' which precedes the play, and more importantly, in the interview material with Churchill, Stafford-Clark and the actors. Here, we gain a contemporary cultural 'signpost' which is already pointing towards History, but which says a great deal about the role playing of women and men in Britain's Thatcherite and post-Thatcherite periods. The transfer of media helps to emphasize contrasts between role playing in life and on stage. The 1992 Marlene, and indeed most of the characters in the play, can be seen to be role playing for lack of any alternatives; the goal(post)s for women's achievements seem to have moved, yet no visible signs or semiotic devices have been left (accidentally or otherwise) to help them out.

Perhaps most telling on the video version is the cast's discussion of the importance of the last line of the play: Angie's 'frightening'. Each participant in the process of bringing the play to life in performance has her or his own view of the meaning of that line, predicated on personal, generational, gender and class positions, as well as by individual approaches to the process of interpretation through 'dramatic analysis'. That line, constructed only of the participial adjective 'frightening', is bewildering in its deliberate lack of specificity. The single word echoes into silence, leaving the field of possible interpretations wide open; it may be resonant only for Angie, or it may send out shock waves for all the women in the play, and in the audience. No easy answers are on offer.

Many branches of performance theory can be seen to inform the play's consideration and representation of women's roles in everyday life, although differences in political views of all involved in the performance project (playwright, director, actors, crew, critics, readers and viewers) will influence the reception of performance theory. This account of the play pays particular attention to visual cues and semiotic performance elements, while other accounts pay more attention to the generational differences in approaches to feminism and the class conflict between characters in the play, for instance.[9]

The video 'text' is, ironically, now the most accessible visual version of the play, and like all video productions of stage plays, it both gains and loses in the translation. The video can be studied, much like the play text, and just as the language of the play can be analysed, so too can the visual 'language' of 'accidental semiotic' signs readable within the video performance. I will concentrate on the theoretical implications which arose out of the practical work of transferring presentation media for this play. In the process, it becomes clear that the play 'speaks' (in many different senses) to a range of issues and ideas and creative methods which are in some ways 'feminist', although the 'behind the scenes' work on the play revealed that Churchill herself, and several cast members, are unsure about the word 'feminist' in relation to what they see as a partially 'realistic' and partially surreal play about women's roles and lives in the 1980s. Now that the play is captured on video, it will move into the new millenium, with or without the blessing of its author or creative team, and the 'feminist' status of the play will be continually re-evaluated.

The space remaining will only accommodate a few brief reflections on contrasting examples of feminist theatre adapted from and for the stage.

BLOW YOUR HOUSE DOWN: FROM 'REAL FICTION' TO FEMINIST DRAMA

Northern English working-class author Pat Barker had not yet won the 1995 Booker Prize for her latest fiction when Northern English working-class playwright Sarah Daniels chose to adapt her 1980s novel, *Blow Your House Down*, for the stage.[10] The play presents a tight-knit group of prostitutes in the north-east of England, struggling to survive both economically and literally, as a stalker kills them off one by one. As such, the play might at first seem an unusual choice for the Live Theatre's production, which opened on Valentine's day, 1995. But this play, which might at one level be described as a 'gritty realist' portrayal of the psychological and cultural impact on the potential victims of a sex-obsessed murderer, takes the form of black comedy. The play is punctuated with potentially painful and downright frightening imagery, all the more effective because the pain and fear affect us at two levels simultaneously: through the developing tension and fear of the likeable set of female characters Daniels provides, and through the sense of connection and solidarity which the medium of humour allows the audience to feel for these otherwise unlikely hero(ine)s. In this play, the pathos of the book is preserved and its impact enhanced by the immediacy of physical proximity between the 'body' of the audience and the bodies of the characters, which are both the physical focus of attention and the symbolic 'subject' of the play.

The 'subject' or 'object' of prostitution has been handled many times before in the theatre, but not too frequently within contemporary feminist theatres. Perhaps the subject strikes a bit too close to home, at least for those of us who study the commercial exchange model of patriarchal commercial societies, considering the economic and cultural pressures on women – not only working-class women – to pay their own full share, while earning less than the traditional male-oriented family wage. The economics of prostitution, from the Bible stories to contemporary newspaper headlines, was handled in experimental form by another UK theatre in 1991, when Jill Greenhalgh directed a non-liner multi-layered performance piece (which could not be usefully called 'a play') for the Magdalena Project. That piece, called *Midnight Level Six*, explored the 'real life' (and death) murder of prostitute Lynette White in Cardiff on Valentine's Day in 1986. Sex and murder are common themes in women's lives, and the abuse of power in gender and class relations is hardly news.

What is striking about Daniels' adaptation of Barker's story, based on 'real' events, is the way in which the language of the play script creates visual images in the mind's eye of the reader. The play is visually gripping, but the real chiaroscuro is projected in the contrast of light humour with the dark and often violent realities of women's lives. The women in this story are, for the most part, more like Churchill's Angie than her Marlene. These women are not concerned with making it big, but rather with making it, with surviving. And while Daniels brings the characters to life with her usual blend of biting wit, street language, and verbal/visual elegance of form, she also leaves a certain rough edge to the play. This is not to be mistaken for pure art. This is a play about life, based on a novel from life, and if we don't like what we see, we had better begin to change the world around us. So, Daniels gives us the young incest survivor Carol, a prostitute who has lost two friends to the murderer and has seen the latter victim, her flatmate and soulmate, Jean, brutally butchered and stitched back together. The seams are, in every sense, allowed to show, and we as readers and audience members are both invited to watch Carol as she looks in the mirror and sees there, not only a reflection of her own image, but also that of Jean; Carol hums 'I see her face everywhere I go' (p. 80), and 'her' is not only Jean but also Carol, and the other women in the play, and – depending on the positioning of the mirror on stage, and our positioning in the audience – perhaps also us.

Daniels is one of Britain's strongest playwrights, irrespective of gender. But in her work, there is no mistaking the gendered realities of the playwright and the characters she creates. She is often compared to Churchill, perhaps because both have had success at the National Theatre, and both have written, often and well, about women. But perhaps it is more important that both writers, though they differ in their own class positions, and their relationships with language and with the concept of 'feminism', share in common a concern for the representation of women in conflict with class and gender, women in conversation with culture.

Churchill's aspiring middle-class heroine Marlene, for instance, is presented in stark contrast to her working-class sister, Joyce; the cast of characters of *Blow Your House Down* is predominantly working class and female, and their class position is the frame for the events of the play and the language in which their stories are told. Churchill looks to women from myth, art and history for the characters who attend Marlene's dinner party, and contrasts them with the more recognizable, though largely less humorous, figures of Marlene, Joyce, and the young girl Angie. Daniels also presents a contrast between the real and unreal; she begins by looking to recent fiction, written by a woman (Barker) and based on 'real life', and adapts that into the body of her play. The play depicts women who are 'real' enough, but also entertains surreal elements: the murdered prostitutes and a young male victim of the fray all reappear, with speaking parts, to the confused young heroine, Carol, and to the audience. This interpolation of forms and styles is familiar in the larger body of Daniels's work, as is the focus in this play on the possibilities for transformation of standard female 'victim' roles through the processes of identification and organization with other women. Without this kind of banding together, Daniels (and Barker before her) seems to suggest, women's lives are truly 'frightening', to borrow the word which ends Churchill's play. What we do with that fear, and how we re-present it on stage, is what matters.

Like the ending of *Top Girls*, which is chronologically more of a beginning, so the close of *Blow Your House Down* is ambiguous; it is not at all clear who lives and who dies, but only that life and death are both real possibilities for these female characters, who have 'won the day' at least in the sense that they finally find ways of supporting each other, come what may.

The transfer, or adaptation, of this story from one medium to another is successful on many counts. The verbal language of *Blow*

Your House Down is deliberately unpoetic, and the visual language of the play (the knives, the men lurking in shadows, the women who are almost visible when they go missing) 'speaks' in a different way. The translation of this book to the stage does not improve the story, so much as communicate it through a different form of language, composed of visual vignettes which are, in 'real terms' and because they reflect so closely on 'real life' for many women, frightening. Humour is a tool which sculpts the double consciousness of the play in performance: it releases some of the tension within scenes, as characters deal with the reality and threat of grisly murder; and it releases tension extrascenically too, as women and men in the audience can laugh away potential over-identification, while remaining fixed by the power of the story and the skill with which it is told, in text and in performance.

But is Barker's story contained in the one Daniels re-presents? And does that matter? Is identifying Barker's version within or beneath or behind the stage version any more relevant, or necessary, an exercise than trying to see from Stoppard's seat in the audience, or Churchill's, or yours, or mine? In this case at least, Barker herself releases us all from the need to ponder her whereabouts in the revised stage/performance 'text'; she granted Daniels complete freedom with text. In so doing, she made the story accessible, though no less 'frightening', to us all.

SMALL DOMESTIC ACTS: GENDER ROLES ON STAGE AND IN EVERYDAY LIFE

One last example reflects a range of different possibilities for gender in performance. The play, Joan Lipkin's *Small Domestic Acts*,[11] sits intriguingly next to those by Churchill and Daniels. It also presents strong female characters. It also experiments with humour in dealing with serious subjects, and experiments with time lines and some overlapping dialogue and scenography. It also examines gender roles and stereotypes in performance. But there are significant differences. Lipkin is Jewish American, born and bred in Chicago and running an alternative performance space (which regularly receives bomb threats) in the basement of a church in St Louis, in the 'Bible Belt' of America. The context for her performance influences the content of her work in immediate ways. This play explores the nature of sexuality by offering a heterosexual couple and

a lesbian couple, faced with a complicated world in which 'feminin-
ity' and 'masculinity' and even 'sexuality' are no longer fixed. The
play follows these four characters – deliberate stereotypes, all –
through the routines of their daily lives, observing what happens
when sexuality, and prejudices about sexuality, shift.

This kind of theatre is confrontational, not very 'British', not everyone's cup of proverbial tea. It was, in this sense, a real challenge
to consider transferring this play, of all plays, to audio tape, primarily for a British audience. But the effort is rewarded if British audiences squirm enough to question the origins of their discomfort.
The transfer to audio loses much in translation: the sight gags, the
visual impact of the sterotyped costumes and presentation of the
characters, and most importantly, our sense of interaction in a live
performance dynamic. But the audio production is a valuable entity
in itself. It makes a new range of demands on its audience. It not
only requires that we imagine what characters might 'look like' but
also where they look, what they choose to see and what they choose
not to see, who the characters look at, and why, and whose version of the play – and of feminism, and of political theatre – they
perceive.[12]

Small Domestic Acts is a decidedly feminist play. It also functions
(even in the audio version) as a cultural looking glass; it offers four
'mirrors', in the form of stereotyped characters with and against
whom we may measure our own views, about sexuality, and about
theatre. We may pretend not to recognize them, but they insist on
seeing us and speaking directly to us, whether we like it or not. By
the end of the performance, we are all part of their story. We have
all met.

Although the main body of this discussion has focused on British
theatre and its stage/world reflections, it seems most appropriate
to open out the context at this 'stage'. Even this brief consideration
of *Small Domestic Acts* opens cultural and theoretical doors. The
play is a provocative counterpart to Ibsen's *A Doll's House*, in its
exploration of characters trapped in 'small domestic acts' and aware
of the need for escape. It echoes strains of *Top Girls* in its focus on
women in the workplace; and it resonates with the theme of class
conflict which threatens to be fatal in *Blow Your House Down*. The
play shares some of the stylistic features and themes familiar from
both Churchill and Daniels, but transcends even the most experimental techniques of these two 'masters' of British feminist theatre,
by breaking a cultural taboo, by means of direct address to the

audience.[13] It is in the moments when characters speak to, and ask questions of, the audience, that the play is transferred from 'theatre' to something closer to life, closer at least to the experience of standing in line behind Tom Stoppard. The difference is: the characters in Lipkin's play don't respect the audience's right not to be recognized, or to be expected to recognize others. Role playing becomes, in this context, not only a gendered phenomenon, but a paradigm emblematic of the fractures and breakdowns of everyday discourse and interaction.

Notes

1. Some preliminary attempts at a definition or set of definitions for British feminist theatres are offered in *Contemporary Feminist Theatres* (London: Routledge, 1993), and are further developed in 'Feminisms and Theatres: Canon Fodder and Cultural Change', in *Analysing Performance*, Patrick Campbell (ed.) (Manchester University Press, 1996).

2. See 'AIDS and Live Art', in *Analysing Performance*, Patrick Campbell (ed.) (Manchester University Press, 1996).

3. Research Theatre International, directed by Beau Coleman with Lizbeth Goodman, based at the Drama Department of the University of Alberta, Edmonton, Canada. Coleman directed the first phase of the work, 'The Wild Woman Project', in 1995. Some of the project's work is currently documented on video; a full documentary in print, video and multi-media is planned for future work on the next phase, 'Embodying Myth Embodying Women'.

   The Magdalena Project, directed by Jill Greenhalgh, based at Chapter, Cardiff, Wales. Annual Magdalena gatherings, festivals and conferences bring together generations of women to work on specific themes, including the notion of gendered language in theatre and the relationship between roles such as motherhood and the roles women create and play in the theatre.

   The Divina Project, co-sponsored by Teatro Settimo and the University of Torino, held annual conferences and festivals in the early–mid-1990s, mainly in Italy, though some of the work toured to the UK. These gatherings were primarily non-theoretical.

   A feature which The Magdalena and Divina Projects share, and which the former was set up to address, is a continuing debate about the relationship between feminist theory and women's theatre practice.

4. Caryl Churchill, *Top Girls* (London: Methuen student edition, 1991); first published by Methuen in 1982. First performed at the Royal Court Theatre, London, 28 August, 1982, directed by Max Stafford-Clark. This production transferred to Joseph Papp's Public Theatre,

New York, in May 1982, and returned to the Royal Court Theatre in July 1982.

5. For a more detailed discussion of this play and its theatrical impact, dramatic imagery, use of overlapping dialogue, and of Churchill's 'role' in the developing feminist literary canon, see chapter 8 of *Literature and Gender*, L. Goodman (ed.) (London: Routledge, 1996).

6. Stafford-Clark and Churchill both took part in the decision to make this change, though they differ in their views on its success. See interviews included on the BBC video: *Approaching Top Girls* (Open University/BBC, 1995). This video became available through Routledge, and can be ordered in NTSC or PAL format from the Open University. The video includes pedagogic exercises and comparative 'behind the scenes' material, along with interviews with Churchill, Stafford-Clark, cast members from both Royal Court productions and a range of academics.

7. These three videos are part of the set, with *Top Girls*, all produced by the Open University BBC in 1995, and all available from Routledge in the Approaching Literature series in 1996. *A Doll's House*, produced by Mags Noble; *Top Girls*, produced by Mags Noble; *The Rover*, produced by Tony Coe; *As You Like It*, produced by Amanda Willett. The last video in this series features Fiona Shaw and Juliet Stevenson, and has been adapted yet again for CD-ROM, by the Shakespeare Multi-Media Research Group of the Open University BBC Interactive Media Centre (1995).

8. Another significant aspect of staging which affected the transfer of media was the interpretation of stage directions and intentions, which Stafford-Clark refers to as 'actioning': see the discussion of this technique in chapter 8 of *Literature and Gender*.

9. See Sheila Rabillard (ed.), *Caryl Churchill: Contemporary Re-Presentations* (Winnipeg: Blizzard Press, 1997).

10. Sarah Daniels, *Blow Your House Down*, adapted from the book by Pat Barker (London: Virago, 1984); the play text is not yet published. The play was first performed at Live Theatre, Newcastle-upon-Tyne, 14 February 1995. Pat Barker won the Booker Prize for fiction for her novel *Ghost Road* (London: Viking, 1995).

11. Joan Lipkin's *Small Domestic Acts* (New York: Applause Books, 1995) was first produced at the AC/DC Performance Series at the St Marcus Theatre, St Louis, Missouri, December 1993. The play text has been published (Applause Books, 1996). A BBC Audio Cassette features a full performance of this play, recorded in St Louis, Missouri, in 1993/4, directed by Anna Pileggi, cassette produced by Tony Coe, academic consultant Lizbeth Goodman.

12. For more extensive discussion of audience interaction and extra-scenic communication, see: 'Death and Dancing in the Live Arts: Performance, Politics and Sexuality in the Age of AIDS', *Critical Quarterly*, vol. 35, no. 2, summer 1993, 99–116.

13. The notion of reflexivity and reflection in performance work by a range of international women performance artists is discussed

further in 'Who's Looking at Who(m): Re-Viewing Medusa', *Modern Drama*, spring 1996, pp. 190–210.

Bibliography

Bassnett, Susan, *Magdalena: International Women's Experimental Theatre* (Oxford: Berg Publishers, 1989).

Burk, Juli Thompson, 'Top Girls in Performance', in: Donkin, Ellen and Susan Clement (eds), *Directing Theatre As If Gender and Race Matter* (University of Michigan Press, 1993).

Campbell, Patrick (ed.), *Analysing Performance* (Manchester University Press, 1996).

Churchill, Caryl, Interview on *Top Girls*, included on the *Approaching Top Girls Video*, produced by the Open University BBC (London: Routledge, 1996).

Cousin, Geraldine, *Churchill: The Playwright* (London: Methuen, 1989).

Fitzsimmons, Linda, *File on Churchill* (London: Methuen, 1989).

Goodman, Lizbeth, *Contemporary Feminist Theatres* (London: Routledge, 1993).

Goodman, L. (ed.), *Literature and Gender* (London: Routledge, 1996).

Goodman, L., *Feminist Stages* (London: Harwood Academic Press, 1996).

Goodman, L. and J. de Gay (eds), *Voices of Women/Languages of Theatre: Magdalena* (Contemporary Theatre Review/Harwood, 1996).

Kritzer, Amelia Howe, *The Plays of Caryl Churchill: Theatre of Empowerment* (Macmillan, 1991).

Owens, W. R. and L. Goodman (eds), *Shakespeare, Aphra Behn and the Canon* (London: Routledge, 1996).

Rabillard, Sheila, *Caryl Churchill: Contemporary Re-Presentations* (Winnipeg: Blizzard Press, 1997).

Stafford-Clark, Max, Interview on Top Girls, included on the *Approaching Top Girls Video*, produced by the Open University/BBC (London: Routledge, 1996).

14

For Christopher Hampton on the occasion of his fiftieth birthday

Translating, Adapting, Rewriting: Three Facets of Christopher Hampton's Work as a Playwright
Albert-Reiner Glaap

Christopher Hampton's work as a playwright is multi-faceted. He has written 'realistic' plays which mirror the nature of our contemporary society, and 'historical' plays which 'use the historical imagination as a means of obtaining perspective on our world'.[1] He is the author of both plays marked by brevity and terseness and extensive plays written for large casts and different settings. Some of his stage plays are modelled on Chekhov and Ibsen, others on Brecht. He has experimented with various techniques, such as the multiviewpoint technique, visual imagery and the structuring of scenes, to name but three. Indeed, Hampton's work is varied. But it is also different from the plays written by some of the other contemporary English dramatists – different in two ways: Hampton tries to write without being influenced by a political or aesthetic ideology; he wants to portray things as they are. In an interview, which I conducted, the playwright stated the following:

> I have always been interested in political issues without being interested in writing prescriptions or somehow answering questions. I am more interested in raising the questions. I think what is confusing for many people who try to assess my work is that it is very hard to find any consistency in it. And that is an unfortunate result of the fact that I am always more interested in doing something different than in anything else.[2]

Indeed, Christopher Hampton's work differs from the mainstream of contemporary playwriting. This is not only true for his subject matter but also for what goes into the making of his plays. He is interested in writing comedy, but it is a kind of 'serious' comedy. In addition to his own original plays, his contributions to the art of translation have also been considerable which mirror the playwright's interest in language generally, and in foreign languages in particular. This is, at least partly, due to the fact that he was brought up in foreign countries and did not come to England until he was ten years old. He was born in the Azores in 1946, educated in Aden and at a British school in Alexandria. During the Suez crisis in 1956, he and his mother fled Egypt. As he grew up outside everyday British life, it is natural that he should keep his distance from involvement in political activities and ideologies which do impinge on the works of some of the other dramatists in contemporary Britain. Christopher Hampton's background and his life outside Britain have made him an ideal mediator between different European cultures. He graduated from Oxford University with a BA in French and German and served as translator for the Schauspielhaus in Hamburg/Germany. For a long time literary texts in French and German have provided a vital source of inspiration for him. He said in an interview:

> I have always felt attracted to French literature. I do know more about it than I do about English literature. I don't quite know why and what the temperamental attraction is. I was very aware of it in the late 1960s and early '70s, when there was a great explosion of writing in this country. Although I liked a lot of the work that was being done, I felt very apart from it.

Hampton worked on some ten translations and adaptations of literary texts in French, German, Russian and Norwegian. The first play he was asked to translate for the Royal Court Theatre was Isaak Babel's *Marya* (1967). His task was to find a way of re-creating a 'speakable' dialogue: 'It was a sort of practical demonstration to me that there is a great difference between accurate translation and translation which is living theatrical dialogue.'

In view of the book's title *Drama on Drama*, this article sets out to answer important questions: What is Christopher Hampton's specific contribution to the contemporary London stage? What are his sources? How does he explore these, meditate on them and use them as springboards for the development of his own plays?

To start with, the title of this essay provides an implicit answer to these questions. By translating, adapting and re-writing both well-known and less known European works he revitalized plays by Chekhov, Molière and Ibsen and discovered for the English stage the novelist Choderlos de Laclos and the plays of Ödön von Horváth who 'through Hampton's efforts [. . .] is now considered, in English, as seriously as Wedekind and Schnitzler in the canon of twentieth-century Viennese drama'.[3] Hampton translated into English Chekhov's *Uncle Vanya* (1970); Ibsen's *Hedda Gabler* (1970), *A Doll's House* (1971), *The Wild Duck* (1979) and *Ghosts* (1983); Molière's *Don Juan* (1972, for BBC/Radio 2) and *Tartuffe* (1984); Babel's *Marya* (1967); Feydeau and Desvallières's *Signed and Sealed* (1976), Ödön von Horváth's *Tales from the Vienna Woods* (1977) and *Don Juan Comes Back From the War* (1978). Apart from translating plays, Hampton worked on plays or literary texts, originally written in French or English, the results of which must be considered as 'adaptations' of the original, like *Les Liaisons Dangereuses*. This play is not a translation because in Choderlos de Laclos's book there is hardly any dialogue; it is an adaptation of a literary novel. 'What I have done is,' says Hampton, 'I have respected the plot, I have not done anything else, really. The purpose was to be faithful, more or less, to the feeling of the original.' The same applies to his dramatization of George Steiner's novel *The Portage to San Cristobal of A.H.*. In addition there is a third category of Christopher Hampton's work as a dramatist, in which a particular play serves as a kind of wall from which to bounce off new meaning, a literary model used as a source of inspiration. *Treats* (1976) was triggered off by Ibsen's *A Doll's House*; *The Philanthropist* (1970) is a rewriting of Molière's *Le Misanthrope*; and *Alice's Adventures Under Ground* (1994) a meditation on Lewis Carroll, the author of the Alice books.

In the following the chapter sets out to give an insight into the processes of translating, adapting and re-writing as different categories of Christopher Hampton's work as a dramatist. Special reference will be made to plays which lend themselves particularly well to an illustration of the different processes.

TRANSLATING

Hampton started being interested in translation when he was very young. As a schoolboy he enjoyed translating poetry, just as a kind of linguistic exercise. When he was asked to do a translation of *Uncle Vanya* and *Hedda Gabler* at about the same time, he decided to do this in cooperation with native speakers of Russian and Norwegian, respectively. In the case of *Uncle Vanya*, the Russian co-translator started off with a literal translation following closely the Russian syntax. 'This gave us an in-comprehensive text,' Hampton reports, 'but she would then explain to me, so that I had a reference when working on the text to see which word was which.' 'With *Hedda Gabler*,' he continues, 'it was a little easier. With a Norwegian dictionary and a text and a literal translation, I worked pretty well from the original, but always with a literal translation at hand.'

If there is what could be termed Hampton's philosophy of translating, it is his attempt to get as closely to the original as possible. In an interview with William J. Free, Hampton explained:

> I actually want to give the audience in its optimum from whatever the original author wished. I don't make any changes at all. I mean, obviously in the Chekhov play and the Horváth as well I do feel that it is my responsibility to make the audience laugh at the point at which the author wished them to laugh and to arrange the work in such a way that the dramatic effect is approximately the same.[4]

Trying to achieve equivalence in difference requires the translator to constantly keep the balance between preserving the original play and making it accessible to audiences who speak a different language. Hampton's opinion has always been that the closer you manage to stick to the original the happier you feel.

As the overall aim of translating plays is to provide a text for actors and not a text for study, the question remains whether it is more valuable to have a translator who knows the target language or someone who can write for actors. It is all a question of 'accuracy against speakability'.[5] Hampton learned translating plays by experiment. When working on *Hedda Gabler*, he looked out for terms which Ibsen used as thematic keywords throughout the play. One of those words was the verb 'dare' which according to Hampton helped him to understand the subject of the play as one of 'failed courage'. He ran into a problem when working on George Steiner's novel *The Portage to San Cristobal of A.H.*[6] The author had insisted on every facet of the book to be exactly (re-)produced and had felt very uncomfortable at the thought of any changes being made.

'Which was fine by me,' Hampton says, 'but in fact it seemed to be – in the end – more of a transcription of the book.'

Tales From the Vienna Woods by Ödön von Horváth,[7] translated by Christopher Hampton, opened at the Olivier Theatre in January 1977 and was directed by Maximilian Schell. This version of the play is somehow indicative of Christopher Hampton's work as translator. Around the end of the 1960s the playwright spent a lot of time in Germany where Horváth was becoming very popular. Hampton had never seen any of Horváth's plays, but when reading them he was immediately impressed. Later, in 1976, when he had been asked to translate a play for the National Theatre and had suggested a stage adaptation of *Les Liaisons Dangereuses*, the theatre did not want that and gave him a list of plays they were interested in. Seeing Horváth's *Tales From the Vienna Woods* on the list, he told Maximilian Schell, the director, that this would be something he was very interested in. Every author presents specific problems to the translator. Horváth, a Hungarian by birth, spoke German at a fairly early stage of his life but did not write German before the age of fourteen. In his case the problem was – according to Hampton – 'that he sort of invents his own language. He says somewhere, in an essay, that he writes plays for characters who would normally talk in dialect, but are trying not to'.[8] Furthermore 'a lot of his characters repeat things that they have heard other people say, but they repeat them slightly wrong. They misquote slightly from the classics. That's a set of problems that has to do with this particular author'.[9] The dialect, and Horváth's individual use of the dialect, was something Hampton did not attempt to imitate in English, because – considering the fact that English dialects are connected with class – 'the result would have been misleading'.[10] Therefore, Hampton tried to render the play in 'a neutral language, differentiated, of course, from character to character'.[11] This he thought would be in line with Horváth's instructions for the production of his play: 'Not a word should be spoken in dialect!'[12] The following scene gives us an idea of Hampton's translation[13] of the Horváth play:[14]

Havlitschek *steht in der Tür der Fleischhauerei und frißt Wurst.*
Das Fräulein Emma: *ein Mädchen für alles, steht mit einer Markttasche neben ihm; sie lauscht der Musik;* Herr Havlitschek –
Havlitschek: Ich bitte schön?
Emma: Musik ist doch etwas Schönes, nicht?

Havlitschek: Ich könnt mir schon noch etwas Schöneres vorstellen,
    Fräulein Emma.
Emma: *summt leise den Walzer mit.*
Havlitschek: Das tät nämlich auch von Ihnen abhängen, Fräulein
    Emma.
Emma: Mir scheint gar, Sie sind ein Casanova, Herr Havlitschek.
Havlitschek: Sagens nur ruhig Ladislaus zu mir.
Pause.
Emma: Gestern hab ich von Ihrem Herrn Oskar geträumt.
Havlitschek: Haben Sie sich nix Gescheiteres träumen können?
Emma: Der Herr Oskar hat immer so große melancholische
    Augen – es tut einem direkt weh, wenn er einen anschaut –
Havlitschek: Das macht die Liebe.
Emma: Wie meinen Sie das jetzt?
Havlitschek: Ich meine das jetzt so, daß er in ein nichtsnutziges
    Frauenzimmer verliebt ist – die hat ihn nämlich sitzen lassen,
    schon vor einem Jahr, und ist sich mit einem andern Nichts-
    nutzigen auf und davon.
Emma: Und er liebt sie noch immer? Das find ich aber schön.
Havlitschek: Das find ich blöd.

Havlitschek *is standing in the doorway of the butcher's, devouring a
sausage.*
Emma, *a girl who's ready for anything, is standing next to him, hold-
ing a shopping-bag and listening to the music.*
Emma: Herr Havlitschek –
Havlitschek: What can I do you for?
Emma: There's something nice about music, isn't there?
Havlitschek: I can think of something a good deal nicer, Fräulein
    Emma.
(Emma *hums along quietly with the waltz.*)
But that needs some work from your end, eh, Fräulein Emma?
Emma: I think you're a bit of a Casanova, Herr Havlitschek.
Havlitschek: You can call me Ladislaus if you like.
Pause.
Emma: I had a dream about your Herr Oskar last night.
Havlitschek: Can't you find something more exciting to dream
    about than that?
Emma: He's got them great big sad eyes, Herr Oskar. It really
    upsets you when he looks at you.
Havlitschek: That's what love does for you.

Emma: How do you mean?

Havlitschek: What I mean is, he fell in love with this bit of shoddy goods, and she just up and left him, must be a year ago now, and went off with some other bit of shoddy goods.

Emma: And he still loves her? I think that's nice.

Havlitschek: I think it's bloody ridiculous.

Hampton was not only confronted with the specific problems mentioned above; he also had to keep in mind that his translation of *Tales from the Vienna Woods* would be the script for the first major production of a Horváth play in English anywhere. Having been brought up in a text-based theatre, he took it for granted 'to examine the text as closely as possible, to try and find out Horváth's intentions and then to embody them in a faithful way'. At the same time Hampton wanted to make the play work out with an English audience. During their ten-week rehearsal Maximilian Schell showed himself extremely meticulous and ready to fight every comma. Needless to say, Hampton's translation resulted in something completely different from, for instance, Tom Stoppard's *On the Razzle* (1981),[15] which is modelled on Nestroy's *Einen Jux will er sich machen*. This play, as Stoppard admits, 'could not be labelled a "translation"'. All the main characters and most of the plot came from Nestroy but almost none of the dialogue attempts to offer a translation of what Nestroy wrote'.[16] Stoppard used the Nestroy play as a kind of basis and wrote something which is not unlike a Stoppard play.

Schell's production of *Tales from the Vienna Woods* (in Hampton's translation) was – in the words of Sheridan Morley, a theatre critic – 'the first gold-plated success the National [has] had since getting established in its new premises'.[17] Whereas Morley found the production 'an absolute triumph of wrapping over contents' and thought that 'the late Ödön von Horváth was fundamentally a writer of scenarios rather than plays', he wanted to make it clear that Christopher Hampton's translation was 'fluent and yet wonderfully spare'.[18]

ADAPTING

In addition to translating plays, Christopher Hampton has also tried his hand at modifying literary works to fit another medium. Two of his more recent adaptations are *Les Liaisons Dangereuses* (1985)[19] and *Alice's Adventures Under Ground* (1994).[20]

   Alice's Adventures Under Ground is a deviation from earlier adaptations. The title is the original title of the first of Lewis Carroll's two Alice books – *Alice in Wonderland* and *Alice Through the Looking Glass*. 'Under Ground' refers to what actually happens: Alice goes down the rabbit hole at the beginning and the whole story takes place 'down there' somewhere in the psyche. As regards Hampton's play, the original notion was that through the personality of Lewis Carroll (pen name for Charles Dodgson) one could shed interesting light on the pieces he wrote – the two Alice books in particular. The playwriting process did not merely involve changing a novel into a play. It was the weaving together of two books in a free associative sort of way. In the introduction to the edition of the play Hampton describes what had been going on in three workshops over two years and he explains how the Alice books had been used:

> We would move chronologically through the two books using only the material which seemed to serve our purpose; we would alternate between scenes confined to Carroll and the child (in some of which Carroll himself would embody some of the characters which seemed closest to him: the Caterpillar, Humpty Dumpty, the White Knight) and scenes in which other adults would invade their privacy.[21]

Scene Eleven of the altogether seventeen scenes is an interlude, the text being taken from Lewis Carroll's letters to Mr and Mrs Mayhew, in which he wrote about the photographs of their children and which reveal the intolerable strains to which 'Carroll subjected himself and others'.[22] Dodgson loved to take photographs of little girls in 'a state of undress'. Thus Hampton's play amounts to a mingling of, and a cross-referencing between, episodes from the Alice books and episodes from Dodgson's life.

   In *Alice's Adventures Under Ground*, Alice's encounters are with representatives of the adult world in the Victorian era, not with animals. The play gives the audience an idea of the Reverend Charles Dodgson, a Platonic paedophile, and his crush on Alice. It reveals some of the irrationalities which the repressive society of that time forced upon people. The National Theatre, where Hampton's adaptation was premièred at the Cottesloe in 1994, declared the play unsuitable for children under 12 years of age.

In the interview I conducted Hampton expatiated on what he and those involved in the workshops had discovered, namely 'that a child of seven was needed'.

I have always been very puzzled by the fact that whenever I had seen any kind of adaptation of *Alice in Wonderland*, I would get angry with the child – she was insufferable. When we were doing our auditions for the first workshop, a very strange thing happened: only when you found a child who was seven years old – which is what the child in the book is – did the character make sense. If you worked with a twelve or fourteen-year-old child you could not understand why this child was asking the questions she asked. Somehow the acuteness of the psychological understanding of the child meant that the piece wouldn't work unless you did it with a child of that age.

Considering that the relationship between the young man – Dodgson was in his late twenties and early thirties when he wrote these pieces – and the small child was to be the central issue of the play, this discovery was very important. The play is about Alice seen through Dodgson's eyes, whereas the stories illuminate Dodgson, the author. It certainly does not suggest that he was a man who behaved incorrectly with little girls. 'One of the things I wanted to do,' says Hampton, 'was to say that the Alice books are not cosy children's books. They are explorations of a troubled psyche in a very restrictive society.'

The play which encompasses all the aspects that go into the making of a Hampton adaptation is *Les Liaisons Dangereuses* which many critics consider to have been his most successful play so far. Like *Alice's Adventures Under Ground* it is not based or modelled on an already existing play. It is not 'drama on drama', it is an adaptation of a literary novel. But whereas Hampton's 'Alice' play is a collage of episodes from Carroll's life and excerpts from his Alice books, *Les Liaisons Dangereuses* is faithful, more or less, to the feeling of the original, that is Laclos's novel, which – as Hampton says – 'has always been one of my favourite novels from the time I first came across it'. This occurred when he was 19 and a university student. Laclos (1741–1803) had become famous for this one novel only, which, in his days, had been a sensation. It was written in 1782 and banned in 1824, because it was said to have scandalized France. The original novel – in the words of Jack Tinker, a theatre critic – consists 'of a series of letters exchanged between a libertine French Vicomte and his former mistress, a Marquise, whose appetite for sexual intrigue and carefully studied corruption is actually more refined and carefully honed than his – fuelled as it is by her female desire for revenge.'[23]

In his epistolary novel Laclos kept all the characters apart so that they could keep on writing to each other. The play, however, brings them together; Hampton replaces the letters with dialogues and invented scenes, but the play retains the irony of the original. Laclos's novel is also a sort of mathematical novel. 'If you analyse the letters,' Hampton says, 'they are actually worked out in a quite interesting mathematical format by Laclos. There are four parts, one part is exactly the same length as the other and so there are various mathematical assets. So I kind of devised a mathematical structure in threes; the scenes come in groups of three.'

Looking at these groups of scenes one notices that they get shorter and shorter in dramatic response to an acceleration all the way through the playscript which is indicative of the technical procedures that Hampton discovered in the novel and which he thought he should embody in the play. This applies also to the characters. 'Again mathematically,' to use his words again, 'I tried to give them, more or less, the same weight in the play as they had in the book. It is quite interesting to count the number of letters attributed to each character. It gives an idea of how to weigh the play.'

At the end of the book, Laclos tips the audience a kind of postmodern wink that the novel has a moralizing ending. The Marquise de Merteuil is found out and denounced, loses her money, gets the smallpox, becomes disfigured and flees the country. In a footnote one reads: 'As a matter of fact even worse things happened to her which I cannot tell you about.' To Hampton this *is* 'a moral ending that Laclos had to put on. I thought I'd just let her get away with it'. And he goes on to say in the interview: 'But it is also clear that she will never recover from it. In a sense, the punishments in the play are worse than all those in the book, because the punishment is self-inflicted.'

Near the end, in Hampton's play, Valmont is killed by the Marquise's latest lover, but the Marquise herself does not succumb to a disfiguring smallpox as in Laclos's novel. Rather, one deduces from the unmistakable silhouette of the guillotine on the back of the wall, just before the characters vanish at the end of the play, that she is finally guillotined for her cruelties, which is a clear reference to the fact that the book was written seven years before the French Revolution.

Michael Billington claims that *Les Liaisons Dangereuses* 'sets new standards in adaptation by retaining the incidents described in Laclos's epistolary 1782 novel while existing as a work of art in its own right'.[24] What has survived in Hampton's play is the acid irony permeating the Laclos novel. In its dramatic tension, however, the play surpasses the original. By having the characters meet, by telescoping and bridging the scenes, by making the scenes increasingly shorter and thereby accelerating the speed the playwright has given *Les Liaisons Dangereuses* is unique qualities. A few scenes are extremely good examples of Hampton's craftsmanship; for instance the second scene, the Vicomte Valmont's first encounter with the virtuous Présidente de Tourvel; or the third scene, in which Valmont uses the naked back of his mistress as a desk to write a letter to Madame de Tourvel whom he hopes to seduce; or Scene Six, in which Valmont seduces 15-year-old Cécile to which, in Scene Ten, the Marquise reacts by merely saying: 'You have rather overstepped your brief.'[25]

In *Les Liaisons Dangereuses* Christopher Hampton takes the audience on an interesting journey. The play starts off on a light note in order to deliver the punches all the more powerfully later on. Hampton explains:

This play, like some of my other plays, starts as sort of a comedy, but ends as a tragedy. At the beginning the audience does not know what to expect; they are enjoying themselves; but then, at a certain point you feel that the audience is feeling bad about having colluded with those on the stage. They begin to understand what the implications are.

This effect is produced by the tightening of dramatic tension in the play. The scenes follow each other more rapidly while the tension increases until it finds release in climactic violence.

RE-WRITING

In 1970, Christopher Hampton wrote *The Philanthropist*,[26] which is modelled on Molière's *Le Misanthrope*. Critics have used different terms and expressions to define both the relationship between these two plays and their specific qualities. Hampton's work has been called a rebuttal of, a riposte to, a meditation on, a re-interpretation of Molière's work. *The Philanthropist*, being a satire on modern intellectual life, or even on English life in the 1960s, different adjectives have been applied to define the specific element of this play: witty, mordent, sardonic, elegant, for instance. It is 'a bourgeois comedy' (which is its subtitle) in prose as opposed to an aristocratic comedy in rhyme, which has been considered an apt description of *Le Misanthrope*.

The Philanthropist is neither only a spin-off from Molière's play, nor merely a collage of dramatized reminiscences of Hampton's time as a student at Oxford from whose New College he had graduated only two years before he wrote this play. *The Philanthropist* is a self-contained piece, a play in its own right. But, as George W. Brandt noted, 'an awareness of *Le Misanthrope* as a kind of shadow behind *The Philanthropist* will add something to our enjoyment. It is like listening to a set of variations with the original melody at the back of one's mind'.[27]

Parallels between the two plays are obvious, because *The Philanthropist* abounds in subtle clues to its French origin. To start with, the title and the name of the central character, which are clear references to the Molière play. 'Phil' means 'lover', and a 'Philanthropist' is a 'lover of mankind' as opposed to a person who dislikes other people, a 'misanthrope', like Alceste, the central character in Molière's play. Rousseau is said to have raised the question, whether Alceste is a true misanthrope, and taking this up, George W. Brandt adds: 'We are similarly tempted to ask: is Philip, the Oxford Alceste, really and truly a philanthropist?' The answer Brandt gives, in either case, is *no*. Alceste, he argues, 'is a disappointed idealist who makes life impossible for himself and all those around him' and 'Philip does not love mankind in an active or even philosophical way; he is just too easy-going to bother, to stand up for himself'.[28] Whatever philanthropist Philip may be, he is also a philologist, and this not only because he is an Oxford don but also because he is a 'lover' of words. Hampton marks him as someone who is interested in words, the development of words and 'all this new work that's being done in structural linguistics'.[29] Already the first scene of *The Philanthropist* teems with examples. Suffice it to give one that is taken from a conversation between Philip, Don, a colleague, and a younger student, called John, whose paper is being discussed:

John: Tell me what you don't like about it.

Don: Well, one thing is that character who appears every so often with a ladder. The window-cleaner. What's his name?

John: Man.

Don: Yes. Well, I take it he has some kind of allegorical significance outside the framework of the play. I mean I don't know if this is right but I rather took him to signify England.

John: No, no, erm, in point of fact he signifies man.

Don: Ah.

John: Yes.

Don: Hence the name.

John: Yes.

Philip: I see.

John: Although now you come to mention it, I suppose he could be taken to represent England.

Philip: Is that two ns?

John: What?

Philip: In Man.

John: No, one.

Philip: Ah, well, you see I thought it was two ns. As in Thomas.

John: Thomas?

Philip: Thomas Mann.

John: Oh.

Philip: So I thought he was just meant to represent a window-cleaner.

John: Well...

Philip: Under the circumstances. I think you've integrated him into the plot very well.

John: Thank you. (*He seems displeased*)[30]

Philip indulges in playing with words, being more interested in how the words are used than in what is being said. The very fact that the whole play takes place in this bachelor don's room is somehow indicative of the ivory tower in which Philip, his colleagues and his students spend their days, involved in their own concerns on which the outside world hardly ever impinges. He alienates almost everyone who is coming his way. This is clearly a reference to modern intellectual life in the Oxbridge circle. Philip becomes increasingly isolated. His love for humanity is not a genuine love. His desire to please makes him suppress his 'ego'; his gentleness, flabbiness and lack of guile make him a modern counterpart to

Molière's Alceste who demands the utmost integrity in all his relationships and openly detests all those who fail to live up to his expectations.

Analogies between the two plays can also be discovered in the other characters. Don, Philip's colleague, corresponds to Philinte, Alceste's friend; Braham to Oronto; Elizabeth, a non-speaking part, plays a role similar to Eliante; Aramint is Hampton's Arsinoe; Celia in *The Philanthropist* replaces Célimène in the Molière play. Moreover, the seven characters in Hampton's play do not merely have specific counterparts in *Le Misanthrope*; each of them embodies one of the seven deadly sins. William J. Free comments on this:

> The notion that human conduct can be understood through these deadly sins is deeply entrenched in our culture, and the motif resonates throughout the play without the playwright's overt attention to it. Hampton uses the game [i.e. which involves the seven deadly sins] to define his characters in relation to the general spiritual malaise which seems to have overtaken them all.[31]

The Philanthropist was one of the first plays in the 1970s. It is both in the tradition of the *bourgeois comedy* and a play in its own right. It was written by a dramatist who spent part of his life outside Britain, belongs to the settled upper middle class, went to a public school, studied at Oxford and in all this was different from many English authors who were highly influential and instrumental in the development of English theatre in that decade. At the same time, Hampton sets new standards by making emotional relationships in modern Britain the subject of *The Philanthropist*. In this play he presents us with a topsy-turvy world in which the harmless do harm and the 'bad' make life enjoyable. Molière's play still works for us. But Hampton's play does not presuppose an intimate knowledge of *Le Misanthrope*. 'It is the extra bit of seasoning', to revert to the aforementioned George W. Brandt, 'to a dish which would be satifying without it – but gains by the extra ingredient'.[32]

Notes

1. Free (1994), p. 124.
2. Glaap (1995), Interview. All further quotations from interviews with Christopher Hampton, for which no bibliographical details are given, are from this interview.

3. Free (1994), p. 122.
4. Free (1994), p. 122.
5. Royal National Theatre (1992), no pagination.
6. Hampton (1983).
7. Hampton (1977).
8. Royal National Theatre (1992), no pagination.
9. Royal National Theatre (1992), no pagination.
10. Hampton (1977), Introduction, p. 6.
11. Hampton (1977), Introduction, p. 6.
12. Hampton (1977), Introduction, p. 6.
13. Hampton (1977), pp. 47–8.
14. Horváth (1961), p. 77.
15. Stoppard (1981).
16. Stoppard (1981), p. 7.
17. Morley (1983), p. 77.
18. Morley (1983), p. 77.
19. Hampton (1985).
20. Hampton (1995).
21. Hampton (1995), Introduction, p. ix.
22. Hampton (1995), Introduction, p. ix.
23. Tinker (1986).
24. Billington (1986).
25. Hampton (1985), p. 69.
26. Hampton (1970).
27. Brandt (1991), no pagination.
28. Brandt (1991), no pagination.
29. Hampton (1970), p. 34.
30. Hampton (1970), pp. 10–11.
31. Free (1994), p. 44.
32. Brandt (1991), no pagination.

Bibliography

Billington, Michael, *Guardian*, 10 January 1986.
Brandt, George W., 'Does the Philanthropist Actually Like People? or: Pardon My French', in: Wyndham's Theatre (ed.), *The Philanthropist* (Programme) (1991).
Free, William J., *Christopher Hampton: An Introduction to His Plays* (San Bernardino, California: The Borgo Press, 1994), no pagination.
Glaap, Albert-Reiner, *Interview with Christopher Hampton*, London, 6 October 1995 (typescript).
Gross, Robert (ed.), *Christopher Hampton: A Casebook* (Garland Publishing: New York & London, 1990).
Hampton, Christopher, *The Philanthropist* (London: Faber & Faber, 1970).
Hampton, Christopher, *Tales from the Vienna Woods* (London: Faber & Faber, 1977).
Hampton, Christopher, *The Portage to San Cristobal of A.H.* (London: Faber & Faber, 1983).

Hampton, Christopher, *Les Liaisons Dangereuses* (London: Faber & Faber, 1985).

Hampton, Christopher, *Alice's Adventures Under Ground* (London: Faber & Faber, 1995).

Horváth, Ödön von, *Geschichten aus dem Wiener Wald*, in: Traugott Krischke (ed.), *Ödön von Horváth. Stücke*. (Reinbeck: Rowohlt, 1961), pp. 51–115.

Morley, Sheridan, *Shooting Stars: Plays and Players 1975–1983* (London: Quartet Books, 1983).

Royal National Theatre (ed.), *Platform Papers. 1. Translation* (London: Publications Department of the Royal National Theatre, 1992).

Steiner, George, *The Portage to San Cristobal of A.H.* (London: Faber & Faber, 1979).

Stoppard, Tom, *On the Razzle* (London: Faber & Faber, 1981).

Tinker, Jack, *Daily Mail*, 19 October 1986.

15

Les Enfants de Parodie: The Enlightened Incest of Anglo-American Musicals

John Elsom

According to the poet Alexander Pope, as quoted by the Anglican clergyman Dr Joseph Spence, the origins of the genre to which musicals are usually said to belong, began in 1727 like this:

> Dr. Swift had been observing once to Mr. Gay what an odd pretty sort of thing a Newgate Pastoral might make. Gay was inclined to try such a thing for some time, but afterwards thought it would be better to write a comedy on the same plan. This was what gave rise to the *Beggar's Opera*. He began on it, and when he first mentioned it to Swift, the Doctor did not much like the project. As he carried it on, he showed what he had wrote to both of us; and we now and then gave a correction, or a word or two of advice; but it was wholly of his own writing. When it was done, neither of us thought it would succeed. We showed it to Congreve, who, after reading it over, said, 'It would either take greatly, or be damned confoundedly'. We were all at the first night of it, in great uncertainty of the event; till we were much encouraged by overhearing the Duke of Argyle, who sat in the next box to us, say, 'It will do – it must do! – I see it in the eyes of them.'[1]
>
> *Spence's Anecdotes* (Scott Library Edition)

Newgate was a notorious prison by the walls of the City of London, where murderers, debtors and highwaymen settled their scores with fortune. *The Beggar's Opera* was a low-life parody of Italian opera, but its triumph at the time, its revivals and the attempts to match its success over the next two centuries led to the development of a new kind of musical theatre, in which some of its original intentions were retained in fragments of form and mood, long after its

231

target had been forgotten. The musical is not easy to define. There are too many exceptions to every rule, but audiences seem to know what to expect when a show is billed as a musical, which suggests that there *is* a genre of that name, though its parameters are marked more by habit and custom than technical distinctions.

One of its traits is 'drama on drama'. Like *The Beggar's Opera*, many musicals imitate or draw their inspiration from another art form. There are 49 productions currently running in London's main theatres, of which 18 are billed as musicals. Of these, five string together well-known pop songs within a framework of a show-business biography, such as *Buddy* (from Buddy Holly), and are often described as 'compilation' musicals. Willy Russell's *Blood Brothers* owes a small debt to Dion Boucicault's *The Corsican Brothers*, but all of the rest, which include *Miss Saigon, Carmen Jones, The Phantom of the Opera* and *Sunset Boulevard*, are openly based on other works. They join a postwar list of similarly derived musicals, such as *Kismet, West Side Story, My Fair Lady* and *Cabaret*, but if this sample still seems too small to support the point, it can be extended back in time to *The Desert Song* (1926), *Chu Chin Chow* (1916) and *The Chocolate Soldier* (1909). Impresarios who scoff at academic criticism should be sternly reminded that even the musical is a triumph of intertextuality.

But the term 'intertextuality' has to be treated with some caution. It became popular during the 1970s to de-mystify the literary process and take away what was then the slur of 'creativity' in which the author tried to play god. Instead of bringing something new into the world, the author shuffled a well-worn pack of ideologically informed cards and although there might be variations in the hands dealt, the chances of pure novelty were considered to be beyond the bounds of possibility. In the case of musicals, there are often no claims for 'originality', quite the reverse. *West Side Story* boasted of its source in *Romeo and Juliet*, *Kismet* in *Prince Igor*. No critic is required to point out the links with other texts which the the author has attempted to conceal: they are plastered across the billboards. There is thus no need for de-mystification, except to satisfy the vanity of the critic. What is of greater interest are the bonds between the musical and the other text/s to which it is indebted.

A musical is not any play with music. It is not an opera, comic opera or operetta. George Gershwin's *Porgy and Bess* (1935) is usually described as a folk opera, to distinguish it from his musicals, but Cole Porter's *Kiss Me, Kate* (1948) is always billed as a musical.

Kiss Me, Kate stays within and owes a debt to *The Beggar's Opera* tradition, but Gershwin had another vision for *Porgy and Bess*. According to his biographer, Robert Kimball, he said that 'If I am successful, it will resemble a combination of the drama and romance of *Carmen* and the beauty of *Meistersinger*.'[2] Echoes of 'One Fine Day' from Puccini's *Madame Butterfly* can be heard in Catfish Row in the opening phrases of Gershwin's 'Summertime'. *Kiss Me, Kate* and *Porgy and Bess* both take other works as their models, but one does so in mockery and the other as a tribute. In the cracks in the pavement which separate *homage* (a tribute) from *pastiche* (a skilful imitation) and *parody* (ironic imitation), the seeds of the genre germinate.

The story of *Kiss Me, Kate* is not only a parody of bad Shakespeare but also of bad musicals based on Shakespeare, of which it is a self-mocking example. It is also show-business on art, the town against the snobs and the New World versus the Old, features which are shared with Gay's Original Mixture. In *Porgy and Bess*, there is little parody but much homage. Gershwin brought the full resources of romantic opera to DuBose Heywood's story about a cripple and a whore who fall in love in the black township of Catfish Row in South Carolina and are cruelly separated. Two duets, 'So In Love' from *Kiss Me, Kate* and 'Bess, You Is My Woman Now' from *Porgy and Bess*, high points from American musical theatre, illustrate the difference. One is sentimental but street-wise, the other passionate but innocent. A similar contrast lies in the songs of travel, in the evangelical optimism with which Porgy starts out for New York to find Bess, 'Oh Lawd, I'm on my way', a journey which is more spiritual and emotional than physical, and the jadedness of 'Another Op'ning, Another Show' and 'We Open in Venice' from *Kiss Me, Kate* where all trips into the unknown seem to arrive at the same place, backstage in some dump of a town.

From these examples, it seems clear why musicals should be less highly regarded than operas. Their aims are not so ambitious or transcendent and might be thought commonplace; but before this assessment deemed to be true, we should reflect that musicals conspire in their own disparagement. They prefer to paddle than drown, stand rather than soar, and their acceptance of human limitations seems to strike a chord in the hearts of their public, who may feel, to misquote *The Wife of Bath*, that operas are for those who would live perfectly 'but, lordings, by your leave that am not I!'. If a musical is too ambitious, it may lack box-office appeal, not because audiences are too stupid, but because they expect a different kind of show. Leonard Bernstein's *Candide* ran for less than three months when it was first staged as a musical in 1957 and was re-classified as a comic opera for its successful revival in 1974.

Musicals inhabit a different emotional territory from operas, though not necessarily an inferior one, and when they are written by composers and librettists who assert the dignity of their trade, the genre can be transformed. I have in mind the most widely acclaimed musical of recent years, *City of Angels*, by Larry Gelbart, Cy Coleman and David Zippel, which won six Tonys from the US critics in 1990 and three Best New Musical awards from their colleagues in London. *City of Angels* is a parody of the *film noir* of the 1940s and the society which produced it, Hollywood. It recouped its US investment stake in less than eight months, but failed to turn this promising start into a downright smash-hit, when it ran for little more than two years in New York. In London it survived for less than a year. Andrew Lloyd-Webber complained to the press that he could not remember the tunes and he was a musician, as well as (it should be added) a rival.

The explanations for this relative lack of success ranged from commercial skulduggery to various ponderings about changes in taste and the decline of the West End. Its director, Michael Blakemore, put forward the idea[3] that audiences today, a post-Presley generation, might not respond to Coleman's pastiche of 1940s bigband jazz and close harmony singing, but there should have been enough people in London who remember Louis Armstrong, Bing Crosby and the Andrews Sisters to fill the hall for a year or so. The slickness of the production, its split-second timing, could be admired for its virtuosity, but was it too 'cold' or, as some suggested, too 'good' for a musical?

If this talk about recoupments and smash-hits seems out of place in a critical essay, I will defend myself by asserting that it is *wholly* appropriate for musicals, which often draw attention to their profit-and-loss accounts and turn them into a metaphor for human survival. 'There's no business like show-business.'[4] They distance themselves from art, particularly 'high art' as patronized by court or state, such as (to take an example at random) Italian opera. But a musical is not only expected to be successful at the box-office, but to *seem* popular too, which is another matter. If its songs are thought to be complicated, they may seem to stray from the genre, a charge often levelled against Stephen Sondheim's musicals.

Cy Coleman's score mocked 1940s film music so skilfully ('Aloura's Theme' with its soaring strings and voices) that its parody could almost be mistaken for honest schlock. Grandiose Hollywood music is as broad a target as Italian opera, but was Coleman's public, like Gay's, ready to laugh at its absurdities? Was it too close to home, breaking another *Beggar's Opera* tradition, for the Italian operas were considered foreign and exotic, before John Gay made them seem more so?

Is there an in-built chauvinism to musicals? Those who consider that the genre is aggressively American in the *Chorus Line* manner, strut, swagger and thrust, might well answer 'Yes'. Musicals often target the art forms of old Europe, aiming their high kicks with New World energy at Ruritanian balls, of which *Call Me, Madam* (1950) and *Can-Can* (1953) are examples. In 1727, Italian opera may have been fashionable, but they were still a continental import and subject to the mockery of *The Spectator*. On his first visit to London, the German-born composer, George Frederick Handel, wrote an opera in the Italian style for the King's Theatre, Haymarket, *Rinaldo* (1711) whose success prompted Joseph Addison to comment that 'the finest writers among the modern Italians express themselves in such a florid form of words, and such tedious circumlocutions, as are used by none but pedants in our own country'. He mocked the live birds in the garden scene, the *recitativos* and the speed in which it was supposed to have been composed, under a fortnight, in the Mannerist tradition, like Vasari, all grace and celerity.[5]

Undeterred by this review, Handel wrote more Italian operas on his return in 1712, also staged at the Haymarket, under the auspices of the trustees of the Royal Academy of Music, who appointed him *Master of the Orchestra*. The arrival of his fellow-countryman to ascend the English throne, George I from Hanover, encouraged him to stay, a privileged guest. Gay contributed to the libretto of Handel's *Acis and Galatea* (1720), but his social position as a wit with no private income nor a reliable patron, was less secure than the Master of the Orchestra's. *The Beggar's Opera* might be described as a librettist's revenge on a composer, for Gay took about 60 popular tunes of the time, gave them new lyrics, and added them to a tale of highwaymen, whores and cut-purses, parodying the shepherds, shepherdesses and lustful deities, which were the stock-in-trade of Italian opera.

His satire operated on several levels. Popular entertainment flexed its muscles against High Art, the urban middle classes challenged the tastes of the court and true Englishmen questioned the credentials of foreigners, one of whom had the temerity to call himself their king. Pope observed that Gay was 'remarkable for an unwillingness to offend the great',[6] but he offended some of them nonetheless, through his political incorrectness. His hero was a highwayman, Macheath, who was not hanged, as he deserved to be, but let off scot-free. The Prime Minister, Sir Robert Walpole, was wary of this affront to law and order, and banned the sequel, *Polly*, which was later published profitably. In it, Macheath escaped to the West Indies where his brigandry remained unnoticed.

> *The Beggar's Opera* was received with greater applause than was ever known. Besides being acted in London sixty-three days without interruption, and renewed the next season with equal applause, it spread into all the great towns of England; was played in many places to the thirtieth and fortieth time; at Bath and Bristol fifty. It made its progress into Wales, Scotland and Ireland, where it was performed twenty-four days consecutively. The ladies carried about with them the favourite songs of it in fans, and houses were furnished with it in screens. The fame of it was not confined to the Author only. The person who acted Polly, till then obscure, became all at once the favourite of the town; her pictures were engraved and sold in great numbers; her life written, books of letters and verses to her published, and pamphlets even made of her sayings and jests. Furthermore, it drove out of England (for that season) the Italian opera, which had carried all before it for ten years.[7]

Pope estimated that Gay made £400 from the first version of *The Beggar's Opera* and £1200 from the second, and guessed that when Gay died in 1732, he was worth 'upwards of three thousand pounds', despite his profligacy. With this example, others became more daring and Sir Robert Walpole curbed their impertinence by introducing a bill into parliament to make all stage performance subject to an official licence, thus starting a tradition of censorship which only ended in 1968. Dr. Samuel Johnson retorted to those who considered *The Beggar's Opera* immoral that the play 'was plainly written to divert'[8] and as such could have no moral purpose, neither good nor bad, an unusually liberal opinion for the time, but it must have been widely shared, for plays with music were exempt from many laws which controlled spoken drama. Even in the 1950s, musicals were forgiven in Britain for being slightly *risqués*, because they were, well, only musicals.

To that extent, the musical had a protected eighteenth-century childhood. Gay selected his airs with exceptional care. They included such early Tudor melodies as 'Greensleeves', street tunes, such as 'Over the Hills and Far Away', and themes taken from such composers as Purcell and even Handel. What they had in common was a deceptive simplicity. They could be sung or whistled in the street, or adapted to suit the accomplished performer. The lyrics, sold in broadsheets, were often more complicated. Many songs were also popular with North American settlers, which may have been where the transatlantic connection began.

Features of eighteenth-century popular music came to be preserved within the genre. Until the mid-1950s, most songs in musicals were ternary in form, verse-chorus-verse, as in *The Beggar's Opera*, not through-composed, as in romantic operas and song cycles. The librettist, Oscar Hammerstein II, complained about this habit of repeating the chorus every sixteen bars or so, saying that it interrupted the stage action. He wanted every song to tell a story. Cole Porter had no such problems. He liked the idea, close to Gay's practice, that a song could be taken from one show and placed in another, for he did not believe that musicals needed to aspire to the heights of dramatic coherence.

Other features were also preserved, not out of obedience, but as a matter of custom. Acts usually began and ended with choruses or duets in which the company joined. There was at least one solo and a duet for the principals in each act, and one solo and a duet for their seconds in each performance. The principals and their seconds were contrasted in an eighteenth-century manner by class distinction of a kind. The seconds in Frank Loesser's *Guys and Dolls* (1950) were Nathan Detroit and Miss Adelaide, the bookie and the chorus girl, who may not have been servants, but were a notch or so below Sky Masterson, the high-rolling gambler, and his Salvation Army moll, Miss Sarah Brown. The duet between the principals, where love is declared, is often used as a *leitmotiv*, sung at first with some self-doubt, as they meet, but with a whole-hearted reprise at the show's climax in the second act. The seconds too have their moments of more down-to-earth glory. In *Guys and Dolls*, the duet between Sky and Sarah is 'I've never been in love before', while the duet between Nathan and Miss Adelaide is 'Sue me'. If the principal's duet in *Kiss Me, Kate* is 'So in Love', that of the seconds is 'Why can't

you behave?'. The titles are self-explanatory. The contrast between
the solos is equally marked. The second female lead's solo is more
worldly (or world-weary) than the principal's, as in 'I'm always
true to you, darling, in my fashion' from *Kiss Me, Kate*, 'Adelaide's
Lament' from *Guys and Dolls* or 'You can always count on me' from
City of Angels. They recall the rivalry between Polly and Lucy for
Macheath's favours and his reply, 'How happy I could be with
either, were t'other dear charmer away.'

The way in which *City of Angels* accepted these conventions but
transformed them can be illustrated from the duet between its two
unlikely principals, which ended the first act with a quarrel and the
second with a declaration of love. The words of 'You're Nothing
Without Me' were inverted to become 'I'm Nothing Without You',
but the leads, Stine and Stone, are aspects of one person and the
duet celebrates a man coming to terms with his *alter ego*. Its 'Hollywood Ending' brings the women into the picture, Stine's estranged
wife, Gabbie, doubling as Bobbie, Stone's lost lover. *City of Angels* is a modern parable in which Personal Integrity is set against
Career Prospects, a more ambivalent than clear-cut dilemma, akin
to those sentiments felt towards Macheath who may have been a
highwayman but less of a rogue than those whom he robs and who
escapes (like Stine) in a 'Hollywood Ending'.

There are two stories in *City of Angels*. One is of the crime novel
which is in the process of being turned into a movie, whose hero,
Stone, a wisecracking gumshoe, is hired by a *femme fatale*, Aloura,
to find her missing step-daughter, Mallory: a plot which recalls *The
Maltese Falcon, Farewell, My Lovely, The Big Sleep* and almost every
film noir of the 1940s and 1950s. The second is of its writer, Stine,
who is trying to devise a screenplay which his producer, Buddy
Fidler, may eventually use, against a galaxy of Hollywood temptations, such as sex, money, politics and too many close-ups. The
stories are tangled together, an episode of one followed by a snatch
of the other, but kept apart visually by lighting and colour, black-
and-white for *film noir*, technicolour for Hollywood. This allows the
plots to be seen side by side, so when Stine re-writes a scene, it
unreels elsewhere.

One gain from this mode of presentation is that it enables 'real-
life' to comment on 'fiction' and vice versa, except that one is scarcely
less artificial than the other. When Stine caves to Buddy's black-
mail, Stone is shocked, 'One small threat and you fold like a card-
table', to which Stine retorts that Stone is nothing more than a 'novel

pain, one speck of lint that fell out the last time that I picked my brain', which cues in the duet, 'You're nothing without me.' When Stine arrived in Los Angeles, a 'stranger in the strangest of lands', he could not at first 'believe [his] luck'. It meant 'lots of work, lots of fun and pots of dough!'. Stone's reaction was cooler and more sceptical. The city of angels was 'where palm trees finger the sky and there's enough sunshine to lay some off on Pittsburgh. But that's all on top. LA, truth to tell, is not much different from a pretty girl with the clap'.

At first, Stine liked Buddy Fidler, 'You can trust a guy that shoots from the hip.' He naively commented that 'at making movies out of books, they say that Buddy wrote the Book', which turned out to be all too true. He winced but smiled at Buddy's perpetual hype, his mixed metaphors (in life as well as art) and spectacularly bad taste; but Stone took exception to the way in which his wisecracks were cut for more close-ups and a crooner, Jimmy Power, was cast for his part. There were other horrors, the removal of every trace of social conscience and the casual treatment of women. 'I'd rather have you shoot yourself', stated Gabbi, Stine's wife and agent, 'than have you prostitute youself', by which she meant the casting couch (with its winners and losers) and its metaphorical equivalent, the talents exploited by power and money.

In the city of angels, bad art, like power and greed, is a destructive force. 'You've got to look out for yourself', sings Jimmy Power and his close harmony team, the Angel City 4, in what begins as an all-American song of self-reliance (as in 'Heart'[9] from *Damn Yankees*, 1955) and ends as a hymn in praise of downright selfishness. His radio show is called 'An Hour of Power'. Many musicals are parables in which the devil has almost the best tunes but where the rights-and-wrongs are presented through the metaphors of show-business. If guts and determination are expressed in the way in which an unknown talent battles his/her way through to become a Star, so Stardom reveals the vanities of fame and wealth, and the hero/heroine returns to more homely satisfactions, perhaps leaving a flashy partner for the girl/boy-next-door.

Stine has similar bimbo-and-wife, money-and-conscience, compromise-and-integrity problems, which we accept at their face value because they belong within the mythology of show-business, a Valhalla where the public may be fickle but always right and the money-men betray artists, not the other way round. The stage may not corrupt its inhabitants more than a bank or a hospital ward, but if this rumour spread, it would lose much of its appeal. State-subsidized theatres have better reputations, but less tawdry glamour, which causes marketing difficulties on both sides, too much respect here, too little there. The raffish patina of the commercial stage was acquired over many centuries, but if we should seek a defining moment when show business detached itself from aristocratic patronage and court influence, we would be drawn inevitably to the first night of *The Beggar's Opera*.

This was where it began, the familiar soap-opera of gambles, disasters and stars-born-overnight. The relationship between angels and punters can be read in Spence's Anecdotes, as the Duke of Argyle examined the audience and Pope kept his eye upon him. In court- or state-subsidized theatres, the fate of a show rests in politics and not in first-night applause, but in show-business, the risk is part of the genre. I suspect that we think less well of a musical where no personal fortunes are at stake.

Gay died in 1732, aged 47. His life was relatively short, unlike that of the actor–manager who took the gamble, John Rich, who staged *The Beggar's Opera* at Lincoln's Inn Fields Theatre outside the centre of town. Its success made 'Gay rich and Rich gay' and turned Rich into the first impresario, more concerned with public taste than fashionable opinion. He had family reasons for distrusting court patronage. His father, Christopher, failed in his attempt to secure the patent house in Drury Lane, and died shortly after. Rich restored the family's fortunes by turning an unfashionable theatre into a popular one by attracting the urban middle classes. He was a mime and magician, who saved British theatre with another eccentric genre, the pantomime.

At each turn of events, we can feel the birth pangs and growing pains of modern show-business. Similar stories are told about *City of Angels*, which opened in an off-centre theatre, the Virginia. It was an elaborate show to stage, which precluded a pre-New York run. No advance notices were leaked to the press, but the backstage gossip which filtered through was less than reassuring. The mechanics of the set protracted the rehearsals. The word went round that at least two of its angels were ready to cut their losses. Blakemore later admitted to a relief that there had been no pre-Broadway run, no panic on the road, no re-writing sessions at night in bedrooms, but it would have been comforting to know that the show had been able even to cheer up Baltimore.

Blakemore is an experienced director, but this was his first musical.

Of the creative team, only Coleman with *Little Me, On the Twentieth Century* and *Sweet Charity* had smelt success on Broadway. In the interval, two of the producers could be heard predicting that the show would not run to the end of the week. For reasons of economy, the first night party was not held at the Algonquin or a glitzy *rendez vous*, but in a nearby diner, where the cast queued to buy cups of coffee. While Blakemore stood in line, someone whispered to him, 'Rich likes it!', not the ghost of old John, but Frank Rich, the critic of the *New York Times*. The producers scrambled to get to the microphone to have the privilege of reading a glowing review from the most powerful butcher on Broadway, which guaranteed a profitable run, but not, as events turned out, as profitable as it might have been.

What went wrong? There could be many reasons. Perhaps its London theatre, the Prince of Wales, was too much in the path of the tourist trade and exposed to Japanese English. *City of Angels* may have bitten the hands of the angels that fed it: it was odd that it was not nursed through the normally difficult weeks in New York after Christmas and that the End of Run notices appeared as soon as its takings dipped below a break-even figure. Blakemore much admired the book's lack of sentimentality, but the public might prefer less austerity and more uncomplicated sex. Elsewhere in London, the RSC brought *The Beggar's Opera* to town in a reverential revival for the umpteenth time.

Perhaps it was too clever, which may have been why the chattering classes liked it but the punters failed to come. If so, *City of Angels* would have something in common with the musicals of Stephen Sondheim, who for 25 years has had a record of near-misses (commercially-speaking) and almost-hits. Before 1970, no song-writer had a better track record than Sondheim, a protégé of Oscar Hammerstein II, a pupil of Milton Babbit, who was part of the *West Side Story* team with Bernstein and Jerome Robbins, and responsible for such hits as *A Funny Thing Happened to Me on the Way to the Forum*, erudite drama on drama, based on the comedies of Plautus. In 1970, he teamed up with Hal Prince, then thought to be the best director of musicals in the world, and wrote the songs for six musicals, including *Company, Follies, A Little Night Music* and *Sweeney Todd*, which had respectable runs of about 18 months, but lacked the remarkable staying power of Marvin Hamlisch's *A Chorus Line*, which ran for more than 14 years, or Andrew Lloyd Webber's *Evita, Cats, Phantom of the Opera* and *Sunset Boulevard*.

Nowadays on Broadway and in the West End, there is little room left for genteel sufficiency. A musical either makes or loses fortunes. It has been hoisted with its own petard. This is not simply a matter of economics. The state-subsidized theatres in London and the not-for-profit companies in the US are in a better position to take the kind of moderate gambles which used to keep many small companies afloat and to act as producing partners for commercial impresarios, as was the case with the RSC and *Les Misérables*, now in its tenth year in London. To attract these vast audiences and to market the shows internationally, the appeal has to be 'broad', which often means that the song-writing skills of a Sondheim are sacrificed to those of the set designer and sound engineer. Parody goes unrewarded. *Sunset Boulevard* does not mock the film on which it is based, but simply sets it to music, intertextuality as an aid to marketing.

After the commercial failure of *Merrily We Roll Along* (1981), his last musical with Hal Prince, Sondheim turned away from Broadway and towards the not-for-profit and state-subsidized theatres for his new shows and old revivals, although some continued to transfer to Broadway for almost respectable runs and win Tony awards, as was the case with *Into the Woods* (1987) and *Passion* (1994). With this shift, there came a change in tone and content. *Sunday in the Park with George* (1984), his first musical with his new director–collaborator, James Lapine, was first staged in the Playwrights Horizon Workshops, before being taken by the Shubert Organisation to Broadway. It attempted to capture in words and music the *pointillist* technique of Georges Seurat, the French Impressionist painter, and to relate it to the life of the artist today and the corrupting effects of the art market in New York. It was staged at the Royal National Theatre in London. Another Sondheim–Lapine musical, *Into The Woods* (1987), explored the Freudian undergrowth of fairy stories. Although the strength of these musicals lay in their songs, these summaries reveal how closely they came to crossing the dividing line between the street-wisdom of the genre and the art-works they parodied.

Sondheim excels in imitating styles of other songwriters. He has described himself as a 'pasticheur'.[10] *Follies* paid its respects to 1930s vaudevilles (with echoes of Romberg, Gershwin, Porter, Berlin and Kern): *Sweeney Todd* was a Victorian melodrama with blood-bath, music hall numbers, ghastly polite. Among the other achievements of his musicals, he has provided a history of two centuries and several continents in terms of popular song-writing. There are hints of Eric Satie in *Sunday in the Park with George*, but how many people whistle 'Gymnopaedie' in the street?

By venturing up-market, Sondheim ran the risk of losing touch with the traditions in which he was so expert. He may have wanted like Bernstein to extend the range of the musical, but in doing so, he threatened to pull it out of shape. In 1995, *A Little Night Music* was staged by the Royal National Theatre and the authority of this state-subsidized company changed the nature of its reception. In the West End, it was received as a charming trifle, but at the RNT, it was treated as a minor masterpiece. There were many anxious faces at the back of the stalls at the Adelphi in 1975, angels watching punters, on whose response the fate of the show rested; but no such worries lent an edge to the revival at the Olivier. This affected the actors, who were not, as we sometimes expect from musicals, too ingratiating, on edge and over-energetic, but calm, relaxed and full of authority.

It reeked of establishment confidence. When that happens, there is a risk that the element of parody, whatever it may be, seems supercilious, *de haut en bas*, which is contrary to the spirit of musicals and how the genre came into being. This may be why Sondheim's recent shows have done less well at the box office, for while audiences may or may not appreciate his skill, they can still resent the direction from which it seems to be coming. Even *Follies*, which contained so many of his most brilliant songs, had a rather tired story about a reunion of vaudeville artistes in their middle age, remembering the follies of their past with or without regret; and the wit stopped when the characters started to speak.

City of Angels by contrast was parody through and through. The book, musical score, lyrics and production mocked an establishment target, Hollywood, from the standpoint of those who (like Stine and Gelbart) had suffered from it, as Gay must have winced at Handel's prolixity. In his introduction to the published text, Gelbart wrote that 'it was a treat for me to be able to write a 1940s movie from the vantage point of the 1980s, and, being able to write about the minefield a screenwriter has to run in Hollywood was for me one from the heart, one that's been dented from time to time by a few real-life Buddy Fidlers, who live to fix what isn't broken, until it finally is'.[11] At the risk of seeming to remystify that which has scrupulously de-mystified, I would like to suggest that this is where an element of originality may lie in the process which used to be called creative. What Gelbart did was to take two Hollywood story patterns and fed into them extracts from his own directly felt experiences, thus bringing the legends closer to his understanding of life, which was what was often meant by creativity (instead of 'something out of nothing') in the days before the Structuralists dispatched the term to a pre-Saussurean limbo.

Anyone who goes to the theatre for any kind of performance has a certain idea of what to expect, which is formed from many impressions, such as critical reviews, word-of-mouth, marketing and the fame of the stars, among which genre is a important factor. You do not go to alternative comedy in the same frame of mind as to a revival of *King Lear*. We have lived through a Modernist age, which favours breaking new ground, but I suspect that originality does not rank highly in our lists of priorities. What we want is something else, a familiar form which helps us to concentrate on areas of our experience. The 'originality' comes in the way in which a good example of a genre, such as *City of Angels*, extends our understanding of what we feel to be its appropriate territory.

Critics can add their empty shells to the various casings. As a former employee of Paramount Pictures, I thought that *City of Angels* was a memorable parody of the Hollywood slave trade, which carried the topical message that if money corrupts, monetarism corrupts infinitely. If it failed to run and run, as it should have done, it may be that it was a bit too painful to watch, those wasted talents, like those of so many others, including all of our own.

Notes

1. From *Spence's Anecdotes*, selected and edited by John Underhill (Scott Library Edition).
2. Robert Kimball, from the introduction to the Glyndebourne Festival recording of *Porgy and Bess* (EMI Records Ltd). See also *The Gershwins* by Robert Kimball.
3. This quotation and later ones are taken from an interview with Michael Blakemore conducted on 21 September 1995.
4. The title of a song from *Annie Get Your Gun* (1946).
5. From the *Spectator*, 6 March 1711.
6. From *Spence's Anecdotes*.

7. From *Spence's Anecdotes*, quoted by Samuel Johnson in *The Lives of the Poets* (1781).
8. From Samuel Johnson, *The Lives of the Poets*.
9. It may be worth noting that 'Heart' is sung by 'Mr Applegate', a Mephistopheles figure, and also pokes fun at US can-do-ness.
10. From Foster Hirsch, *Harold Prince*, P120 (Cambridge University Press, 1989).
11. Page 7, Introduction to *City of Angels* (Applause, 1990).

Select Bibliography

Abel, Lionel, *Metatheatre* (New York, Hill & Wang, 1963).

Bas, Georges, 'Orphée et Eurydice dans *The Sea* d'Edward Bond', *Etudes Anglaises*, 33, 1980, pp. 171–82.

——, 'Théâtre, histoire et politique dans une pièce radiophonique: *Pearl* (1978) de John Arden et la question irlandaise', *Etudes Anglaises*, 39, 1986, pp. 424–37.

Blau, Herbert, *To All Appearances: Ideology and Performance* (London & New York: Routledge, 1992).

Boireau, Nicole, 'Jeux et enjeux dans les pièces en un acte de James Saunders', *Coup de Théâtre*, 13, 1994, pp. 67–87.

Cohn, Ruby, *Retreats from Realism in Recent English Drama* (Cambridge University Press, 1991).

——, *Anglo-American Interplay in Recent Drama* (Cambridge University Press, 1995).

Dällenbach, Lucien, *Le récit spéculaire: Essai sur la mise en abyme* (Paris: Seuil, 1977).

Egan, Robert, *Drama within Drama: Shakespeare's Sense of His Art in* King Lear, The Winter's Tale *and* The Tempest (New York: Columbia University Press, 1975).

Essif, Les, 'Introducing the "Hyper" Theatrical Subject: The *Mise en Abyme* of Empty Space', *Journal of Dramatic Theory and Criticism*, 9, 1994, pp. 67–87.

Forestier, Georges, *Le théâtre dans le théâtre sur la scène française du XVIIe siècle* (Genève: Droz, 1981).

Genette, Gérard, *Palimpsestes* (Paris: Seuil, 1982).

Hallyn, Fernand, *Onze études sur la mise en abyme – Romanica Gandensia* (Gent, Belgique, 1980).

Homan, Sidney, *When the Theater Turns to Itself: The Aesthetic Metaphor in Shakespeare* (London & Toronto: Associated University Press, 1981).

Homan, Sidney, *The Audience as Actor and Character: The Modern Theater of Beckett, Brecht, Genet, Ionesco, Pinter, Stoppard and Williams* (London & Toronto: Associated University Press, 1989).

Hornby, Richard, *Drama, Metadrama, and Perception* (London & Toronto: Bucknell University Press, 1986).

Hutcheon, Linda, *Narcissistic Narrative: The Metafictional Paradox* (Wilfrid Laurier University Press, 1980).

——, *A Theory of Parody* (London: Methuen, 1985).

——, *A Poetics of Postmodernism: History, Theory, Fiction* (London: Routledge, 1988).

Issacharoff, Michael, 'Inscribed Performance', *Rivista Di Letterature Moderne E Comparate*, 39, Fasc. 2, 1986, pp. 93–105.

——, 'Labiche et l'intertextualité comique', *Cahiers de l'Association Internationale des Etudes Françaises*, 35, 1983, pp. 169–82.

Landow, George P., *Hypertext: The Convergence of Contemporary Critical Theory and Technology* (Baltimore & London: Johns Hopkins University Press, 1992).

Levy, Shimon, *Samuel Beckett's Self-Referential Drama: The Three I's* (London: Macmillan, 1990).

Ogée, Frédéric et Rouyer, Marie-Claire, *R. B. Sheridan: The Critic* (Paris: Didier Erudition, 1995).

Pavis, Patrice, *Le théâtre au croisement des cultures* (Paris: Corti, 1990).

Ricardou, Jean, *Nouveaux problèmes du roman* (Paris: Seuil, 1978).

Rouyer, Marie-Claire, 'Identité et identification dans quelques exemples de théâtre dans le théâtre: de la comédie classique emboîtée au "one-man-show"', *Cahiers du CERT*, 6, 1979, pp. 68–98.

Schmelling, Manfred, *Métathéâtre et intertexte: Aspects du théâtre dans le théâtre* (Paris: Lettres Modernes, 1982).

Schlueter, June, *Metafictional Characters in Modern Drama* (New York: Columbia University Press, 1979).

Sommi (de'), Leone, *Quatre Dialogues en Matière de Représentations Théâtrales* (Paris: Rampazzio & Associés, 1992).

'Theatre on Theatre', a special issue of *Modern Drama*, 30, March 1987.

Todorov, Tzvetan, *Poétique de la prose* (Paris: Seuil, 1971).

Törnqvist, Egil, *Transposing Drama: Studies in Representation* (London: Macmillan, 1991).

Vanden Heuvel, Michael, *Performing Drama/Dramatizing Performance: Alternative Theater and the Dramatic Text* (Ann Arbor: The University of Michigan Press, 1991).

——, 'Complementary Spaces: Realism, Performance and a New Dialogics of Theatre', *Theatre Journal*, 44, 1992, pp. 47–58.

Wilshire, Bruce, *Role Playing and Identity: The Limits of Theatre as Metaphor* (Bloomington: Indiana University Press, 1982).

Wilson Ann, 'Fool of Desire: The Spectator to the Plays of Sam Shepard', *Modern Drama*, 30, 1987, pp. 46–57.

Index